# ATTILA

*Also by John Man*

Gobi: Tracking the Desert
Atlas of the Year 1000
Alpha Beta
The Gutenberg Revolution
Genghis Khan: Life, Death and Resurrection

# ATTILA

## The Barbarian King
## Who Challenged Rome

## JOHN MAN

## BANTAM PRESS

LONDON  •  TORONTO  •  SYDNEY  •  AUCKLAND  •  JOHANNESBURG

TRANSWORLD PUBLISHERS
61–63 Uxbridge Road, London W5 5SA
a division of The Random House Group Ltd

RANDOM HOUSE AUSTRALIA (PTY) LTD
20 Alfred Street, Milsons Point, Sydney,
New South Wales 2061, Australia

RANDOM HOUSE NEW ZEALAND LTD
18 Poland Road, Glenfield, Auckland 10, New Zealand

RANDOM HOUSE SOUTH AFRICA (PTY) LTD
Endulini, 5a Jubilee Road, Parktown 2193, South Africa

Published 2005 by Bantam Press
a division of Transworld Publishers

Copyright © John Man 2005

Maps by Hardlines

A catalogue record for this book is available from the British Library.
ISBN 0593 052919 (cased)
0593 054210 (tpb)

Typeset in 11½/14½pt Sabon by
Falcon Oast Graphic Art Ltd

Printed in Great Britain by
Mackays of Chatham plc, Chatham, Kent

1 3 5 7 9 10 8 6 4 2

For ATS

# CONTENTS

# CONTENTS

# MAPS

# ILLUSTRATIONS

*First section*

Lajos Kassai on horseback. Courtesy Lajos Kassai.

Xiongnu textile: author's photo; view of the Kozlov dig: from S. I. Rudenko, *Die Kultur der Hsiung-Nu und die Hügelgräber von Noin Ula*, 1969; author by a Xiongnu grave/pair of stirrups: author's photos; earring from the headdress of a Xiongnu noblewoman, 4th to 2nd century BC: Inner Mongolia Museum, Huhehaote; textile with a man's face: from S. I. Rudenko, op.cit.

Arkhip Ivanovich Kuindzhi *Morning on the Dnieper*, 1881: © State Tretyakov Gallery, Moscow; 'Devil's Ditch': author's photo; skull of a Hunnish noble lady, mid 5th century AD, found in Ladenburg (Baden), on loan from the Kurpfälzisches Museum, Heidelberg, Ladenburg, Lobdengaumuseum/akg-images; Hunnish cauldron: photo A. Dabasi/Hungarian National Museum.

City walls, Istanbul: © Adam Woolfitt/CORBIS; relief depicting a barbarian fighting a Roman legionary, 2nd century AD/Louvre, Paris, Lauros/Giraudon/Bridgeman Art Library; medals of Valens and Gratian: © Kunsthistorisches Museum, Vienna; coin portrait of Theodosius II: British Museum, Department of Coins & Medals.

Fibula and necklace: photo A. Dabasi/Hungarian National Museum; two swords from Pannonhalma: photo Nicola Sautner © University of Vienna; Peter Tomka: author's photo; Hun diadem, 5th century: Römisch-Germanisches Museum/Rheinisches Bildarchiv der Stadt Köln.

*Second section*

Lajos Kassai on horseback/portrait: author's photos; Pettra Engeländer: Caro Photoagentur.

Porta Nigra, Trier: David Peevers/Lonely Planet; Honoria, obverse of coin, 5th century AD: British Museum, Department of Coins and Medals; Aetius from an ivory diptych panel, 5th century AD: Monza cathedral treasury; martyrdom of St Nicasius on the central portal lintel of Reims cathedral: © Archivio Iconografico, S.A./CORBIS; Frankish soldier, detail from the missorium of Theodosius, 388 AD: Werner Forman Archive/Academia de la Historia, Madrid; Pouan treasure: Musées d'Art et d'Histoire, Troyes.

Raphael *The Meeting of Leo the Great with Attila*, 1511-14: Vatican Museums and Galleries, Bridgeman Art Library/Alinari; Attila outside Aquileia from the *Saxon Chronicle of the World*, Gotha: akg-images.

Still from Fritz Lang's *Nibelungen*, Part II: bfi; Attila from a stained-glass window, 1883, Lesparre-Médoc: akg-images/Jean Paul Dumontier; 'Hun or Home?', First World War poster: private collection, Barbara Singer/Bridgeman Art Library.

Death of Attila from a 14th-century manuscript of the *Saxon Chronicle of the World*, MS germ 129 f, 53: Berlin, Staatsbibliothek.

# ACKNOWLEDGEMENTS

I would like to thank Todd Delle, Arizona; Borsó Béla, Ilona and Dori, Szár; Yuliy Drobyshev, Institute of Oriental Studies and Institute for Problems of Ecology and Evolution, Moscow; Pettra Engeländer, Seeburg, Berlin; Gelegdorj Eregzen, National Museum of Mongolian History, Ulaanbaatar; Peter Heather, Worcester College, Oxford; Barry Groves, archery expert; Kassai Lajos, Kaposmérõ, Kaposvár; Kurti Bela, Szeged; Tserendorj Odbaatar, National Museum of Mongolian History, Ulaanbaatar; Szegedi Andrea, for her excellent driving and translation; Dr Peter Stadler, Naturhistorisches Museum, Vienna; Graham Taylor, Karakorum Expeditions, Ulaanbaatar; Peter Tomka, Xántus János Muzeúm, Györ; Karin Wiltschke, Naturhistorisches Museum, Vienna; Doug Young, Simon Thorogood and their colleagues at Transworld; and, as ever, Felicity Bryan.

# INTRODUCTION:
## A BEAST, CORNERED

HE'S HISTORY'S BOGEY-MAN, 'GOD'S SCOURGE', A SYMBOL OF brute destructiveness, a cliché of extreme right-wing-ness. Beyond that, he's known only to those who study the collapse of the Roman empire in the fifth century. Even to them, he is scarcely more than a predator, the grimmest of those many barbarians tearing at the flesh of the empire in its death agony.

But there is a lot more to Attila than clichéd barbarism. This is the story of a man of astonishing ambition, who deployed forces the like of which no-one had ever seen before. With his Hun army of mounted warriors, strengthened by a dozen allied tribes and contingents of siege machines, he was for a while the Genghis Khan of Europe. From his base in what is today Hungary, he created an empire that reached from the Baltic to the Balkans, from the Rhine to the Black Sea. He struck deep into the Roman empire, threatening its very roots. Hun warriors who had once crossed the Balkans on their way to Constantinople could later have watered their horses in the Loire, in the heart of Roman Gaul within a three-day gallop of the Atlantic, and then the next year bathed in the Po, on a campaign that might have led to Rome itself. Constantinople and Rome did not fall. But Attila's achievements ensured that his name lived on, and lives on today, not just as the supreme barbarian, but as a hero.

This is my attempt to explain Attila's rise, his brief moment of glory, his sudden extinction, and why he is such an enduring presence.

It takes time to build up an image in the round, because he rose and operated in several worlds, all interfused in complicated ways.

The first world was the one from which he sprang, a way of life which dominated much of Asia for 2,000 years. This was the way of the nomadic herders, or pastoral nomads, to give them their formal name; in particular their military aspect, the mounted archer. From China to Europe, cultures outside the Eurasian heartland were at risk of sudden invasion by these centaur-like people, able to shoot with extraordinary accuracy and power while at full gallop. This book is in part a portrait of their most devastating manifestation before the rise of the Mongols 800 years later.

But Attila's Huns were not the pastoral nomads – the mounted archers – their forebears had once been. By the time they became known to the West, they were already victims of their own success. Most nomadic invasions were self-limiting, because pastoral nomads, when migrating or at war, could not at the same time create the military hardware they needed to extend their instant empires or build the necessary administrative infrastructure and skills to rule the lands they conquered. It happened in China, and in the West as well: for nomads, the sequel to conquest was either stability and a softer life, or retreat and dissipation.

So it was with the Huns. They swept like a tidal wave from the ocean of green, the grasslands of Asia, into the Hungarian plain, and broke upon the rocks of several other worlds of forests and cities – Rome; its eastern sister, Constantinople; and a dozen other tribes, all of them manoeuvring in alliance and rivalry. The Huns were the new bullies on the block, and for a time swaggered their way to power. But, like many nomad groups before them, they were increasingly caught in a contradiction, feeding off settled, agricultural peoples, but biting, indeed destroying, the hands that fed them.

The dilemma faced by Attila runs as a recurrent theme through this book. He was the leader of a people on the cusp of change. Their grandparents had been pastoral nomads; they themselves were betwixt and between: part nomad, part settled, unable to return whence they had come, unable to sustain their old way of life. Their sons faced a stark choice: to become partners of, or conquerors of, the greatest military power ever known – Rome – or perish.

His problem was to find a place for the Huns in the world of the collapsing Roman empire. Unless he entirely re-created his people's culture, behaved himself, built cities and joined the western world, his empire would never be secure from the threat of war and possible defeat. That was what his successors, the Hungarians, did, almost 500 years later. It was easier for them, because by then Europe had settled down a bit; but, even so, it took them a century. Attila was not the ruler to make such changes. He was, finally, more robber baron than empire-builder.

He is therefore remembered as our worst nightmare, matched in folk memory only by Genghis Khan. Actually, for Europeans, Attila is by far the worse of the two: Genghis never reached Europe, though his heirs did, and even they got no further west than Attila's homeland; Attila led armies two-thirds of the way across France and well into Italy.

A destroyer he certainly was, but not uniquely so: many leaders of many ages have become robber barons and murderers. They still emerge today – an Amin here, a Saddam there. Their murderous impulses constantly threaten to break through our civilizing constraints, as they did in Nazi Germany, in Rwanda, in the Balkans; and, in lesser ways, in Vietnam, Northern Ireland – any place where hatred of a feared or despised 'other' becomes dominant. This murderous hatred is the force exemplified by Attila in our minds. He is our own dark side, the ogre, Mr Hyde, *Beowulf*'s Grendel waiting to emerge from the swamp of our unconscious and destroy us all. That is the prejudice expressed by the Christian writers who recorded his assault on their world, and the prejudice willingly embraced by most of us ever since.

Fortunately, there is an equal and opposite human impulse: the desire for peace, stability and reconciliation. Attila had this urge, too, employing secretaries to exchange letters in Greek and Latin, sending and receiving ambassadors galore. The Huns had no tradition of diplomacy, yet Attila could play at peace and politics as well as at war.

So, as the lights go on, the shadows fade, and the preconceptions flee. He is not all bogey-man. Indeed, to Hungarians he is a hero. All Hungarians know that their nation was founded by Árpád, who led his Magyar people over the Carpathians in 896. The event is celebrated in every Hungarian schoolbook history. Yet, deep in the Hungarian psyche, there lurks the shrewd suspicion that Árpád was only reclaiming land staked out 450 years before by Attila. This is the foundation myth, as told in the most impressive of medieval Hungarian chronicles. Until recently, Hungarian histories routinely reproduced a pseudo-biblical family tree, according to which Attila begat four generations of descendants, the last of whom begat Árpád – even though this genealogy requires each sire to have produced his heir at the age of 100. Deep down, the Hungarians feel that Attila was a Hungarian at heart, and honour him for it. Attila – the stress in Hungary is on the first syllable, which is rounded until it is almost an O, Ottila – is a common boy's name. The nation's most famous poet of the last century was Attila Jószef (1905–37) – or, rather, Jószef Attila, because the Hungarians put the given name last. Many towns have streets named after Attila or Jószef Attila. To anyone coming from western Europe, it seems distinctly odd, rather like naming sons and streets and squares after Hitler. It is, of course, a question of winner takes all: *our* conquering hero is *your* brutal oppressor, now as always. Now that Mongolia's national hero, for 70 years *persona non grata* under communism, has been rehabilitated, Mongolians name their sons Genghis. Hungarians, who suffered brutally under Mongol troops in 1241, do not.

Attila will never elsewhere enjoy the respect conferred on him in Hungary, but he deserves to be examined in more depth. I can't do this in the usual way of historians, by re-assessing the written evidence, because written evidence is hard to come by. Ammianus Marcellinus, the fourth-century Greek historian from what is now Syria, covered a good deal of the background; Jordanes, an untutored Goth who became a Christian, turned out a rambling history that badly needed editing; Priscus, more a bureaucrat than a historian, left the only account of Attila at home. After these, we have only a few Christian chroniclers, more interested in seeing the ways of God among men than in recording events objectively. From the Huns themselves – nothing. The Huns did not write, and so all the written sources are by outsiders, none of whom spoke Hunnish, few of whom knew the Huns at first hand, and almost all of whom were keen to portray only the worst side of their subject. The best I can do is recruit archaeologists, historians, anthropologists and one notable sportsman to add to the unreliable primary sources. Even so, trying to see Attila is like peering at a filthy old portrait by the light of a few candles.

It is worth trying, nevertheless, because these flickerings reveal new insights and some high drama that help us go beyond myth and cliché. Attila remains an archetype of oppression and pillage, quite rightly, and possessed many of the traits common in today's pseudo-Attilas: he too was devious, ruthless, sometimes charming but never reliable, good at finding yes-men to do his bidding, self-deceptive – and fortunately, in the end, an engineer of his own destruction. But in other ways Attila was one of history's great originals. Never before had such a force sprung upon the West from the world of nomadic horsemen. Never before had there been such a threat from a single leader, let alone one so admired by his own people and so adept at turning enemies into allies; nor would there be another such after him until the rise of the master strategist and empire-builder, Genghis Khan, 750 years later.

In the end, his reach vastly exceeded his grasp. He could never really have taken over the Roman empire. This makes him a failure in the eyes of historians, who tend to see him as no more than a pillager on a vast scale, the most extreme expression of anti-Roman barbarism. But there are other ways of assessing his historical significance. Though the Huns vanished from the earth, their disappearance was like that of gunpowder in a social and political explosion from which Europe's nation-states emerged. It all happened in very slow motion, over centuries, and much of it would have happened anyway; but from the post-Roman mess a new world emerged that bore scarcely a trace of one of the major causes of the bang, except in memory. Something enormous had vanished, the ruins of which were all around; and ever since, people have sought a focal point to simplify, explain and dramatize the cataclysm. Attila fits the bill perfectly, filling several roles at once: a force for historical change; a personality who straddled most of Europe; the ultimate destroyer; a divine scourge of sinful Christians – and always, to some, a hero.

# I

# THE MENACE

# 1

# THE STORM BEFORE THE WHIRLWIND

IN 376 DISTURBING NEWS REACHED THE EMPEROR VALENS IN Constantinople. Valens, co-ruler with his brother of the Roman empire, was familiar enough with troubles on his frontiers, but there had never been anything like this. Far to the north, beyond the Balkans, on the marshy northern banks of the Danube, refugees were gathering by the thousand, destitute and starving, fleeing their farms and villages in terror, rather than face – what? They hardly knew; only that, in the words of the historian Ammianus, 'a hitherto unknown race of men had appeared from some remote corner of the earth, uprooting and destroying everything in its path like a whirlwind descending from high mountains'.

It was an apt image. These aliens were mounted archers who whirled into battle at the gallop, circling in to loose a rain of arrows before veering away to safety. They were horsemen such as no-one had ever seen before, riding as if *nailed* to their horses, *forged* into their saddles – writers struggled to find suitable images – so that man and mount seemed one, like the centaurs of old come to life. They had blown in from the voids of Inner Asia, driving the residents ahead of them like cattle. It would take some years for the 'unknown race' to appear en masse, under their most effective and devastating leader, but already their eruption across the steppes of today's southern Russia and Ukraine had shunted tribe against tribe, the last of which now clamoured on the Danube's banks. Something had to give.

Valens' immediate concern was not the thud of alien hooves but the horde of refugees. They were Goths, members of a huge Germanic tribe that had wandered into eastern Europe and southern Russia two centuries before, and had now divided into western and eastern branches. These first refugees were western Goths, known as the Visi- ('wise') Goths, as opposed to the Ostro- ('Eastern') Goths, who, as Valens would soon discover, were hard on the heels of their distant kin.

Valens, approaching 50 and with twelve years of ruling behind him, knew a good deal about the proud and inde- pendent Visigoths, and had reason to be wary of them and their leader Athanaric. Wanderers no more, they had settled in what is now Romania and turned themselves from nomads into farmers, from marauders into disciplined foes. Thirty years before, they had supposedly become allies of the empire, having been bribed into supplying soldiers for the armies of Rome and Constantinople. But they would not stay put, and ten years ago Valens himself had gone to war with the intention of penning them into their homeland. Things hadn't gone to plan. The Goths could be broken in battle, but they had the annoying habit of holing up in the mountains of Transylvania, and as guerrillas they were unbeatable. Three years into the war, Valens – bow-legged, paunchy, with a lazy eye – needed to bolster his shaky authority with a show of dominance. But Athanaric said he had sworn a terrible oath to his father never to set foot on Roman soil; so, instead of summoning his opponent to discuss terms, Valens had to talk peace on a boat in the middle of the Danube, as if emperor and barbarian leader were equals. They agreed that good fences made good neighbours, that the Danube was the natural fence, and that neither side would cross it.

What a difference seven years made. Here were the Visigoths, down and out, about to ignore the terms of the treaty by invading not as warriors but as a whole nation of asylum-seekers: families, children, sick and aged, by the wagonload. What if Valens took a hard line, forced the refugees to stay where they were and revelled in Athanaric's despair? It could not be that simple, because this was not Athanaric's doing. Rumour of the alien menace had inspired rebellion among the threatened Visigoths, and Athanaric was no longer a force. It was a new leader, Fritigern, who was now begging for imperial permission to cross the rain-swollen Danube, dreaming of a new life for his people in the welcoming and fertile valleys of Thrace.

The chances were they would come anyway; so Valens judged it best to turn the crisis to some advantage. Fritigern, smart enough to unite his desperate people and keep on the right side of Rome, made no threats; indeed, he promised not only to live peacefully, but also to supply more men for the imperial army. Both rulers knew there was a precedent: years before, a previous colony of Goths had been allowed to travel 150 miles south of the Danube to settle in Adrianople, today's Edirne, and had proved exemplary citizens. Advisers urged Valens to see his former foes not as refugees but as recruits for the emperor's overstretched army. Valens agreed, provided the Goths gave up their arms. Officials journeyed north, not to oppose, but to help, with transport, food and allocations of land in the frontier provinces.

So as the spring of 376 turned to summer the destitute Visigoths came plodding over the low-lying northern banks, past shallow lakes and marshes, taking to the river in boats and dug-out canoes hastily made from tree-trunks, hauling rafts bearing their wagons and horses. Here the river, clear of the Iron Gate gorge that cuts through the Carpathian and Balkan mountains, runs broad and gentle for 400 kilometres before splitting up into its reedy delta. The challenge for the refugees was not the strength of the current, but the rain-swollen breadth of water, 2 or 3 kilometres across. Many, drawn by the sight of the low hills opposite, tried swimming, only to be carried slowly downriver to their deaths in the flood plain.

How many were on the move? The imperial officials wanted to know to calculate food supplies and land grants. It was hopeless. Ammianus quoted Virgil:

> To try to find their number is as vain
> As numbering the wind-swept Libyan sands.

Perhaps they did not try very hard. The commanding officers were not the empire's finest. Flawed, sinister and reckless, according to Ammianus, they hatched schemes to profit from the unarmed refugees. One scam involved rounding up dogs, which they offered as food if in return they received one Visigoth as a slave: hardly treatment to inspire lasting friendship.

Besides, this was no promised land. So many people all at once would have overwhelmed the Thracian countryside. They had to be kept where they were. The southern banks of the Danube turned into a vast holding camp for the be-draggled and tunic-clad refugees. To the Visigoths, it seemed that they had fled one frying-pan only to land in another. They muttered about taking direct action to seize the lands they thought they had been promised. The flawed, sinister and reckless regional commander, Lupicinus, ordered up more troops from Gaul to quell disorder.

But time was running out. The Visigoths' eastern cousins, crowds of Ostrogoths also fleeing the unnamed menace to the east, arrived at the Danube, saw it weakly held, and crossed, without waiting for permission. Pushed and reinforced by the new influx, Fritigern led his own people 100 kilometres south, to the local provincial capital, Marcianople (the ruins of which lie half-exposed near Devnya, 25 kilometres inland from the Bulgarian Black Sea resort of Varna). There Lupicinus, whose every act seemed to lead to disaster, invited the Visigothic leaders to a lavish dinner, ostensibly to discuss an aid package, while outside the walls the mass of their people, kept at bay by several thousand Roman soldiers, seethed with rumour and resentment. Suspecting their chief had been lured to his downfall, the Visigoths attacked a contingent of Romans and seized their weapons. When news of this foray reached the dinner table, Lupicinus had some of Fritigern's attendants killed in revenge, and probably had plans to kill them all. But that would have been suicidal. The rioters were now an army. Fritigern had the presence of mind to point out that the only way to restore peace was for him to return to his people, sound, healthy and free. Lupicinus saw he had no choice, and released his guest – who at once, as Ammianus says, 'took horse and hurried away to kindle the flame of war'.

Across Lower Moesia – northern Bulgaria today – outraged Visigoths robbed, burned and looted, seizing yet more weapons. A pitched battle ended with more Romans dead, more arms seized, and Lupicinus cowering in the sacked streets of Marcianople. The empire had overcome similar disasters, as Ammianus recalls – but that was before the old spirit of high morals and self-sacrifice had been undermined by a craving for ostentatious banquets and ill-gotten gain.

And, he might have added, sheer stupidity: for Valens, afraid that Goth would side with Goth, ordered the long-established and peaceful Visigothic colony in Adrianople to leave, at once. Adrianople, dominating the main pass out of the Balkan mountains on the way to Constantinople, was not a city to risk. He intended to secure the place, and achieved the exact opposite. When the Goths asked for a two-day delay to pack, the local commander refused, encouraging locals to drive them out by pelting them with stones. At this the colonists lost their tempers, killed a number of their oppressors and, quitting the city, threw themselves into the arms of their fellow Goths.

In the autumn of 377 the rival armies reached stalemate, with the main force of Goths seeking safety in the steep valleys of the Balkan range and the Romans in the parched grasslands of Dobruja, which today backs the Black Sea coast of Romania and Bulgaria. The Goths continued to pillage – the only course open to homeless refugees with families to feed – then broke through the Roman blockade to loot their way south into present-day Turkey. Ammianus paints a scene of anarchy anticipating future Balkan horrors: babies killed at their mothers' breasts, women raped, 'men led into bondage, crying out that they had lived too long and weeping over the ashes of their homes'.

What, meanwhile, were the prospects for reinforcement? Not good. Though the empire had perhaps 500,000 men under arms, half of these were frontier garrisons watching for trouble in the *barbaricum*, while only half formed mobile field armies. Besides, many of the troops were non-Roman mercenaries, and any order to move inspired desertions. Troops could come only from the Gaulish frontier, under the command of Valens' young nephew Gratian, who had been co-ruler and emperor of the West for the last two years. Still only eighteen, he had a growing reputation as a leader, but it was all he could do to keep the peace along the Rhine and the Danube. The plan to shift troops from Gaul to the Balkans leaked across the frontier, inspiring German raids that demanded Gratian's attention all that winter. It was not until early 378 that he set out to aid his uncle.

If at this point you had asked a Roman or a Greek what was at stake, you would have been told that two worlds stood face to face: the barbarian and the civilized. In fact, in western, central and southern Europe, we are dealing with many worlds. The empire of Rome, Gaul and Constantinople; barbarian tribes fighting each other and the empire; and the untamed forested borderlands of the north-east.

To its citizens, the Roman domain was their world, their foundation, their pride, their very life. As republic and then as empire, it had been there for over 700 years, as we know from archaeological research – even longer for Romans, whose history was rooted in legendary beginnings: for them AD 377 was 1130 AUC, *ab urbe condita*, 'from the foundation of the city'. Rome's cultural roots were deeper still, for it was the heir of ancient Greece. It was Rome's manifest destiny, as the rock of civilization and good government, to rule the shores of the Mediterranean, to reach southwards down the Nile and northwards across the Alps, to Gaul, the Rhine, the North Sea and beyond, even to the remote northern reaches of the islands off Europe's coast, where Hadrian finished building his rampart against the highland barbarians in 127. In the third century there had even been a brief advance across the Danube, into present-day Romania, when it seemed for a while that the true frontier in eastern Europe would be the Carpathians.

But expansion had its limits, dictated by non-Roman peoples and by geography. The north-east had a formidable barrier of forest. *The Forest*. To feel the trepidation inspired by the word demands an imaginative leap back to a time when much of Europe beyond the Rhine was still an untamed landscape, its vast, dark woodlands hardly touched. For non-forest people, it was the epitome of danger, the grim and forbidding abode of evil spirits. To Romans, the Ciminian forests of Etruria were bad enough; but those north of the Alps were the very essence of barbarism. In AD 98 Tacitus painted a picture of the landscape in his *Germania*. Beyond the Rhine, he says, the land was *informis* – unshaped, hideous, dismal: the word has all these senses. The Hercynian forest, named after an ancient Greek term for the forest of Bohemia in today's Czech Republic, was by extension the tree-covered region that stretched from the Rhine to the Elbe. Pliny claimed that its huge oaks had never been cut or lopped since the world began. People said it took 9 days to cross north to south, and 60 days for the 500-kilometre east–west journey – not that, in the words of Julius Caesar, 'anyone in Germany can say that he has heard about the end of this forest'. Here lived beasts unknown elsewhere, some dangerous – elk with horns like tree-boughs, brown bear, wolf and aurochs, the European bison. Rome and Greece looked back to legends of Arcadian groves, recalling a time when even Greece was forested; but not to anything so uncharming and impenetrable as this.

To Romans, the inhabitants of this wilderness were them-selves wild, men descended from a primal deity, Tuisto, who had sprung from the soil like a tree. They wore cloaks pinned with thorns and lived on wild game, fruit and milk products. In all this huge area there was, they said, not a single town. Villages, linked by tracks, were of mean wooden houses. The picture was not all bad, of course. Tacitus was eager to point out that, in contrast to the sturdy simplicity of the forest peoples, Rome had become soft and corrupt. It was best, though, for civilized folk to steer clear; those who dared to probe risked a terrible fate. In AD 9, Publius Quintillius Varus had led 25,000 men into the Teutoburg forest, in north Germany somewhere between the Rhine and the Weser, where they were ambushed and slaughtered by Cheruscan spearmen materializing from among the swamps and trees. Varus saw the devastation and fell on his sword.

Of course, things had moved on in 300 years. The clan warriors of Tacitus' day, typified by the image of a hot-blooded, blond, beer-swilling giant, had long since vanished or amalgamated into larger units, the Saxons, Franks and Alemanni from which future nations would arise. Already the forests were patched by the clearings and farms of a dozen tribes; but, by comparison with today, they remained largely intact. This was the primeval world of magic and power, the source of life and death, the habitation of prey and predator, where children were lost and witches found and spirits in-habited trees. It is recalled in 'Little Red Riding Hood' and 'Hansel and Gretel' and the other fairy tales collected by the Grimm brothers in the nineteenth century, and later still in the Mirkwood of Tolkien's *Lord of the Rings*.

If the forest dictated the outermost limits of empire, the retreat from beyond the Danube had marked the beginning of its collapse. By the late fourth century, there were no thoughts of retaking trans-Danubian Dacia and of conquering the German forests. Soon Britain would be abandoned, Hadrian's frontier wall left an empty monument to former greatness. Once all had been governed from Rome, by the emperor and the Senate. Now the Senate was a husk and real power was wielded by the army, while the emperor did his best from some campaign HQ, or from his residences in Trèves and Milan and Ravenna.

The real cancer in this vast body was the emerging problem of division. When Constantine founded his 'New Rome' in

330, it was to have been the heart of his new religion, Christianity, and the symbol of a new unity. In fact, from then on the Latin-speaking western empire began to part company with its Greek-speaking (though frequently bilingual) eastern wing. Rome's decline was mirrored by Constantinople's rise.

Constantine chose well when he decided to develop a small, ancient town on a rocky peninsula in the Black Sea into his new version of Rome. It was said, of course, that God had guided him, though it didn't take omniscience to see that the peninsula was a much better base than Rome from which to secure the empire's shaky eastern frontier. The little town of old Byzantium had occupied the tip of this rocky nose. Constantine enclosed five times that area behind a wall 2 kilometres long, and built into his new capital a triumphal arch, the first great Christian church and a marble-paved forum, its 30-metre porphyry column from Egypt topped by an Apollo with the head of Constantine himself. A hippodrome for processions and races was connected via a spiral staircase to the reception halls, offices, living areas, baths and barracks of the imperial palace. Within a century there would be a school, a circus, 2 theatres, 8 public and 153 private baths, 52 porticoes, 5 granaries, 8 aqueducts and reservoirs, 4 senatorial and judicial meeting halls, 14 churches, 14 palaces and 4,388 houses in addition to those of the common people. By then there were walls almost all around it, seaward as well, except along the Golden Horn river, which was protected by an immense chain (it was broken only once, in 1203, by soldiers of the Fourth Crusade, who loaded a ship with stones, fixed a huge pair of shears on the prow, drove at the chain and snipped it).

The beauty of the city and the speed of its construction made Constantine's capital a glory. But within a generation it had achieved the opposite of what its founder intended: not unity but division, confirmed by the emperor Valentinian. He was an impressive character – champion wrestler, great soldier, energetic, conscientious in defence of the realm; and he decided the interests of the empire would be best served by the creation of two sub-empires, each of which could look to its own defence. In 364 he made his brother Valens the first eastern emperor, while he, Valentinian, kept control of the West. It might have worked, had the threats to unity been containable. They were not. The empire, though still nominally united by history and family, had begun to split: two capitals, two worlds, two languages and two creeds (each fighting its own sub-creeds of paganism and heresy).

This was no firm foundation for confronting enemies within and without. To the east lay the great imperial rival, Persia; in Africa, Moorish rebels; and right across northern Europe and the frontiers of Inner Asia the *barbaricum*, inhabited by those who spoke neither Greek nor Latin. With continual barbarian incursions across the Rhine and Danube, Rome – the term sometimes included Constantinople and sometimes didn't, depending on the context – tried to defend itself with a range of strategies from outright force to negotiation, bribery, intermarriage, trade and, finally, controlled immigration. This last was in the end the only possible way to stave off assault, and yet it also led inexorably to further decay. Barbarians were good fighters; it made sense to employ them, with confusing consequences for both sides. Enemies became allies, who often ended up fighting their own kin. Peace came always at the price of continued collapse: the army was strengthened by an influx of barbarians, but taxes rose to pay for them; faith in government declined, and corruption spread. By the late fourth century the empire's borders resembled a weakening immune system, through which barbarians crept, in direct assault or temporary partnership, while the army – the ultimate arbiter of political authority and the guardian of the frontiers – were like the blood platelets of this ageing body, always rushing to clot some new wound, and never in sufficient numbers.

Not all the empire's enemies were on or beyond its borders. Since Constantine's decision to adopt Christianity earlier in the century, his new capital had been the heart of division over and above the usual political squabbles about succession. Christians naturally fought against paganism, which proved remarkably resilient. In addition, Christians squabbled with each other, for these were the early days of church doctrine, with rivals arguing fiercely over the nature of a god who was somehow three-in-one, and somehow both human and divine. No-one could understand these mysteries, but that didn't stop rival believers stating firm opinions, fighting for some new orthodoxy, and branding their opponents unorthodox and heretical.

The most challenging heresy was named after the Alexandrian priest Arius, who claimed that Jesus was wholly human – God's adopted son, as it were – and thus by implication not divine, and therefore inferior to his father. This idea appealed to eastern emperors, notably Valens, perhaps because it did not appeal to the western ones. It was in this form that Christianity first reached the Goths, whose converts became stubbornly Arian.

This, then, was the glorious, vast and diseased structure that Valens was once again preparing to defend as he marched north from Constantinople in the early summer of 378, planning to join up with his co-emperor and rival, his ambitious nephew Gratian.

Now Valens' battered ego took the reins. He, who had demanded Gratian's help, had become jealous of his nephew's success, and eager for a victory of his own. Marching north to Adrianople in July, he was told by his scouts that a Goth army was approaching, but that it consisted of only 10,000 men, a force rather less than his own of some 15,000. Outside Adrianople, he made his base near the junction of the Maritsa and Tundzha rivers, around which over the next few days arose a palisade and a ditch. Just then an officer arrived from somewhere up the Danube with a letter from Gratian urging his uncle not to do anything hasty until the reinforcements arrived. Valens called a war council. Some agreed with Gratian, while others whispered that Gratian just wanted to share in a triumph that should belong to Valens alone. That suited Valens. Preparations continued.

Fritigern, laagered in his wagons some 13 kilometres away up the Tundzha, was himself wary of giving battle. Around him were not just his warriors, but their entire households as well: perhaps 30,000 people, with an unwieldy corps of wagons, all arranged in family circles, impossible to re-form in less than a day. To fight effectively – away from the en-cumbering wagons – he would need help; and so he had sent for the heavily armoured Ostrogothic cavalry. Meanwhile he played for time, sending out scouts to set fire to the sun-scorched wheat fields between his encampment and the Romans' – and a messenger, who arrived in the imperial camp with a letter: yes, 'barbarian' leaders were quite capable of using secretaries fluent in Latin to communicate with the Roman world. This missive was carried by a Christian priest, who would probably have become an aide to the Visigoth in the hope of converting him. The letter was an official plea to revert to the status quo: peace, in return for land and protection from the whirlwind approaching from the east.

Valens would have none of it. He wanted the fruits of victory: Fritigern captured or dead, the Goths cowed. He refused to reply, sending the priest away on the insulting grounds that he was not important enough to be taken seriously.

Next morning, 9 August, the Romans were ready. All

non-essential gear – spare tents, treasure chests, imperial robes – was sent back into Adrianople for safety, and the horsemen and infantry set off to cover the 13 kilometres to the Visigothic laagers. It was a short march, but a gruelling one, over burned fields, under a scorching sun, with no streams in sight to refresh the heavily armoured troops.

After a couple of hours the Roman horsemen and infantry approached the Visigothic camp and its huddles of wagons, from which rose wild war cries and chants in praise of Gothic ancestors. The sweaty approach had caused the Romans to straggle, with one wing of the cavalry out in front and infantry behind blocking the way of the second. Slowly they pulled themselves into line, clattering their weapons and beating their shields to drown out the barbarians' clamour.

To Fritigern, still awaiting help, these were unnerving sights and sounds. Again, he played for time, sending a request for peace; again, Valens sent the envoys away as of too low a rank. Still no sign of the Ostrogothic cavalry. Time for another message from Fritigern, another peace proposal, raising the stakes, suggesting that if Valens would supply someone of high status he would himself come to negotiate. This time Valens agreed, and a suitable volunteer was on his way when a band of Roman outriders, hungry for glory, perhaps, made a quick lunge at the Visigothic flank. The volunteer diplomat beat a hasty retreat – just in time, for at that moment the Ostrogothic cavalry came galloping in along the valley. The Roman cavalry moved forward to confront this new menace.

That was what Fritigern had been waiting for. His infantry burst from the wagons, firing arrows, throwing spears, until the two lines clashed and locked in a heaving scrum of shields, broken spears and swords, so tightly packed that soldiers could hardly lift their arms to strike – or, having done so, lower them again. Dust rose, covering the battle-ground in a choking, blinding fog. Outside the mêlée, there was no need for the Visigothic archers and spearmen to aim: any missile thrown or fired at random dropped through the dust unseen, and had to find a mark.

Then came the heavy cavalry, with no opposing Roman cavalry to stop them, trampling the dying, their battle-axes splitting the helmets and breastplates of infantrymen weakened by heat, weighed down with armour and slipping on the blood-soaked ground. Within the hour, the living began to stumble away from the Roman lines over the corpses of the slain. 'Some fell without knowing who struck them,' writes Ammianus. 'Some were crushed by sheer weight of numbers, some were killed by their own comrades.'

As the sun set, the noise of battle died away into the silent, moonless night. Two-thirds of the Romans – perhaps 10,000 men – lay dead, jumbled with corpses of horses. Now the dark fields filled with other sounds, as the cries, sobs and groans of the wounded followed the survivors across the burnt-out crops and along the road back to Adrianople.

No-one knows what happened to Valens. At some time during the battle he had been lost or abandoned by his body-guard and found his way to the army's most disciplined and experienced legions, holding out in a last stand. A general rode off to call in some reserves, only to find they had fled. After that, nothing. Some said the emperor died when struck by an arrow soon after night fell. Or perhaps he found refuge in a sturdy farmhouse nearby, which was surrounded and burned to the ground, along with all those inside – except one man who escaped from a window to tell what had happened. Thus the story came to Ammianus. There was no way of proving it, for the emperor's body was never found.

The violence continued, and the empire had no answer to it. The Visigoths knew from deserters and prisoners what was hidden in Adrianople. At dawn they advanced beyond the battlefield, hot on the heels of the survivors seeking refuge. But there was no safety to be had; for the defenders, scrabbling to prepare for a siege they never expected, fearful of weakening their defences, refused to open the gates to their fleeing fellows. By midday the Visigoths had encircled the walls, trapping the terrified survivors against them. In desperation, some 300 surrendered, only to be slaughtered on the spot.

Luckily for the city, a thunderstorm washed out the assault, forcing the Visigoths back to their wagons and allowing the defenders to shore up the gates with rocks and make ready their trebuchets and siege bows. When the Visigoths attacked the next day, they lost hundreds crushed by rocks, impaled by arrows the size of spears and buried under stones tipped from above.

Giving up the assault, they turned to easier targets in the countryside, looting their way across 200 kilometres to the very gates of Constantinople. There the rampage died, killed by the sight of the vast walls, and then by a horrifying incident. As the city mounted its defence, a Saracen contingent suddenly erupted from the gates. One of these fearsome warriors, carrying a sword and wearing nothing but a loincloth, hurled himself into the fray, sliced open a Gothic soldier's throat, seized the corpse and sucked the streaming blood. It was enough to drain what remained of the Goths' courage and force a retreat northwards.

The war dragged on for four more years, ending in a treaty that gave the Goths almost exactly what had been agreed in the first place: land just south of the Danube and semi-independence, with their soldiers fighting for Rome under their own leaders. It would not last, for the Goths were a nation on the move, the greatest of the many barbarian migrations that would undermine the empire. A Visigoth who fought at Adrianople could have lived through another revolt, a slow advance deeper into the empire, the brief seizure of Rome itself in 410, a march over the Pyrenees and a final return over the same mountains to find peace at last in south-west France.

And all this chaos – the refugee crisis, the rebellion, the disaster of Adrianople, the attack on Constantinople, the impossible peace, the slow erosion by barbarians – had been unleashed by the 'unknown race' to the east. Still no-one in the empire or even the nearer reaches of the *barbaricum* knew anything of them.

Perhaps they should have done. For, as Ammianus mentions in passing, among the cavalry that had come to Fritigern's rescue was a contingent of these lightly armed horse-archers, no more than a few hundred, probably operating as outriders for the main Goth force. It was their arrival the previous year that had forced the Romans to withdraw, allowing the Goths to break through into Thrace. No doubt they had been doing very nicely as freebooters and spies, harassing enemy flanks. If they had been in the battle outside Adrianople, no-one would have taken much notice of these few coarse creatures with their minimal armour; but they were seen afterwards, during the looting. Then they vanished, for few cities had fallen and the pickings would have been meagre. They left, however, with another sort of treasure: information. They had seen what the West had to offer. They had witnessed Rome's worst day since the defeat by Hannibal at Cannae 160 years before. They might even have guessed that Rome would in future rely more on heavy cavalry, which, as they knew, was no match for their own type of warfare. They had seen Rome's wider problems: the difficulty of securing a leaky frontier, the impossibility of gathering and moving large armies to fight fast-moving guerrillas, the arrogance of the 'civilized' when confronting the 'barbarian'. While the whole Balkan sector of the empire collapsed into rioting, these swift mounted archers galloped back northwards and eastwards with their few stolen items, and their vital intelligence: *the empire was rich, and the empire was vulnerable.*

These lightly armed, fast-moving horsemen were the first Huns to reach central Europe. It was their relatives who had unleashed the whirlwind that had blown the Goths across the Danube. Shortly, under the most ruthless of their leaders, they too would cross the river, with consequences for the decaying empire far in excess of anything wrought by the Goths.

# 2

# OUT OF ASIA

NO-ONE KNEW WHERE ATTILA'S PEOPLE CAME FROM. PEOPLE SAID they had once lived somewhere beyond the edge of the known world, east of the Maeotic marshes – the shallow and silty Sea of Azov – the other side of the Kerch straits that links this inland sea to its parent, the Black Sea. Why and when had they come there? Why and when did they start their march to the west? All was a blank, filled by folklore.

Once upon a time, Goth and Hun were neighbours, divided by the Kerch straits. Since they lived either side of the straits, the Goths in Crimea on the western side, the Huns over the way on the flat lands north of the Caucasus mountains, they were unaware of each other. One day a Hun heifer, stung by a gadfly, fled through the marshy waters across the straits. A cowherd, in pursuit across the marshes, found land, returned, and told the rest of the tribe, which promptly went on the warpath westward. It is a story that explains nothing, for many tribes and cultures depicted their origins in terms of an animal guide. A suspiciously similar tale had long been told of Io, a priestess changed into a heifer by her lover Zeus. Io, as heifer, was driven out of Inner Asia by a gadfly sting, crossing these very straits, swimming over seas, via Greece, where the Ionian islands were named after her, until she arrived at last in Egypt; and it was as a bull that Zeus carried Io's descendant Europa off to establish civilization in the continent named after her. So such tales about the Huns satisfied no-one. To fill the gap, western writers came up with a dozen equally wild speculations. The Huns were sent by God as a punishment. They had fought with Achilles in the Trojan war. They were any of the Asian tribes named by ancient authors, 'Scythian' being the most popular option, since the epithet was widely applied to any barbarian tribe. The fact is that no-one knew – but no-one liked to admit his ignorance. It was important, too, for authors to show off their knowledge of the classics, for, as every literate person knew, it was literature that marked the civilized from the barbarian. If as a Roman you mentioned Scythians or Massegetae, at least you knew your Herodotus, even if the Huns were a blank.

The Huns' tribal victims were no better informed. According to the Gothic historian Jordanes, a Gothic king had discovered some witches, whom he expelled into the depths of Asia. There they mated with evil spirits, producing a 'stunted, foul and puny tribe, scarcely human and having no language save one which bore but slight resemblance to human speech'. They started on their rampage when huntsmen pursued a doe (no heifer, gadfly or cowherd in this version) across the Straits of Kerch, and thus came upon the unfortunate Goths.

Academics don't like holes like this, and come the Enlightenment a French Sinologist, Joseph de Guignes, tried to fill it. De Guignes – as he is in most catalogues; or Deguines, as he himself spelled his name – is a name that usually appears in academic footnotes, if anywhere. He deserves more, because his theory about Hun origins has been a matter of controversy ever since. At present, it's making a comeback. It may even be true.

Born in 1721, de Guignes was still in his twenties when he was appointed 'interpreter' for oriental languages at the Royal Library in Paris, Chinese being his particular forte. He at once embarked upon the monumental work that made his name. News of this brilliant young polymath spread across the Channel. In 1751, at the age of 29, he was elected to the Royal Society in London – one of the youngest members ever, and a foreigner to boot. He owed this honour to a draft displaying, as the citation remarks, 'everything that one might expect from a book so considerable, which he has ready for the press'. Well, not quite. It took him another five years to get his work on the press, and a further two to get it off; his *Histoire générale des Huns, des Turcs et des Mogols* was published in five volumes between 1756 and 1758. The gentlemen of the Royal Society would have forgiven the delay, for de Guignes seemed about to emerge as a shining example of the Enlightenment scholar. He should have become a major contributor to the cross-Channel exchange of knowledge and criticism that led to the translation of Ephraim Chambers' *Cyclopedia* in the 1740s and its extension under the editorship of Denis Diderot into the great *Encyclopédie*, the first volume of which was published in the year of de Guignes' election to the Royal Society. In fact, de Guignes never escaped the confines of his library, never matched the critical spirit of his contemporaries. His big idea was to prove that all eastern peoples – Chinese, Turks, Mongols, Huns – were actually descendants of Noah, who had wandered eastwards after the Flood. This became an obsession, and the subject of his next book, which sparked a sharp riposte from sceptics, followed by an anti-riposte from the impervious de Guignes.

He remained impervious up to his death almost 50 years later. His history was never translated into English.

But one aspect of his theory took root, and flourished. Attila's Huns, he said, were descendants of the tribe variously known as the 'Hiong-nou' or Hsiung-Nu, now spelled Xiongnu, a non-Chinese tribe, probably of Turkish stock. After unrecorded centuries of small-time raiding, these people founded a nomadic empire based in what is now Mongolia in 209 BC (long before the Mongols came on the scene). He does not argue his case, simply stating as a fact that the 'Hiong-nou' were the Huns, period. 'First Book,' he starts: 'History of the Ancient Huns.' At one unproven stroke, he had vastly extended the range of his subject by several centuries and several thousand kilometres.

It was an attractive theory, because something at least was known about these people in the eighteenth century, to which a good deal more has since been added; so much, indeed, that it is worth looking more deeply at the Xiongnu to see what the Huns may have lacked and may have wished to regain as they trekked westward to a new source of wealth.

The Xiongnu were the first tribe to build an empire beyond China's Inner Asian frontier, the first to exploit on a grand scale a way of life that was relatively new in human history. For 90 per cent of our 100,000 years as true humans, we have been hunter-gatherers, organizing our existence around seasonal variations in the environment, following the move-ments of animals and the natural flourishing of plants. Then, about 10,000 years ago, the last great ice sheets withdrew and social life began to change, relatively rapidly, giving rise to two new systems. One was agriculture, from which cascaded the attributes that came to define today's world – population growth, wealth, leisure, cities, art, literature, industry, large-scale war, government: most of the things that static, urban societies equate with civilization. But agriculture also provided tractable domestic animals, with which non-farmers could develop another lifestyle entirely, one of wandering herders – pastoral nomadism, as it is called. For these herders a new world beckoned: the sea of grass, or steppe, which spans Eurasia for over 6,000 kilometres from Manchuria to Hungary. Herders had to learn how best to use the pastures, guiding camels and sheep away from wetter areas, seeking limey soils for horses, making sure that cattle and horses got to long grass before sheep and goats, which nibble down to the roots.

The key to the wealth of the grasslands was the horse, tamed and bred in the course of 1,000 years to create a new sub-species – a stocky, shaggy, tough and tractable animal that became invaluable for transport, herding, hunting and warfare. Herdsmen were now free to roam the grasslands and exploit them by raising other domestic animals – sheep, goats, camels, cattle, yaks. From them came meat, hair, skins, dung for fuel, felt for clothing and tents, and 150 different types of milk product, including the herdsman's main drink, a mildly fermented mare's-milk beer. On this foundation, pastoral nomads could in theory live their self-contained and self-reliant lives indefinitely, not wandering randomly, as outsiders sometimes think, but exploiting familiar pastures season by season.

Pastoral nomads were also warriors, armed with a formidable weapon. The composite recurved bow, similar in design across all Eurasia, ranks with the Roman sword and the machine-gun as a weapon that changed the world. The steppe-dwellers had all the necessary elements – horn, wood, sinew, glue – to hand (though they sometimes made bows entirely of horn), and over time they learned how to combine them for optimum effectiveness. Into a wooden base the maker would splice horn, which resists compression, and

forms the bow's inside face. Sinews resist extension, and are
laid along the outside. The three elements are welded together
with glue boiled from tendons or fish. This quick recipe gives
no hint of the skills needed to make a good bow. It takes years
to master the materials, the widths, the lengths, the
thicknesses, the taperings, the temperatures, the time to set
the shape, the countless minor adjustments. When this
expertise is applied correctly with skill and patience – it takes
a year or more to make a composite bow – the result is an
object of remarkable qualities.

When forced out of its reverse curve and strung, a powerful bow stores astonishing energy. The earliest known
Mongol inscription, dated 1225, records that a nephew of
Genghis Khan shot at a target of some unspecified kind and
hit it at a distance of some 500 metres; and, with modern
materials and specially designed carbon arrows, today's hand-
held composite bows fire almost three-quarters of a mile.
Over that kind of distance, of course, an arrow on a high,
curving flight loses much of its force. At close range, say
50–100 metres, the right kind of arrowhead despatched from
a 'heavy' bow can outperform many types of bullet in
penetrative power, slamming through half an inch of wood or
an iron breastplate.

Arrowheads had their own sub-technology. Bone served
well enough for hunting, but warfare demanded points of
metal – bronze or iron – with two or three fins, which would
slot onto the arrow. The method for mass-producing socketed
bronze arrowheads from reusable stone moulds was probably
invented in the steppes around 1000 BC, making it possible
for a rider to carry dozens of standard-sized arrows with a
range of metal heads. To produce metal arrowheads pastoral
nomadic groups had metallurgists, who knew how to smelt
iron from rock, and smiths with the tools and skills to cast
and forge: both specialists who would work best from fixed

bases and who, during migration, needed wagons to transport their equipment.

Thus, towards the end of the first millennium BC, steppeland pastoral nomadism was evolving into a sophisticated new way of life, supporting herders, some of whom doubled as artisans – carpenters and weavers as well as smiths – and most of whom, women included, doubled as fighters. As opposed to the static, agricultural societies south and east of the great deserts of Central Asia, these were people committed to mobility. Expertise with horses, pastures, animals, bows and metallurgy threw up leaders of a new type who could control the flow of animals and access to the best pastures, and thus marshal the resources for conquest. As their steppeland economies flourished, these leaders welded together intertribal alliances, armies and, finally, from about 300 BC, several empires. But this evolution produced a different type of society. Empires gather wealth and have to be administered. They need headquarters – a capital – and other smaller towns, all forming an urbanized stratum on top of traditional nomadic roots. Among these empires, the first and possibly the greatest before the rise of the Mongol empire was that of the Xiongnu.

The Xiongnu originally lived in the great northern loop of the Yellow River, in the area known today as the Ordos, in the Chinese province of Inner Mongolia. They might have been little more than one of the many troublesome but transitory barbarian kingdoms that rose and fell in Inner Asia, had it not been for a peculiarly ruthless proto-Attila named Motun (also spelled Modun or Mao-dun), whose rise in 209 BC was recorded by the first major Chinese historian, Ssu-ma Ch'ien. Motun had been given as a hostage to a neighbouring tribe by his father, Tumen (a name, incidentally, that in Mongol means 'ten thousand', in particular a unit of

The Huns' Distant Roots

- - - - - Motun's empire, 174 BC

Area of inset

Urals

Huns

S t e p p e

? ? ?

Lake
Baikal

Noyan Uul    Xiongnu
Heartland
1st century BC

Xiongnu emigration after 89 AD

G o b i

Tien Shan

CHINA

R. Dniester

R. Danube

Carpathian Mountains

R. Tisza

390
Hungarian
Plain

Pannonia

Visigoths

Ravenna

Balkan
Mountains

Marcianople

378

Rome

Adrianople    Thrace
Constantinople

Visigoths
396-8

R o m a n    E m p i r e

Mediterranean    Sea

Western Empire    Eastern Empire

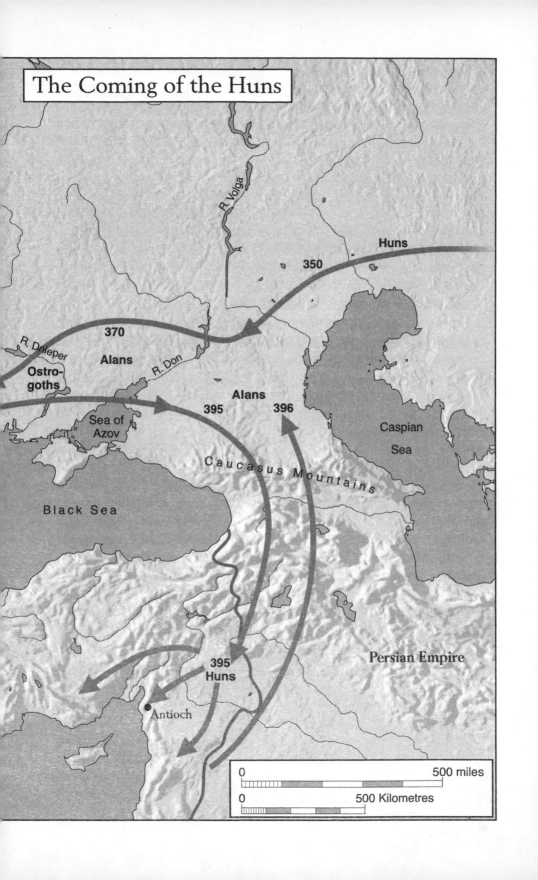

# The Coming of the Huns

R. Volga

Huns

350

370

R. Dnieper

Alans

Ostro-
goths

R. Don

Alans

395

Alans

396

Sea of
Azov

Caspian
Sea

Caucasus Mountains

Black Sea

Persian Empire

395
Huns

Antioch

0                                    500 miles

0                          500 Kilometres

10,000 soldiers: apparently the Xiongnu spoke some sort of proto-Mongol-Turkish, before the two languages began to evolve separately). Ssu-ma Ch'ien, writing in the following century, tells the story of what happened next, slipping out of his usual staid style and drawing, perhaps, on some Xiongnu foundation epic sung by bards to explain their nation's rise. Tumen favoured another heir and wished Motun dead. He therefore attacked his neighbours, expecting that Motun would be killed. But the prince staged a dramatic escape, stealing a horse to gallop back to his father, who greeted him with forced smiles and the gift of his own troops, as befitted his status. This was Motun's chance to take his revenge on his father. Planning to make every one of his men guilty of regicide, he drilled them into total obedience. 'Shoot wherever you see my whistling arrow strike!' he ordered. 'Anyone who fails to shoot will be cut down!' Then he took his band hunting. Every animal he aimed at became a target for his men. Then he aimed at one of his best horses. The horse died in a hail of arrows; but some had hesitated, and they were executed. Next he took aim at his favourite wife. She died, and so did those who wavered. Then Motun shot at one of his father's finest horses. More arrows, another death, and this time no waverers. Now Motun knew all his men could be trusted. Finally, 'on a hunting expedition, he shot a whistling arrow at his father and every one of his followers aimed their arrows in the same direction and shot the chief dead', filling him so full of arrows that there was no room for another. Next in line was a neighbouring ruler, whose skull became Motun's goblet, the usual symbol of power for nomadic rulers.

Now the Xiongnu had a solid base on which to build a steppe empire that eventually reached 1,000 kilometres north to Lake Baikal and almost 4,000 kilometres westward to the Aral Sea. Furs came from Siberia, metals for arrowheads and scaled armour from the Altai mountains, and of course a stream of silk, wine and grain from north China's Han rulers, who were happy to trade and provide gifts if that was what it took to keep the peace. On the firm foundation of Motun's 35-year reign, the Xiongnu elite built a rich and varied life in the valleys of northern Mongolia and southern Siberia. Ivolga, just south-west of Ulan-Ude, was then a well-fortified Xiongnu town, with carpenters, masons, farmers, iron-workers and jewellers among its residents. Some of the houses had underfloor heating, Roman-style. To the west, in today's Kansu and Sinkiang, the Xiongnu controlled 30 or so walled city-states, one of which had 80,000 inhabitants. Trade, tribute, slaves and hostages all flowed towards the centre, Motun's capital, west of Ulaanbaatar, not far from the old Mongol capital of Karakorum. Here came the envoys and tribal leaders, in three great annual ceremonies, complete with games like those held at today's national festival in Mongolia.

To administer all this, Motun used officials who wrote Chinese. The Chinese historian Pan Ku recorded several of his letters. In one, Motun actually seems to suggest a marriage of political convenience with the Han emperor's mother, Lü. 'I am a lonely widowed ruler, born amidst the marshes and brought up on the wild steppes,' he moaned in mock-mournful style. 'Your majesty is also a widowed ruler living a life of solitude. Both of us are without pleasures and lack any way to amuse ourselves. It is my hope that we can exchange that which we have for that which we are lacking.' Empress Lü told him he must be joking. 'My age is advanced and my vitality weakening. Both my hair and teeth are falling out, and I cannot even walk steadily. The *shan-yü* [as the Xiongnu emperor was known] must have heard exaggerated reports.' Motun sent an envoy to apologize. So much for the Xiongnu being nothing but crude barbarians.

Motun's success was something new in the long history of

China's dealings with the northern barbarians. In response, the first emperor of the Jin dynasty, which ruled from 221 to 206 BC, joined up several local walls to create the first Great Wall, not so much as a defence against invasion as to define the area of Chinese control over peasants, trade and soldiery. This was the outward and visible sign of the division that had arisen between herder and farmer, mobile and settled, civilized and barbarian. Indeed, from then on the Wall would define the very essence of Chinese culture in Chinese eyes. Today the remains of its several manifestations still loom across northern China, running through desert or dividing wheat-fields, mostly eroded stumps except today's Great Wall, built of stone in the sixteenth century, the last assertion of an ancient prejudice. In the words of Ssu-ma Ch'ien, inside the Wall 'are those who don the cap and girdle, outside are the Barbarians'. The nomads were literally 'beyond the pale', the wrong side of civilization's palisade.

In 1912, a Mongolian mining engineer named Ballod was surveying the pine-covered Noyan Uul hills 100 kilometres north of the Mongolian capital, Ulaanbaatar – or Urga, as it was in those pre-revolutionary times. He came across a mound that had been opened some time in the past. Thinking these were old gold-workings, he dug further, and found a few bits of metal, wood and fabric. He realized he had found not a mine, but a *kurgan*, a burial mound. He sent some of his bits to the museum in Irkutsk – and then nothing happened for twelve years, which was not surprising, given the First World War and revolution in both Russia and Mongolia. Ballod died; his find remained in limbo. Then, early in 1924, the famous Russian explorer Petr Kozlov arrived in Ulaanbaatar with an expedition returning from Tibet. The times being harsh, Ballod's widow sold the remaining bits of her husband's trove to Kozlov. Intrigued, Kozlov despatched a colleague, S. A. Kondratiev, to check out the site. It was February and the ground frozen, but Kondratiev's workers hacked into Ballod's mound and found a timber-lined shaft. Kozlov changed his plans. By March he knew he had a major discovery: these hills were one huge Xiongnu burial site covering 10 square kilometres, with 212 tumuli. A few test shafts revealed that the graves had been robbed, but had then become waterlogged and subsequently deep-frozen – which was fortunate, because everything the robbers had not taken had been deep-frozen as well. Kozlov's team excavated eight mounds. Removing a 9-metre-deep over-burden of rocks and earth, they found sloping approaches to 2-metre-high rooms made of pine logs, carpeted with embroidered wool or felt. Inside each was a tomb of pine logs, and inside that a silk-lined coffin of larch. The con-struction of the rooms was superb, with silk-covered wooden beams neatly inlaid into side walls and supports set in well-made footings. A piece of decorated pottery from *kurgan* no. 6 revealed when at least one grave was made: it listed both the maker and the painter, and was dated 'September of the fifth year of the Chien-ping' (corresponding to 2 BC).

Every grave was a mess, with treasure troves of objects, over 500 in all (most of them now in St Petersburg), all strewn about by the robbers among human and animal bones: not a single skeleton had been left intact. The remains are not up to Tutankhamen standards, because almost all the gold had been taken, but enough had been left to show that these were wealthy people, who had more on their minds than war and the next lambing season. They loved handi-crafts, of the easily carried and durable sort, and their community had the time and skills to produce them. Here are some of the things they admired: patterned felt, lacquered wooden bottles, bronze pots, spoons of horn, knee-length underpants of wool and silk, silk socks, Chinese- and

Mongolian-style wrap-around robes, buckles, silk caps, fur hats, jade decorations, bronze bridle decorations, fly-whisks, axle-caps, fire-sticks (they made fire by friction, rubbing a round stick on a board), clay pots, bronze pestles, horse decorations, bronze staff-ends, golden jewellery, seals, silver plates with yaks and deer in bas-relief, felt carpets embroidered with animal motifs (some interwoven with silk), silk flags, and many tapestries wonderfully embroidered with turtles, birds and fish, and men's portraits, and horsemen, and Chinese lions. The women did their hair in plaits – for the plaits were still there, bound up just as they were when they were cut off and thrown onto the floors and sloping entrance corridors in the rituals of mourning.

Of course, many of these products of leisure and wealth would have been won by force, or the threat of it. Power sprang from bowstrings and hooves. Ssu-ma Ch'ien tells of a Chinese eunuch who, having fled to join the Xiongnu, put things bluntly to his former countrymen: 'Just make sure that the silks and grain-stuffs are the right measure and quality, that's all . . . If there is any deficiency or the quality is no good, then when the autumn harvest comes we will take our horses and trample all over your crops.' But the transfer was not all one way. The Xiongnu may have been experts in extracting golden eggs, but they took care not to kill the goose. Trade flourished. The Chinese needed horses and camels from the steppes, sable and fox furs from the Siberian forests, jade and metals from the Altai mountains. Trade, moreover, was only one way of ensuring peace: the Chinese tried everything else as well. Motun was given a royal bride in the hope that he would produce compliant heirs. 'Whoever heard of a grandson trying to treat his grandfather as an equal?' argued one official to the emperor. 'Thus the Xiongnu will gradually become your subjects.' And daughters, even with handsome dowries, were a lot cheaper than armies.

(Tough on the poor girls, though. One princess wrote a poem mourning her fate: 'A domed lodging is my dwelling place, with walls made of felt. Meat is my food, with fermented milk as the source. I live with constant thoughts of my home, my heart is full of sorrow. I wish I were a golden swan, returning to my home country.')

Walls, marriages, trade – and gifts as well. In 50 BC the Chinese imperial court bestowed on one visiting Xiongnu king 'a hat, a girdle, clothes and underwear, a gold seal with yellow cords, a sword set with precious stones, a knife for wearing at the girdle, a bow and four sets of arrows (with 12 in each set), 10 maces in a case, a chariot, a bridle, 15 horses, 20 *ghin* of gold, 200,000 copper coins, 77 suits of clothes, 8,000 pieces of various stuffs, and 6,000 *ghin* of cotton-wool'. All this was the equivalent of the Danegeld with which the English tried to pay off the exacting Vikings; but it was also designed to sap nomad strength with luxuries, as one defecting Chinese official warned his new bosses: 'China has but to give away one-tenth of her things to have all the Xiongnu siding with the House of Han. Tear the silk and cotton clothes you get from China by running among thorny bushes just to show that they hold together worse than woollen and leather clothing!'

Noyan Uul, The Lord's Mountain: the name drew me. On a trip in the summer of 2004, I had my chance. A hundred kilometres from Ulaanbaatar? As I arranged car and driver, I thought it would be an easy jaunt. Surely anyone in the travel business would know how to find such a significant site. Not so, on either count. Memories have faded, and Noyan Uul is on no tourist route. You may find a passing reference to it in a guide book, but no help at all in getting there.

I found help in Ulaanbaatar's Museum of Mongolian History, in a rather odd form. The resident Xiongnu expert sounded odd, because that was his name: Od. Actually, Odbaatar, but Mongolians generally shorten their names to the first element. At first glance I thought he was odd in other ways as well: unusually slight of build, with soft and gentle features, like some furry animal caught away from its nest. He shook hands over-delicately, then held his hands together as if in deference. Wrong again. His modesty disguised not just rare expertise but surprising toughness. He was nursing a dreadful injury: while helping a friend with some building work, he had sliced his forearm on some broken glass, nearly severing a tendon. I had almost opened him up again.

Noyal Uul was only one of several Xiongnu finds, he said. Archaeologists had found sixteen Xiongnu cemeteries, on one of which (Gol Mod, 450 kilometres west of UB) a French–Mongolian team has been working since 2000. But, under Od's guidance, it was Noyan Uul, the royal cemetery, that sprang to life, because the museum displays photographs of the site, a model tomb, bits and pieces left over from Kozlov's pillaging dig, bow ends of horn, a silk carpet showing a yak fighting a snow leopard, an iron stirrup (to which we shall return later), an umbrella, three pigtails.

'Ah, yes.' I recalled my reading. 'People cut off their hair in ritual mourning, didn't they?'

'I think maybe not mourning. Maybe ritual killing. One pigtail, one person. It is hard to say because the victims were not usually buried with the king. Not many bones. But I saw one skull in Gol Mod with a hole in it, as if, like . . .'

'A pick-axe?'

'Yes, pick-axe.'

'Od,' I said on impulse, 'I'm going to Noyan Uul tomorrow. Can you come with me?'

He was intrigued. He had never been there, and wasn't sure if we could find our way. Od's boss added another member to the expedition: Erigtse, a graduate student whose dissertation was on Noyan Uul. He looked like a Mongolian Indiana Jones: burly, with broad, weathered features and a crew-cut.

Next morning we were off, heading north in a solid Russian UAZ 4 × 4. There were six of us: the driver, two hardy Australian women along for the experience, the two Mongolian academics and me. After two hours, we were off what passes for a surfaced road and on a track, heading up the valley of the Sujekht river, rolling like a dinghy in a swell towards the forested ridges of the Noyan Uul mountains.

The rutted, boggy track rose through stands of birch and knee-high shrubs, grasses, and yellow flowers. The track was well worn – by hunters, I suggested. 'Gold-diggers!' shouted Erigtse, over the engine. Of course – the man who found the graves had been a gold-miner. They were not the only ones. The track levelled out, and there was a truck-load of Russian and Mongolian scientists, their vehicle parked wheel-deep in shrubs. They were an expedition come to study plant successions. In this borderland, they wanted to know: was the steppe moving north, or the forests south? The answer might reveal interesting things about climate change – but also, if they could collect some peat samples from deeper down, about the past, and why this place was chosen as a royal burial site.

Where were the graves, the mounds?

Erigtse pointed to a grove of birch trees.

I couldn't see anything but trees. It was like trying to recognize someone hidden by a duvet.

'Before, there were no trees,' said Erigtse. 'These are maybe thirty years old. There are fires, people cut.'

It struck me that, seen in an action replay over decades, this wilderness was not a wilderness at all. It was a flickering series of woodlands and glades, their comings and goings regulated by hunters, woodcutters, looters and now archaeologists and botanists, and perhaps soon the occasional tourist. Old trees were rarities – the only one in view, a gnarled and fire-blackened fir, nothing out of the ordinary, had been honoured with pieces of blue silk, as if this mere centenarian were a Methuselah of trees.

Hidden by the slender birches and a blanket of shrubs was a circular mound, and in the other side of the mound was a hole. This – Kozlov's tomb no. 1 – looked like an overgrown and abandoned well, a square pit lined with decaying timbers. No-one but Erigtse could have seen through the plant cover to point out where Kozlov's men had cut through the mound and revealed the entrance-path, where the coffin had been carried and the goods placed in reverence, before slaves had reburied it all, and built the burial mound, and left the place to be found by looters.

There were other mounds dotted through the woodlands, all practically invisible. You simply wouldn't know they were there, but in a half-hour walk we came across dozens of them – Erigtse knew of 100 or so – mostly only a metre or two high, and 10 metres apart. Some were bigger. One, no. 24, was a crater that must have taken weeks to excavate. It is still 6 metres deep and a stone's throw across, with the entrance-road running into it much as Kozlov's team had dug it, like an ancient sunken lane. The monarch of no. 24 had had a lavish send-off.

It was not the mounds that set me thinking so much as the site. I had been on the mountain where most Mongolians and most scholars believe Genghis is buried. The Xiongnu came from north and west of UB, the Mongol homeland was to the east, and the two cultures were separated by over 1,000 years. But I would bet on a connection. Burkhan Khaldun, 200 kilometres to the east in the Khenti mountains, and Noyan Uul have this in common: they are impressive mountains, but easily accessible for people on horseback (it's no good having a holy mountain too remote and difficult to get to); they are on the borderline between northern forests and southern steppes; the burial sites are at the head of a river valley and up on a flat place, before the going gets tough to the summit; and both proclaim a sense of belonging: this is ours, and here we lie, for ever. Are these coincidences? I think not. It seems likely that the Mongols, as they rose to unity and then to empire under Genghis, would have known of these tombs, maybe even knew their contents, and said to themselves: Aha, *that's* how you bury kings!

But what of the possible link *westward*?

'Erigtse,' I asked, as we prepared to lumber down over the grasslands and onto the road back to UB. 'Do you think the Huns were the Xiongnu?'

'Oh yes. We say Hun-nu.' He pronounced the *h* like a Scottish *ch*, as in *loch*, usually transliterated as *kh*. '*Khun* is, you know, our word for "man", "person". I think they used the same word as we do. They were the enemies of China, so our word *khun* became *xiong* in Chinese.' (It sounds like *shung*, which is not too far from *khun*.) 'It means "bad". And *nu* means "slave". Xiongnu – Bad Slaves.'

If the Xiongnu were indeed the Huns, Noyan Uul is part of what Attila's forefathers left behind. They forgot about holy mountains and royal burials on hills, for after two centuries of wandering there would have been no sense of belonging anywhere. They had become less than the first Xiongnu. They had become rootless nomads.

For 150 years the Xiongnu remained unsapped by Chinese luxuries and untamed by Chinese princesses. Eventually the Han wearied of Xiongnu demands, and started a long-drawn-out series of campaigns to defeat them. A brief revival of Xiongnu fortunes in the first century AD ended with a north–south split, the southerners joining the Han, the northerners retaining their independence in Mongolia, where in

AD 87 a diverse group of clans from Manchuria, the Hsien-pi, seized the Xiongnu chief and skinned him, taking the skin as a trophy. A final battle scattered the northerners in 89. By the mid-second century they were all gone, drifting westward, as many vanquished tribes did, into the void of Central Asia and beyond, towards some new source of wealth. From Rome's point of view, according to which inland Eurasia was divided into arcs of increasing barbarism, marked off by the frontier, rivers, tribes and trade areas, they would emerge from the outer darkness; but to nature the stripes are horizontal, marked by forest, grassland and desert. Mountains and inland seas distort the bands, forcing the grassy highway to meander or cutting it briefly. But the Xiongnu knew the way: along the Gansu Corridor between the Gobi and the Tibetan highlands, then north-west where the railway line now runs to Ürümqi, and out of the reach of China through the Dzungarian Gap between the Altai and Tien Shan. The journey had its dangers, both from other tribes and from nature. The Dzungarian Gap is notorious for its brutal wind, the *buran*,[1] remarked by later travellers braving the same 80-kilometre corridor of corrugated badlands. Friar William of Rubrouck noted its dangers on his way to meet the Mongol khan in 1253. Douglas Carruthers, British explorer and travel writer, passed through in 1910. 'At night we heard a distant roar as the imprisoned winds of the Djungarian deserts escaped through this narrow defile,' he wrote in *Unknown Mongolia*. 'Great cloud-banks swept through the "straits" as if rushing through some gigantic funnel.' A winter *buran* could flip yurts from their moorings, deep-freezing their inhabitants with a wind-chill factor that takes the temperature down to −50°C.

---

[1] Often translated as 'snowstorm', a *buran* is rather more than that, which is why it became the name of the Soviet space shuttle.

A tough journey, but one that had been done before many times by tribes moving west, and would be done again, by herds and wagon-trains alike. It was on the far end of these steppelands that Friar William saw the Mongols' tent-bearing wagons 10 metres across, with axles like masts, hauled by teams of up to 22 oxen, riding the prairies like galleons. The Xiongnu did not have similar resources, but they were just as competent. They would surely have come through in the summer, with their flocks well fattened by spring pastures, before putting them to graze on the 2,000-kilometre steppe of Kazakhstan.

Two hundred years later, as de Guignes noted, there emerged from the far end of Central Asia a tribe, much degraded by comparison, but with a similar lifestyle – nomads, tent-dwellers with wagons, mounted archers – and a vaguely similar name. That was enough for de Guignes, and for his successors, the weightiest of whom was Edward Gibbon in his *Decline and Fall of the Roman Empire*. In Gibbon, de Guignes found magisterial backing. The Huns who threatened Rome were descendants of the tribe that threatened China, made 'formidable by the matchless dexterity with which they managed their bows and their horses; by their hardy patience in supporting the inclemency of the weather; and by the incredible speed of their march, which was seldom checked by torrents or precipices, by the deepest rivers, or by the most lofty mountains'. Gibbon used words and phrases as artillery, blasting doubt before it had a chance to grow. For the next two centuries, it was taken as a matter of fact that the Huns were the Xiongnu, reborn in poverty. The 1911 edition of the *Encyclopedia Britannica* relies on the carelessly misspelt 'de Guiques'. Experts like the French historian René Grousset and the American William McGovern, both writing in the 1930s, simply referred to the Xiongnu as the Huns, period, without bothering to argue the case. Albert Herrmann's *Historical Atlas of China* of 1935 has a spread on the 'Hsiung-Nu or Huns'. About the same time, it occurred to more sceptical scholars that there was absolutely no evidence to bridge the gap between the two. Indeed, the difference between the sophisticated nobility buried in Noyan Uul and Attila's impoverished hordes is striking. The theory fell into limbo. As Edward Thompson, one-time Professor of Classics at Nottingham University, baldly wrote in his 1948 book on the Huns, 'This view has now been exploded and abandoned.'

But it has recently regained lost ground. The two tribes were briefly so close in time and space that it is hard to believe they were separate. The remnants of the Xiongnu, fleeing along trade routes that led through the Ili valley in southern Kazakhstan in about 100, reached the Syrdar'ya river by about 120. In round figures, that's 2,800 kilometres in 30 years, or a mere 90 kilometres a year. In 160, the Greek polymath Ptolemy mentions the 'Khoinoi', commonly equated with the Chuni, the initial *ch* sounded as in the Scottish *loch*, which makes them sound pretty much like 'Huns'. These people he placed between two other tribes, the most distant of which, the Roxelani, probably lived on the Don, thus putting the Huns just north of the Sea of Azov – the 'Maeotic marshes' mentioned later by Roman authors. The gap has narrowed to 2,000 kilometres and 40 years – a gap easily crossed at the slow pace of 50 kilometres a year.

There is a further piece of evidence for the link. In 1986 a joint Russian–Mongolian expedition excavated a grave site in the far west of Mongolia, in the Altai mountains. Their report refers to the find as a 'Hun' site, reflecting the Mongolian eagerness to equate Xiongnu and Hun, but it is clearly Xiongnu. The five graves were remarkable because they had not been thoroughly vandalized. All contained wooden coffins, and four of the five held the remains of bows: bits of bone or horn, which were used as 'ears' at the end of the limbs and to reinforce the central section. From the end-bits, which were of different lengths, the authors concluded that the bows were asymmetrical, the upper limb being longer than the lower limb. Later Hun bows were asymmetrical; indeed, it was their most obvious trait, for reasons that remain obscure. The end-bits themselves – the 'ears' – also suggest a link with the Huns, because the later Hun bows had highly developed ones.

The mystery would have been soluble if the Altai graves had contained the bows themselves. But they didn't. Perhaps they had simply rotted away? That doesn't seem right: wooden coffins surviving for some 2,000 years, and bits of birch-bark in one of them, but no wooden bows? It gets odder. The four graves had in turn three ears, three ears, two ears and four ears, and each grave also contained a varying number of the horn strips used to reinforce a bow's wooden body. Many bits, no complete bows. In fact, no complete bow has ever been found in a Hun grave or cache. Even when a pair of apparently matching bone laminations was found – at a fourth-century site near Tashkent – a close look revealed that the two long bone strips had been carved by different makers, for different bows. There can be only one conclusion: the bits found in graves do not belong together, or to any particular bow. As one of the greatest of experts on the Huns, Otto Maenchen-Helfen, concluded: 'The people buried the dead warrior with a sham bow.' Once suggested, the idea is obvious. *Of course* they buried sham bows, or broken ones. Bows took expert bowyers years to make. In many cultures loyal subjects buried goods with their kings reflecting their royal status; but bows, which everyone had to have, were not high-status objects. The graves in western Mongolia were for lower-ranking officials, who would have wished to pass on their prize possessions to their surviving relatives. Who in their grieving families would waste such a precious, life-and-death object by burying anything but a few unused bits and pieces?

Perhaps, then, what we see in Xiongnu graves is a Hunnish bow in the process of evolution; and this, if true, would argue for a direct link between Hun and Xiongnu.

If Hun and Xiongnu are not quite joined by archaeology, what about folklore? If there was a link, isn't it odd that the Huns did not seem to have a folk memory of it? The Xiongnu's Turkish successors in Mongolia were happy to claim them as ancestors until they, too, were driven westwards in the eighth century; but Attila, much closer to the Xiongnu in time, apparently never did. He had his bards, but no eye-witness recorded them singing of conquering forebears.

Again, the argument can be made to run both ways. Sometimes folkloric information is astonishingly enduring – the Trojan war remained alive in oral accounts for centuries before Homer wrote it down. Sometimes it fades fast, especially during a long migration. I once worked with a small tribe in the Ecuadorian rainforest who had moved into their area at some indeterminate time in the past few centuries – that much is certain, because they had either never learned stone-age crafts or had forgotten them while on the move, using the stone axes made and dumped by a previous culture. The Waorani are not short of legends, but all they say about their own origins is that they came 'from down-river, long ago'. The Mongols, too, forgot their origins: their great foundation epic, *The Secret History of the Mongols*, says only that they sprang from a wolf and a doe, and had crossed an ocean or lake to arrive in Mongolia perhaps 500 years earlier. The Huns seem to have forgotten much faster – in 250 years – recalling nothing of their forebears; nothing, at least, that anyone recorded.

Perhaps there was something more active than mere forget-fulness at work as Xiongnu turned to Hun. Once reduced from imperial grandeur to impoverished bands, perhaps the Huns became ashamed of their decline, and simply refused to mention their former greatness to their children. I have never heard of such a process being recorded; but then, it wouldn't be, would it? One generation of taboo – 'Don't mention China!' – would be enough.

In researching Hun origins we get very little help from language. Though Attila employed interpreters and secretaries, no-one wrote Hunnish, only Latin or Greek, the languages of the dominant culture, with its inbuilt prejudice against barbarian tongues. Scholars have been free to im-provise, a favourite solution being Gibbon's, that the Huns were actually Mongols. (They weren't: the Mongols did not move into Xiongnu territory until half a millennium after the Xiongnu had gone.) Some experts have claimed certain words as Hunnish; all are disputed; no single word that is absolutely, undoubtedly Hunnish has survived.

But we have Hun names, or think we do. First we must strip away veils of obscurity, for Huns, Goths, other Germanic tribes, even Romans all adopted names from each other's cultures; and Hun names acquired Latin or Greek end-ings; and they were often spelled differently by different scribes. Still, there is behind these veils a core of names that offer clues about the language. Attila's uncle Octar was also written Oiptagos, Accila, Occila, Optila and Uptar (*ct* shifted to *pt* in the Balkan dialect of Latin). But *öktör* means 'powerful' in old Turkish. A coincidence? Scholars think not. The names of other characters in this story also suggest Turkish roots: Attila's father Mundzuk ('Pearl' or 'Decoration'), his uncle Aybars ('Moon Panther'), his senior wife Erekan ('Beautiful Queen'), his son Ernak ('Hero'), a shadowy king Charaton/Kharaton ('Black' something, possibly 'Clothing'). The -*kam* ending on a few names seems to recall the Turkish for 'priest' or 'shaman'. Of course, names are shifty, easily absorbed from another culture, as biblical names have been absorbed into English. But there is enough, in the words of the greatest of Hun archaeological experts, István Bóna, 'to correct a great and widely-held error perpetrated by some modern researchers: because of some Mongoloid features in selected skulls, they confuse race with language, and turn the Huns into thorough-going Mongols'.

To tally the possible, the probable and the certain: the Huns were probably of Turkish stock, probably spoke a Turkish language (which shared roots with Mongolian), were possibly a remnant of migrating Xiongnu, had no connection with China apart from some cultural overlap, and were certainly nothing whatever to do with the Slavic and Germanic tribes into whom they so rudely barged.

In the evolution of the warrior nomad, there remained a vital step. To be truly effective, a bowman needs a delivery system. For this, the Scythians and Chinese developed the two-wheeled chariot: a fast, stable and manoeuvrable firing platform, always provided that you, the archer, had a driver; and always provided that your society had access to wood and carpenters, mines and skilled metalworkers. Thus they were the preserve of well-organized, semi-urbanized peoples. Nomads, riding perhaps bareback, almost certainly without stirrups, could only occasionally match the skills and resources of charioteers.

To reach a peak of effectiveness, warrior nomads had to await the arrival of the stirrup, in particular the iron stirrup, an invention that, in combination with the saddle, was as influential as the composite bow in the development of warfare. This is a murky subject. Prevailing orthodoxy claims that stirrups developed surprisingly late and spread surprisingly slowly, perhaps because expert horsemen can manage without them, perhaps because chariots provided a partial solution to the problem of wielding a bow. The earliest stirrups, first recorded in India in the second century BC, were supposedly made of rope, as supports for the big toe. The idea was carried to China and Korea, where iron stirrups emerged in the fifth century AD. From there, iron stirrups spread westwards, the first evidence for them being dated to the early sixth century. But dig deeper, and orthodoxy vanishes in a puff. Stirrups should be older, they really should. The idea is so obvious, after all. And they really should not have come from India. A simple toe-stirrup is a help in mounting, but only if you have bare feet, which is all very well in India, but not in Central Asia, where horses were first domesticated. The combination of leather boots, iron-working and horses should have inspired the creation of the iron stirrup by 1000 BC, along with arrowheads. Perhaps it did; but it doesn't show up in the archaeological record until Turks came to dominate Mongolia in the sixth century. The earliest example I have seen is a reference by the great scholar Joseph Needham, in his *Science and Civilisation in China*: a pottery figure showing a Chinese horseman with stirrups, dated AD 302. If the Chinese had stirrups, so, surely, did their enemies. Yet they do not appear in paintings of mounted archers. (There is a theory that explains this, according to which iron stirrups were the invention of fat and lazy town-dwellers who could not leap nimbly into the saddle, namely the Chinese, at which point the nomads saw the stirrup's advantages, and adopted it. There's no evidence to back this. Do you believe it? I don't.)

It's a mystery, which deepened when Od was taking me round the Museum of Mongolian History. For there among the Xiongnu relics was an iron stirrup, not from Noyan Uul, but from a Xiongnu grave in Khovd province, in the far west.

Yet from the royal graves of Noyan Uul not a single stirrup. Indeed, as Od e-mailed me, 'We excavating a lot of graves, unfortunately we couldn't find more [stirrups].' This is all very strange. Perhaps the western graves were made later, when the Xiongnu had been defeated and were on the move westwards? In which case, are we to assume that the Xiongnu, iron-workers and horse-riders *par excellence*, had no stirrups when they were powerful, yet had them when they were not? And, if they had them at all, why did the idea not diffuse instantly to everyone else?

Including, of course, the Huns, who should have known about and used the stirrup, whether or not they were Xiongnu originally. Yet from Hun archaeological finds, which have produced bits, saddles and bridle ornaments, we have not a single stirrup. Nor is there any mention of them in the (admittedly inexpert) Latin and Greek sources. Yes, Huns could have ridden without stirrups, or used rope or cloth ones, but why, when they had metalworkers for arrowpoints and swords and cooking-pots, would they reject iron stirrups? The mystery remains.

In any event, by about AD 350 the pastoral nomads of Inner Asia had an advantage over infantry, heavy cavalry and chariots. The Huns had the hardware for conquest, and could operate summer or winter, each warrior supplied with two or three remounts, each carrying his bow as his prize possession, along with dozens of arrows and arrowheads for hunting and fighting, each ready to protect wives, children and parents in wagons. They were something new in history, something with potential beyond the Xiongnu: a juggernaut that could live off the land if necessary, or by pillage. Pillage was a lot easier. Like sharks, they had become expert predators, honed to fitness by constant movement, adapted to roam the inland sea of grass, blotting up lesser tribes, until they emerged from the unknown and forced themselves onto the consciousness of the sophisticated, urbanized, oh-so-civilized Europeans. Our first view of the Huns, therefore, is from outside, and as full of loathing, prejudice and error as you might imagine.

The Greeks were appalled by the barbarian menace from the steppes, exemplified by the Scythians. The very word 'barbarian', said to derive from the incomprehensible *bar-bar-bar* noises these outsiders made in lieu of language, summarized a prejudice, an expression of xenophobia that buttressed the Greeks' own sense of identity and self-worth. It was an idea that lumped all non-Greeks together in undifferentiated otherness, people who were cruel, stupid, unrefined and oppressed, and who, of all things, gave power to women. Euripides personified barbarism in Medea, who supposedly came from the far side of the Black Sea: a domineering, passionate, child-murdering witch. Much of this was self-serving nonsense, for the Scythians developed a sophisticated, complex culture that lasted for some 700 years.

Rome inherited the same prejudices, and took action accordingly. The whole length of the imperial frontier, over 4,000 miles, was secured by roads, walls, towers, forts and ditches, from the Atlantic coast of Africa, up the Middle East, down the Euphrates, back to the Black Sea and beyond. In western Europe, Rome had the benefit of two great rivers, the Rhine and the Danube, which virtually bisect the continent from north-west to south-east. From the early years of the first millennium, the two rivers became the Roman equivalent of the Great Wall, with Dacia the Roman equivalent of the Ordos, the borderland sought by the dominant culture as a buffer zone, but from which it had been driven by the barbarians. Europe's geography was less convenient than China's. Rhine and Danube almost join, but their upper reaches form a right-angle north of the Alps which is hard to defend. As the empire grew stronger, successive emperors cut the corner with forts, towers and eventually a stone wall that ran for almost 500 kilometres across southern Germany, with another wall, Hadrian's, marking the frontier against the northern barbarians. A wall also blocked the 80-kilometre corridor between the Danube and the Black Sea. The Rhine–Danube wall, though, was abandoned under the onslaught of 260, and the empire retreated again to the rivers.

In forming their view of Attila's people, then, the Romans tapped into attitudes inherited from the Greeks. These were the vilest creatures imaginable. They came from the North, and everyone knew that the colder the climate was, the more barbaric the people were. To paraphrase Ammianus Marcellinus, who never saw a Hun himself, they were squat, with thick necks, so prodigiously ugly and bent that they might be two-legged animals, or the figures crudely carved from stumps which are seen on the parapets of bridges. There was nothing like them for cruelty and ugliness, the one accentuating the other, because they cut their baby boys' cheeks so that, when they became men, their beards grew in patches, if they grew at all. They knew nothing of metal, had no religion and lived like savages, without fire, eating their food raw, living off roots and meat tenderized by placing it under their horses' saddles. No buildings, of course, not so much as a reed hut; indeed, they feared the very idea of venturing under a roof. Once they had put their necks into some dingy shirt, they never took it off or changed it until it rotted. Granted, they were wonderful horsemen; but even this was an expression of barbarism, for they practically lived on horseback, eating, drinking and sleeping in the saddle. Their shoes were so shapeless, their legs so bowed that they could hardly walk. Jordanes, the Gothic historian, was no less insulting. These stunted, foul and puny tribesmen, offspring of witches and unclean spirits, 'had, if I may say so, a sort of shapeless lump, not a head, with pin-holes rather than eyes'. It was amazing they could see at all, given that 'the light that enters the dome of the skull can hardly reach the receding eyeballs . . . Though they live in the form of men, they have the cruelty of wild beasts.' These are judgements that have echoed down the ages. Practically everyone is happy to quote everyone else, including Gibbon, in condemning the Huns as smelly, bandy-legged, nasty, brutish and revoltingly short.

Almost all of this was nonsense.

As the Huns emerged from somewhere north of the Caspian to approach the Black Sea in the mid-fourth century, they were, in Roman eyes, at the very limit of the known world. But with spotlights borrowed from anthropologists and archaeologists it is possible to highlight a few of their defining traits. As visitors to the Huns found later, they had beards, grew crops, were perfectly capable of building houses, and included as high a proportion of handsome men and beautiful women as everyone else. Certainly, the men would have commanded respect, because they would have been formidably hardy, weather-beaten, with slab-like shoulders from daily use of their powerful bows. But, as in today's Mongolians, there was probably enough of an admixture of other races to make some of them extremely appealing. No-one who saw the Huns face to face mentioned any children with facial scars; the men's beards may have been thin, as Attila's was, and some adults may have had scarred faces, but that was nothing to do with cruelties inflicted in childhood; they were self-inflicted as part of mourning rituals.

No metal? No cooked food? You would think the evidence of metalworking would have struck home with the first Hun arrows, followed quickly by the evidence for cooking. Their bulkiest possessions were huge cooking-pots, cumbersome bell-shaped things with hefty handles, up to a metre in height and weighing 16–18 kilos: cauldrons big enough to boil up clan-sized casseroles. Dozens of them have been found, in the Czech Republic, Poland, Hungary, Romania, Moldova – and

Russia, where half a dozen have turned up scattered over a huge area, one near Ul'yanovsk on the Volga, another 600 kilometres further north, one even from the Altai mountains only 250 kilometres from the Mongolian border. They look like enormous vases, with cone-shaped stands. They are crudely cast in two or three moulds, the stand sometimes being made separately, then roughly soldered together, the joints and rough spots left unfiled. The contents of the alloys vary greatly: most of the metal is local copper, with additions of red oxide of copper and lead, but hardly any of the tin which, when mixed with copper, makes bronze. To any good metal-caster, they would seem amateurish, not a patch on Chinese bronze pots or those made by the Xiongnu. But these were people on the move, which makes the cauldrons interesting. Hun metalworkers had the tools to melt copper (it takes a furnace to create a temperature of 1,000°C) and some large, heavy stone moulds. The cauldrons alone – leaving aside the decorated saddles and horse harnesses – disprove the idea that these were just primitive herders who knew nothing but fighting and ate raw meat. It takes a large, well-organized group and surplus food to support and transport metalworkers, the tools of their trade and their products.

No religion? More rubbish. It has to be, because *H. sapiens* evolved as an incurably religious creature. It seems likely that the urge to explain and control the natural world is so fundamental to human intelligence and society that no group, however basic, has ever been found to lack the conviction that we spring from the universe's hidden essence, remain part of it, are subject to it, can influence it and will return to it.[2]

---

[2] This sweeping generalization is a hypothesis, unproven. I have some evidence, derived from the tribe I worked with in the Ecuadorean rainforest in the early 1980s. The Waorani were then among the simplest of societies known to anthropologists, with no chiefs, shamans or elaborate rituals; with extremely simple music, no clothing but strings of cotton round their waists (into which

The Huns were no exception, and the Romans knew it really; by 'no religion' those who said it meant not a *proper* religion, like theirs, whether Christianity or the civilized paganism inherited from the Greeks. 'Superstition' didn't count. What the Huns believed, exactly, and how they worshipped are entirely unknown, but there can be no doubt that they were animists, awed enough by the forces of nature, by wind, snow, rain, thunder and lightning to imagine spirits in them all. It is fair to guess that, like the Mongols a few centuries later, they saw the origins of these forces in the overarching sky, worshipped heaven above as the fount of all, and sought to control their own destiny through worship and sacrifice. We modern Europeans unthinkingly recall this sky-god in every *Good Heavens! Ciel!* and *Himmel!* we utter. Turkish and Mongol tribes, who lived cheek-by-jowl before the Turks headed west late in the first millennium, had a name for their sky-god: Tenger or Tengri, in two of several common spellings. Tenger turns up all across Asia, from the Tengri desert of Inner Mongolia to an eighth-century bas-relief in eastern Bulgaria. In Mongol, as in many other languages, *tenger* means simply 'sky' in its mundane as well as its divine aspect. The Mongols' Blue Sky – Khökh Tenger – is a deity as well as a nice day.

---

the men tucked their penises), no art other than body decoration and their few wonderful artefacts (notably 3-metre blowguns and the best hammocks in Amazonia). But they did have stories, and folklore, and a cosmology, with an afterlife – a heaven where people swung in hammocks and hunted for ever, a limbo for those who returned to this world in animal form, and an underworld of the 'mouthless ones' – and spirits both good and evil, and a myth of creation, overseen by the creator, Waengongi. A 'primitive' tribe who were monotheists! That was a surprise. The idea of one god is supposed to have evolved from polytheism as a higher form of religion. It proved very handy for American missionaries when they arrived with news of what their version of Waengongi had told them. (The 'primitive' four lines up is ironic: the Waorani were experts in their way of life, and as bright and as dim, as wary and as curious, as charming and as offensive and as thoroughly human as the rest of us.)

(English has the same ambivalence: *Heavens above, the heavens opened.*) The Xiongnu also worshipped Tengri. A history of the Han dynasty (206 BC – AD 8), written towards the end of the first century by the historian Pan Ku, in a section on the Xiongnu, says, 'They refer to their ruler by the title *cheng li* [a transliteration of *tengri*] *ku t'u* [son] *shan-yü* [king]' i.e. something like 'His Majesty, the Son of Heaven'. In early Turkish inscriptions, the ruler has his power from Tengri; and Tengri was the name given to Uighur kings of the eighth and ninth centuries. The Huns could not have been outside Tengri's wide reach. Whether or not they were Xiongnu remnants, whether or not they retained the same name for their god, they surely brought a similar belief-system with them, and a similar faith that shamans, with their chants and drums and spirit-guides, could open a hotline to heaven.

The evidence is in the few records. In 439, just before fighting the Visigoths outside Toulouse, the Roman general Litorius decided to please his Hun auxiliaries by performing what the Romans called the *haruspicatio*, a ceremony of divination. Attila, who had seers at his court, did the same thing before his great defeat 12 years later. What was true in the mid-fifth century must have been true at earlier times, for divination had a history dating back millennia. Indeed, it was fundamental to Chinese culture, inspiring the earliest Chinese writing: in the Shang dynasty around 1500 BC, shamans saw meanings in the heat-cracks of scorched turtle-shells, and turned the shells into memo pads by scribbling their interpretations on them. Later, many Central Asian groups, including the Mongols, adopted scapulimancy – the practice of reading omens in the heat-cracked shoulderblades of cattle. No-one recorded such a ceremony at Attila's court, but the Huns' origins make it highly likely that their shamans used scapulimancy in their divinations.

\*

There is one characteristic that would have struck you as an outsider, once you had become accepted enough by a few important families to be received informally. Some of the children had deformed heads. They seemed to have grown upwards and backwards to form a loaf shape. This was not the result of disease. There was nothing wrong with these children; the opposite, probably, because they would have seemed to live a more privileged life than most. It would no doubt have been easily explained to you, once you had mastered Hunnish. Unfortunately, there were no visitors on that level of intimacy, certainly none who spoke Hunnish and recorded the results of their conversations. The only way anthropologists know of this habit is from finding a number of skulls, mostly of children, with this odd deformity.

I had my introduction to artificial cranial deformation in Vienna's Kunsthistorisches Museum, the Museum of Art History, where Peter Stadler is the resident expert in the barbarian tribes of the Carpathian basin and Karen Wiltschke is the physical anthropologist with a specialist interest in this arcane area. We talked in the museum's collection of skeletons, none of them set up on wire like anatomical specimens, but lying loose in boxes stacked two or three deep, piled on top of each other in columns, 150 to a column, 80 columns of them lining four walls and the side of a corridor – 25,000 boxed skeletons, with another 25,000 waiting to be inventoried. Of these, some 40–50 have skulls that are artificially deformed. Since they date from the early fifth century, they are mostly Hun skulls, and many are those of children. From the scanty evidence, it appears that both boys and girls were given distorted crania, which they preserved as adults if they survived. Some didn't, of course, which accounts for the lower percentage of adults among the remains.

Cranial deformation has been quite common throughout history. An extraordinary study of the subject was published in 1931: *Artificial Cranial Deformation: A Contribution to the Study of Ethnic Mutilations*. Its author, Eric Dingwall, had an odd fascination for ethnic mutilations, among other things. In the fine tradition of English eccentricity, he lived in a flat in St Leonard's surrounded by a prize collection of chastity belts, working on psychical research and, in an honorary capacity, on the arcana section of the Cambridge University Library, until his death in 1986. He also wrote one of the first studies on female circumcision. Female circumcision – genital mutilation, as it is now called – is with us still; cranial deformation has all but vanished. The differing fates of the two practices have uncomfortable implications for the human character, female genital mutilation being painful, crude, secretive and swift (though its effects are anything but swiftly over), while cranial deformation is painless, demands long-term care and remains openly evident throughout the subject's life. It arose in scores of societies all over the world. Neanderthalers distorted skulls 55,000 years ago, and the technique has been with *Homo sapiens* throughout our history, a 'curious and widespread custom', as Dingwall noted, providing examples from Asia, Africa, Indonesia, New Guinea, Melanesia, Polynesia and all the Americas as well as Europe. As he remarks, it can have nothing to do with rites of puberty or initiation rituals, because it can only be done in early childhood, when the skull is still soft and growing. In the Americas, indigenous groups in Chile and the north-west used to flatten their babies' heads by tying boards against them, most notably the Chinook, who are therefore also known as Flathead Indians. Other cultures used fabric bandages to create a cylindrical, loaf-like skull. It is not hard to do. All it takes is a headband wrapped tight, but rewrapped every few days to preserve pressure, to prevent inflammation and to allow for washing. This was the technique used by aboriginals in New South Wales, Australia, some 13,000 years ago, and probably by the ancient Egyptians to give Nefertiti, Akhenaten's queen, her elegant attenuated skull. It was a common practice in rural France in the seventeenth and eighteenth centuries.

Why, for heaven's sake? That is one possible answer: in some cases, it might well have been for the sake of heaven, a sign that a child was destined for the priesthood. But the reasons seem to be mainly social. Among the Chinooks, it was considered proof of good nurturing; mothers who could not be bothered were considered neglectful, and their round-headed children risked being teased by their flat-headed peers. In other cultures, in which mothers or nurses had the time to provide the necessary attention, a long head was a sign of status. In the case of the Huns, it was more subtle than that. Several busts of Nefertiti accentuate her elongated head; but no-one remarked that Attila had a deformed head, or that his sons did, or any of his generals, or his envoys, or his queen, so either they kept their heads covered – and why would they do that, if the deformation were a mark of high status? – or status alone was not the reason behind head-binding.

There is a pattern to be explained. As Karen Wiltschke said, 'The further east you go, the greater the percentage of deformations.' But then, during the 20-year span of Attila's empire (433–53) and immediately afterwards, other tribes in the Huns' short-lived realm also adopted the practice. Take the great Ostrogothic leader Theodoric, who was born in Pannonia (today, western Hungary and eastern Croatia) a year or two after Attila's death and ended his days as king of post-Roman Italy. On his coins he is shown with an elongated head, which must have been given him soon after his birth in about 454 – presumably because that was the fashion taken over from the most successful of the barbarian invaders, who in turn brought the habit with them from the east.

We are left with a puzzle. From archaeology we know that the Huns bound the heads of some of their children, who retained their deformed skulls as adults. Yet no outsider recorded seeing any such thing. All we can do is guess at an explanation. Perhaps these buried skulls were in life kept discreetly under hats, known only to the tribe itself, hidden from outsiders. Perhaps the long-heads were an elite, a sort of freemasonry, whose secrets were passed from father and mother to son and daughter. There was among hunting societies such a freemasonry: the community of shamans, who could in their trances take wing upon the beat of drums and become hawk, eagle, gander or duck to roam at will in the realms of power and insight. From the shamans and their visions came the knowledge of a people's strength and an enemy's weakness, of the right time to fight, of the way fate would turn, of the cause of diseases and their cures. Such things were not to be revealed to strangers.

Look at Attila's forebears in a wider context. Into the Black Sea, draining western Russia and eastern Europe, flow four great rivers, looking on the map like flashes drawn to an oddly shaped lightning conductor. From west to east, they are the four Ds: Danube, Dniester, Dnieper and Don, marking regions of increasing obscurity to the Romans, from the semi-Romanized Dacia (present-day Romania), across the nomad-lands of southern Russia to the impenetrable and unknown valleys of the Caucasus. Jutting down in the middle of this twilight world, like a lamp from a shadowy ceiling of barbarism, was the Crimea, which had been a Greek base for centuries, and remained in imperial hands in Roman times. To Roman writers, as to the Greeks, the Black Sea and its river-bastions were buffers between civilization and the barbarian wilderness, with the Crimea as a transition zone for those approaching by sea. Here, Herodotus had known Scythians who lived between the two worlds, Hellenism and tribalism.

But inland, away from the Greek coastal colonies, lay the very un-Greek world of the Pontic steppe, the vast, treeless, gently rolling grassland of Kazakhstan. Now, it has become a Russified version of the mid-West, tamed by the plough. Then, it was to westerners the heart of barbarian darkness, and to uncounted tribes for two millennia a new homeland or a temporary sanctuary in their slow surge westward. It was from beyond even these remote areas that the Huns came, from a world of myth and shadows, an opening break on a vast billiard-table, which sent tribes ricocheting off each other into the Roman world.

What set them in motion? Why would a small tribe in the depths of Asia suddenly explode onto the world stage? Once, it was fashionable to ascribe large migrations and nomadic assaults to climate change and the pressure of population, as if the 'heartland' were in fact a vast heart beating to some hidden ecological rhythm, pumping out an arterial flow of peoples westwards. But climate alone is not a sufficient explanation, for to a lesser tribe it might have been as fatal as a drought to impoverished Ethiopians.

Actually, there is a heart beating on the far side of Eurasia. It is China, the history of which is a series of dynastic heart-beats that has continued, with each beat lasting anything from decades to centuries, for over 2,000 years. The emergence and collapse of dynasties over such a period is unique in some four millennia, and many historians have spent their lives trying to spot an underlying pattern in this remarkable sequence. If there is one, it seems to have some-thing to do with the idea of unified rule, in pursuit of which dynasties have followed each other, their life-histories driven by complex interactions involving – among other elements – agriculture, rivers, canals, walls, peasant uprisings, the raising of armies, barbarian incursions, taxation, civil service, power politics, corruption, revolution, collapse and the emergence of some new challenger from outside the established order. For us right now, the point is that sometimes nomad rulers entered the Chinese heart and sometimes the Chinese core took over the barbarian frontier. Every pulse would shake up the borderlands, and send another tribe or two westwards, usually out of time, out of history. As it happened, the fourth and early fifth centuries in north China were chaotic, a time labelled by some historians the Sixteen Kingdoms of the Five Barbarians, the chaos diminishing somewhat when a Turkish group, the T'o-pa, established a kingdom known as Northern Wei in 396. Did the chaos, much of it unrecorded, send shock waves of refugees westward, forcing the Huns to move? No-one has a clue.

I'm not even sure it matters. A cold snap in central Asia or an invasion by this or that group of nomadic refugees cannot explain why the Huns were inspired to conquer, and the others weren't. Why the difference? Their success owes nothing to climate or the historical process, and everything to their fighting skills, which are examined in the next chapter.

Let's speculate about their reasons for moving on the basis of what they lacked and what they had:

• They lacked luxuries.
• They had the power to rob.

Pastoral nomads produce more than enough for the necessities of life, but *always* lack luxuries, if you adopt the standards of the upper echelons of settled societies. Their very survival demands it. Herds must be led to new pastures, tents put down and up, pack animals and wagons loaded. Possessions threaten mobility, and thus survival. Life on these terms is a life without trimmings. It is wonderful for building character. You can see the results in Mongolia today, out in the countryside no more than two or three hours from the capital. At best, these are proudly independent people: men tough as their horses, wielding their pole lassos like circus riders, red-cheeked children and sturdy women, all with strong hearts and fine teeth, tributes to a sugar-free diet. But a quick visit in summer makes for a romantic view of the pastoral nomad. Tourists easily buy into this latter-day version of the noble savage, who drives his herds between known pastures, living in an age-old seasonal rhythm. But strip away the wind-powered generator, the motorbike and the TV; set aside the school in the nearest town, where children can stay; return in winter, go back in your imagination a century or two, imagine a life without fresh fruit or vegetables (a problem even today in remote areas), and you will see how nasty and brutish this life can be. Winters are lethal. An ice storm that seals up the grass kills horses and sheep by the thousand. Not long ago, such a catastrophe would leave families starving, without milk, meat or dung-fuel. At one level, suffering and its corollaries – fortitude, strength, sturdy in-dependence – were a source of pride; at another, of envy. No wonder pastoral nomads looked outwards.

In fact, looking outwards was built into the way of life. Pastoral nomads were self-sufficient for a few months, a year perhaps, but not in the long term. The evidence is there today in Mongolia, as it was in the thirteenth century, as it had been in the rise and fall of every nomad kingdom since before the Xiongnu. To survive on the steppe, you need a tent, and to support a tent you need wooden lattice walls and wooden roof supports. Wood comes from trees, and trees come from forests and hills, not rolling grasslands. In addition, if you could afford one, a two-wheeled wagon came in handy to carry the young and the old, the tents and cauldrons and other possessions. Wagons, too, were made of wood. For both tents and wagons, steppe herdsmen needed forests. To get wood you need axes, which means iron, either made by local blacksmiths or acquired by trade. Already, we are looking at a society more varied and adaptable than that of 'pure' pastoral nomadism. And that is just for survival. In addition, nomads, being as human as the rest of us, want refinements unavailable on the grasslands, like tea, rice, sugar, soft and varied fabrics, especially silk: in brief, the goods produced by farmers and more complex, urban societies.

Pastoral nomads do not live in constant, random wanderings. Many herding families may lead remarkably stable lives for years, decades, even generations, because flocks depend on knowing where and when to find pastures; and the need to guarantee them, year after year, demands co-operation and unwritten laws. But, in the long term, change is inevitable. Seasons vary, disease takes its toll, clans breed, and grow, and split, and dispute pastures. Throughout history, the steppe-land has heaved with changes of its own, let alone the changes imposed on it by settled societies round its edge.

Apply all this to the area from which the Huns came, the Pontic and Caspian steppes. It was a cauldron, a slow-motion seething of intermixed and successive peoples. Imagine, then, our small group of Huns, buffeted from established pastures by a few bad years or the ambitions of long-forgotten neighbours. They move into new pastures, unwelcome as gypsies, despised, a threat to and threatened by new and suspicious neighbours, lacking both a homeland and the soft textiles, the carpets, the exotic drinking cups and the jewellery that ease and enliven nomadic life. Strip away the hospitality that acts as a security blanket for nomadic travellers and the reassuring knowledge of local pastures. Wouldn't you, in these circumstances, yearn for all that you lack?

The Huns were refugees wanting a base, a regular source of food, a renewed sense of identity and pride in themselves. These were lacks that could be satisfied in only three ways: by finding unoccupied land (no chance); or by some new arrangement with established groups (tricky, with little to offer in return); or by force. The future life they faced would be very different from that of the traditional pastoral nomad, for once on the move, with no pastures to call their own, trying to muscle in on the territories and trading arrangements of others, with force as the only means of doing so, they were seated on a juggernaut that would never find rest. For now, with every kilometre westward, they would find pasturage increasingly reduced by settled communities. They would, inevitably, become dependent on the possessions of others. These might have been acquired by trade; but the Huns were less sophisticated than their new neighbours. With little to offer other than wool, felt and domestic animals, their only remaining option would have been theft. They would turn from pastoral nomads into a robber band, for whom violence would be as much a way of life as it became for wandering Vikings.

The Huns were on the move westward, away from the grasslands of Kazakhstan and the plains north of the Aral Sea, wanderers who faced a choice between sinking into oblivion or climbing to new heights by conquest. Conquest demanded unity and direction, and for that we come at last to the final element in their rise to fame and fortune: leadership. It was leadership that had been lacking before; leadership that eventually released the Huns' pent-up power. Some time in the fourth century the Huns acquired their first named leader, the first to bring himself and his people to the attention of the outside world. His name was something like Balamber or Balamur, and hardly anything at all is known about him except his name. It was he who inspired his people, focused their fighting potential to attack tribe after tribe, each of whom had their own strengths, and each some weakness. For the first time, a great leader released the tactical skills and established a tradition of leadership that would, in the end, produce Attila.

In AD 350 the Huns crossed the Volga. A few small, violent bunches of mounted archers led their wagons and winding columns of horses and cattle into the grassland country which survived little changed until Anton Chekhov saw it as a boy in the 1870s, an experience he described in one of his first great works, *The Steppe*. The view that stretched out before the Huns, the 800-kilometre sweep of grassland from the Volga to the Crimea, was recorded by the young Chekhov (in Ronald Hingley's translation) before the plough claimed it. This is a new day, as seen through the eyes of Chekhov's young hero, Yegorushka:

> Now a plain – broad, boundless, girdled by a chain of hills – lay stretched before the travellers' eyes. Huddling together and glancing out from behind one another, the hills merged into rising ground extending to the very horizon on the right of the road, and disappearing into the lilac-hued distance. On and on you travel, but where it all begins and where it ends you just cannot make out. First, far ahead where the sky met the earth – near some ancient burial mounds and a windmill resembling from afar a tiny man waving his arms – a broad, bright yellow band crept over the ground . . . until suddenly the whole wide prairie flung off the penumbra of dawn, smiled and sparkled with dew . . . Arctic petrels swooped over the road with happy cries, gophers called to each other in the grass, and from somewhere far to the left came the plaint of lapwings . . . Grasshoppers, cicadas, field crickets and mole crickets fiddled their squeaking monotonous tunes in the grass.
>
> But time passed, the dew evaporated, the air grew still and the disillusioned steppe assumed its jaded July aspect. The

grass drooped, the life went out of everything. The sunburnt hills, brown-green and – in the distance – mauvish, with their calm pastel shades, the plain, the misty horizon, the sky arching overhead and appearing so awesomely deep and transparent here in the steppe, where there are no woods or high hills – it all seemed boundless, now, and numb with misery.

In the mid-fourth century this grassland was dominated by the Sarmatians, a loose confederation of Iranian people who had taken it over from the Scythians more than 500 years before. Much is known about the Sarmatians, because some of their art treasures were found in western Siberia and handed over to Peter the Great of Russia. They liked to make plaques of coloured enamels set in metal showing fighting animals – griffins or tigers against horses or yaks: a style that spread westward to the Goths and other Germanic tribes. The Sarmatians specialized in fighting with lances, their warriors protected by conical caps and mailed coats; no match for the Hun tornado.

One group of Sarmatians were the Alans, a wide-ranging sub-federation known as As to the Persians. (It is from their name, by the way, that 'Aryan' is derived, *l* shifting to *r* in some Iranian languages; thus the tribe so admired by Hitler turns out not to be Germanic at all.) Now we are getting into a region and a tribe that became known to the Romans. Seneca, Lucan and Martial mention them in the first century AD. Martial, a sharp-tongued master of epigrams, skewered a certain Caelia and her wide-ranging sexual habits by asking how a Roman girl could give herself to Parthians, Germans, Dacians, Cilicians, Cappadocians, Pharians, Indians from the Red Sea, the circumcised members of the Jewish race and 'the Alan with his Sarmatian mount', yet cannot 'find pleasure in the members of the Roman race'. The Alans raided south into Cappadocia (today in north-eastern Turkey), where the Greek historian and general Arrian fought them in the second century, noting the Alan cavalry's favourite tactic of the feigned retreat (to be perfected later by Hun archers). Ammianus says they were cattle-herding nomads who lived in wagons roofed with bark and worshipped a sword stuck in the ground, a belief which Attila himself would adopt. They were terrific riders on their tough little horses. The Alans, more European than Asian, with full beards and blue eyes, were lovers of war, experts with the sword and the lasso, issuing terrifying yells in battle, reviling old men because they had not died fighting. They were said to flay their slain enemies and turn their skins into horse-trappings. Theirs was an extensive culture – their tombs have been found by the hundred in southern Russia, many of them commemorating women warriors (hence, perhaps, the Greek legends of Amazons). It was also a flexible one, happy to assimilate captives and to be assimilated. Indeed, perhaps adaptability was their main problem in the mid-fourth century: for they lacked the unity to counter the Hun style of mounted archery.

The Huns blew them apart, clan by clan. The Alans would soon form fragments of the explosion of peoples which usually goes by its German name, the *Völkerwanderung*, the Migration of the Tribes. However, while good assimilators, they also had a talent for retaining their own identity. In the slurry of wandering peoples, the Alans were like grit, widely mixed, but always abrasive. Within a couple of generations, different clans would become useful recruits for the Huns, and also allies of Rome. Their remnants in the Caucasus would transmute into the Ossetians of southern Russia and Georgia: the first two syllables of this name recall their Persian appellation, As, with a Mongol-style plural -*ut* (so the current name of the little Russian enclave known as North Ossetia–Alania doubly emphasizes their roots). At the other end of the empire, they would join both the Goths on their march into Spain – some derive the name Catalonia from a combination of Goth and Alan – and the Vandals, who swept them up on their flight to North Africa in about 420. We shall be hearing from the Alans again later in this story.

Across the Dnieper lived the Ostrogoths. They were settled farming folk, but their venerable chief, Ermanaric,[3] would have been something of a role model for an aspiring Hun leader. He was the central figure of an estate that straggled from the Black Sea to the Baltic, from its core, which Ermanaric ruled directly, out to an ever looser network of vassals, allies, tribute-payers and trade partners. According to one story, Balamber made his move because Ermanaric was not the man he had been. One of his vassals had turned traitor and fled, leaving his unfortunate wife, Sunilda, to suffer Ermanaric's revenge. She was tied torso and legs to two horses, which, when whipped to a gallop in opposite directions, tore her in half. Her two brothers tried to assassinate the old king, but managed only to wound him, after which, in Jordanes' words, 'enfeebled by the blow, he dragged out a miserable existence in bodily weakness'. Balamber, with his Hun and Alan cavalry, smashed Ermanaric's army just north of the Black Sea in about 376. The loose federation of tribes collapsed like a burst balloon; the old Ostrogoth committed suicide; and Balamber took a Gothic princess in marriage to seal the takeover.

At the Dniester, the Visigoths of today's Romania were next in line, as Valens was about to discover. These had become a proud and sophisticated people, now settled in towns, with a respect for law and order administered by their ruler, whom they called a judge. When a Roman envoy referred to the

[3] Ermanaric's name probably derives from Hermann-Rex, King Hermann, the Gothic having adopted the Latin word and turned it into *reiks*, which, when retransliterated, became *ric*. It was a common ending for the names of Gothic aristocrats.

Visigothic ruler as 'king', he objected: a king ruled with authority, he said, but a judge ruled with wisdom. Rome, having given up thoughts of direct rule, treated the Visigoths as trade partners, valuing the supply of slaves, grain, cloth, wine and coins. Some of them were Christian. A generation before the Huns arrived, a Greek bishop, Ulfilas, had devised an alphabet for Gothic and translated the Bible. But Christianity never won over the 'judge' or the other aristocrats, who were keen to preserve their own beliefs – the very essence of their own sense of identity – in the face of the new cultural imperialism flowing from Constantinople. After Valens acknowledged Visigothic independence under Athanaric in 369, it seemed both would benefit: their agreement established a mutual trade link, mutual respect, a buffer state for Rome against the barbarian hordes of Inner Asia, freedom for Athanaric to do whatever he wanted without fear of great-power intervention. What he wanted was an end to Christianity. This he achieved by means of a sinister ritual reimposing the old Gothic religion, which (as the historian Tacitus implies) was centred on an earth-mother goddess, Nerthus. Athanaric's officials wheeled a wooden statue of the goddess to the tents of Christian converts and ordered them to renounce their faith by worshipping the statue, on pain of death. Most chose to live, apparently, except a fanatic named Saba, who was set on martyrdom. When he was declared a fool and thrown out of his village, he taunted his fellow tribesmen until they threw him in a river and drowned him by pressing him down with a piece of wood. He became, as he would have wished, the first Gothic saint.

Rome and Christianity could be resisted, then; but not the advancing Huns. Athanaric tried, setting up a line of defence along the Dniester, but it was easily bypassed when the Huns ignored the Gothic army, crossed the river by night and made a surprise assault on the Goths from the rear. After a hasty retreat across present-day Moldova, the Goths started to build a rampart along the Moldovan border, the River Prut. It was at this point that Gothic morale collapsed, driving them across the Danube into Thrace and starting the train of events that led to the battle at Adrianople.

Behind them, advancing from the Ukrainian lowlands, came Attila's immediate forebears, on a 75-kilometre march over the Carpathians, winding uphill along the road that now leads from Kolomyya through the Carpathian National Nature Park. It was the regular route for invaders, one used again almost 1,000 years later by the Mongols. You climb easily to 931 metres (3,072 feet) over the Yablunytsia Pass (good skiing in winter, pretty alpine walks in summer), then drop to the Romanian border, and, leaving the Transylvanian highlands on your left, follow the snaking, narrow road along the River Theiss onto the Hungarian grasslands.

Here, as the wagon-train and herds spread out over the Carpathian basin, old pastoral and fighting skills again came into their own.

# 3

# THE RETURN OF THE MOUNTED ARCHER

'A VILE, UGLY AND DEGENERATE PEOPLE': THESE ARE THE WORDS of Ammianus, writing from within the Roman empire, the epitome of civilization in his own eyes and those of his readers. No wonder he was prejudiced; he was describing the most effective enemy ever to assault the empire. We, with the privilege of hindsight and security, should set prejudice aside, show some respect, and seek to understand why Attila's people had such an impact.

Their power lay in four elements:

- an ancient skill, mounted archery;
- a new version of an ancient weapon, the recurved bow;
- a new tactical technique;
- leadership.

The man himself is the subject of later chapters. What we are interested in right now is his raw materials: the skills and ambitions of mounted pastoral nomads armed with bows. Mounted archery was the military technique that could hold to ransom urbanized cultures across all Eurasia for the best part of 2,000 years, until gunpowder blew the horseback archer from history as utterly as it blew the Japanese samurai and the Swiss pike-man. Within a very short time, the skills that had defined nomadic warriors from Manchuria to the Russian steppes had fallen from use and almost from memory, enduring only in the accounts of those who had been on the receiving end of nomad arrows and in the minds of armchair strategists. The mounted archers themselves left no manuals. No-one after they vanished had a clue about how actually to do mounted archery – how to slide arrows from quivers, load them and fire them, time after time, while sitting on a galloping horse, let alone doing so in formation. No-one tried it.

Until now. Mounted archery is back, bringing a new understanding of how these warriors gained their supremacy – and there is more to it than that skill alone. Almost all Eurasian pastoral nomads were master-horsemen and master-bowmen, and none matched the Huns in their destructive ability. Nor was leadership enough on its own to explain Hun success. Attila had something extra to underpin his victories, something particular to the Huns. Only with the revival of mounted archery has it become possible to say what that magical element was.

The revival of the old skill is entirely due to one man: Lajos Kassai, who is, I suspect, the first true mounted archer in Europe since the departure of the Mongols in 1242. The Mongols left from Hungary; it was in Hungary that Attila had his base; so it is fitting that Kassai is a Hungarian – and particularly fitting that he is based a day's gallop both from the Mongol line of advance and from Attila's fifth-century headquarters. What follows is the story of his life's work: as you read, track the tight interlocking of skill, toughness, dedication and self-assurance. This is what mounted archery gives now, and what it once gave the Huns. Kassai jokes about being Attila reincarnate – 'I feel I was born in the twentieth century by some administrative error' – but it's not entirely a joke, if it's young Attila under consideration, rather than King Attila.

I heard of Kassai because anyone who knows anything about Huns and mounted archery mentions him. If I had been in the world of horses and bows, I would have heard of him in Colorado or Berlin. As it was, I first heard the name from museum people in Vienna and in the northern Hungarian town of Győr, and again from a lover of Andalusian horses in northern Hungary who knew Kassai was shortly to demonstrate his skills at a sporting festival in Budapest. Kassai Lajos – if you put the given name second, in the Hungarian style – comes out as Cosh-eye Lah-yosh: the rhythm and the soft *sh* sounds turned the name into poetry. By now he was becoming an obsession with me.

I and my interpreter Andrea Szegedi found him at the fair on Margaret Island in the Danube. He was dressed in a simple wrap-around costume, nomad-style, a Hun reborn, with three assistants selling his own brands of bow. Could we have a word? A nod, that was all, not even a smile. In a refreshment tent, he fixed me with intense, steady blue eyes in a face blank of expression. I was unsure of myself, not knowing anything about mounted archery, or how long we had, or whether I would see him again. He might have tried to put me at my ease with some polite phrases. Not a bit. It was unsettling – and became more so when I tried for some soundbite responses.

Where, for instance, did his interest in mounted archery come from?

'Something inside me.' He replied in halting English,

nailing me with a fierce gaze. 'What do you mean?'

'Well, just, why the interest?'

He switched his gaze to Andi, and went on in Hungarian, just as abruptly. 'It was from the inside. I have to do it. That's all.'

'I understand interest from others is growing?'

'They come from everywhere, from the US, from Canada, to learn.'

'Why do people love it?'

'If I can't tell you why I do it, I can't tell you why they love it.'

I saw why he had no patience with me. I was an outsider, the questions were dumb, and he was fiercely concentrated, not on me, but on what he was about to do, on its brutal physical and emotional demands. It was like approaching a top tennis player just before a Wimbledon final and expecting deep answers about the inner game of tennis. Besides, there was much more going on, which I was too busy with camera and tape-recorder to notice. Andi was a medical student: short-cropped hair, good on a horse, tall, lithe as a thorough-bred herself, and thoroughly, impregnably professional – or so I thought, until she talked later about the impression he made.

'Yes, he could look scary. But his mood changed in a second. He has this nice smile. Then he was really funny. He swore. Like something was "bitchily good", as we say. Then sometimes the way he looked . . .' She was driving us along a flat, straight road over the *puszta*, but her mind was not on grasslands. 'We have an expression, that when someone looks at you like that they can see your bones. That was how it felt. He could see my bones. He just looked at me and asked me a really simple question, and I had to think really hard, because he was looking into my eyes, and he was amazing.' She paused. 'He really was. Honestly.'

Clearly, there was more to Kassai than the scattered responses that came my way during that interview. It took me another meeting on his home ground, more talk, and respectful observation to understand. Mounted archery is his life's work. To explain it to me would have taken weeks. Fortunately, he has already taken the time by writing his story in a book, *Horseback Archery*. But even that tells only half the story. The other half emerges in action, in teaching, in the commitment that others give him. There could be no real understanding of him except in action, any more than there can be a real understanding of what it takes to be a mounted archer unless you become one.

He is a man whose life perfectly matches what he feels is his destiny. From this flows a steely self-assurance, a rock-solid sense of identity and purpose, hard-won in a world that he sees as obsessed by change, growth, novelty and ambitions which, once realized, must be replaced by new ambitions. Kassai, like a monk, heard the call, followed, and arrived at his goal. But, unlike a monk, he did not find the way and the goal through a teaching, or an organization, or a Master. They are his alone. And both have involved an extraordinary combination of physical and mental work. There is something of the Zen warrior in him, the fighter who achieves internal balance to hone his martial skills – except that he had to become his own Master, invent his own religion, as it were. It has taken him over 20 years.

I asked again: Why? He says he has no choice in the matter, as if mounted archery were in his very genes. Of course, it couldn't be, because the skills of the mounted archer were not around long enough to work their way into the genetic code. For nomads, the roots lay not in nature but in nurture, in skills implanted in childhood and perfected over decades. Kassai did not have that advantage. He grew up in a world of collective farmers and city-dwellers and factory-workers.

Perhaps, as a child, he experienced another sort of nurture, some unconscious need to escape the oppression imposed by the Soviet-backed counter-revolution, the drabness of communism.

Escape lay in his imagination, sparked off in his childhood by a novel about the Huns, *The Invisible Man*, by Géza Gárdonyi. It is the story of a Thracian slave, Zeta, who travels to Attila's court with the Greek civil servant Priscus (the invisible man himself, whose real-life eye-witness account of the journey in 449 is the subject of a later chapter). Zeta has many adventures, falls in love with a flighty Hun girl, rejects another who loves him despite rejection, campaigns with Attila, fights in the great battle of the Catalaunian Plains, witnesses Attila's funeral, and finally flees to safety with the girl he recognizes at last to be his own true love. It's all rather overblown, with a great many exclamation marks, but it's a good, quick, vivid read for children, and is justly famous in Hungary. Never out of print since its publication in 1902, it reflects and intensifies Attila's popularity and the widespread belief that the Huns were the Hungarians' true ancestors, never mind that everyone also knows perfectly well that their real ancestors arrived as Magyars over 400 years later.

Here's a taste of it, in its English translation, unfortunately entitled *Slave of the Huns*, describing in lurid and exaggerated terms Attila's hordes preparing for their advance westward:

Young people exercised out in the fields in huge swarms. Horns blared out signals. A long falling note meant a retreat. Two long rising notes meant an about-face in mid-gallop and shoot. This manoeuvre I simply could not master. The Huns had been practising from childhood on; when the horses were galloping so fast that they were swimming through the air, the riders would turn themselves round, lie on their stomachs and shoot their arrows far behind them. Some even shot lying on their backs.

For weeks, the hordes continue to arrive, the Alans with their javelins, Nubades in wolfskins, bearded Blemmyes, painted Gelons armed with scythes, the thundering carts of the Bastarnes, Akatiri with bows half again as tall as themselves, haggard, large-boned Skirians, and Heruls and Kvads and Ostrogoths, and on and on for pages,

> ten thousand here, twenty thousand there, fifty thousand of the Jazyges alone, eighty thousand Gepids, sixty thousand Goths. We counted them for a week, just by taking their leaders' word for how many there were. When we passed the half million mark, we left off. To this day I don't know how many people were gathered . . . there must have been more than a million horses and thousands upon thousands of carts.

Heady stuff to a boy yearning for action and freedom, happy to be swept along by a novelist's exaggerations. 'Yes, our ancestors the Huns were the greatest horseback archers of the world,' says Kassai. 'I imagined the wild gallops, the horses foaming at the mouth, the drawn bows. What a sensation! I wanted to be like them, a terrifying, fearless warrior.'

The first step was to become an archer. As a child and then as a young man, living near Kaposvár, 40 kilometres south of Lake Balaton, he made bows by the dozen, gathering information and experience. He tried different types of wood for their power and speed of reaction, the best ways to laminate tendons (on the back of the bow, to resist stretching) and horn (on the belly, to resist compression), arrows for weight and rigidity, arrowheads for their penetration. He became a good shot, building up on rapid fire as well.[1] This is demanding enough in itself. The muscles and sinews of the forearm and shoulder must turn to iron. The three fingers of the firing-hand must get used to the bowstring's constant abrasion, for in the heat of battle mounted archers could not use either the protective leather tab of modern archers or the thumb-ring employed later by Turks. If you train from childhood, the fingers adapt by growing calloused skin, but Kassai did not have that advantage; he binds his fingers with tape.

But all of this was mere archery. He still had not ridden. Having tried a few formal riding lessons, he realized that there was no-one from whom he could learn to ride like a nomad. Practically the only place he could have learned today is Mongolia, where children as young as three are tied onto horses until the two become one. It was too late, and Mongolia too far away, for Kassai; he was grown up, and would have to teach himself. This he did in his twenties with the aid of a spirited creature called Prankish, who baptized him with fire, sweeping him off by galloping under low branches, dragging him by the stirrup, and falling on him in mud. 'The only time I sensed the countryside was when I had my head buried in it.'

One day, a wild gallop ended at a steep hillside. Prankish stopped. In unexpected stillness, Kassai looked around. He was in a dead-end valley, with sides so steep and close it seemed that if he reached out he would touch them. It felt like finding his place in the world, a place where, in words that are emotive even in translation, 'accepting the sweet solitude

---

[1] Establishing a tradition since taken to an extreme by one of Kassai's friends, an Italian, Celestino Poletti, who, using one of Kassai's bows, holds the world record for firing as many arrows as possible in 24 hours. This must be one of the craziest of human achievements. He stood there firing one arrow every 5 seconds, 11 arrows a minute, 700 an hour, round the clock until he had shot 17,000 arrows.

of a voluntary exile, I could retreat from this noisy century and develop mounted archery to perfection'.

Not that it was yet a place to live or ride in, for it was densely forested, its open spaces overgrown with weeds, its lowest area a mess of mud and reeds. It belonged to a state farm, but as farmland it was useless; so he rented 15 hectares and set about adapting it for horseback archery.

This was a long, slow process. A valley like that, where nature ruled, deserved the respect due to a sovereign entity. A man might befriend it for the brief term of his earthly existence, but he must cause no permanent damage. He must attend to the winds, the waters, the plants, the movements of animals and people. How does the wind blow around the contours of the hills? Which way does the water flow? What happens when there is a lot of rain, or a long drought? Where does the snow melt first and last? Which way do horses walk, and where do they like to lie? Where do they graze in the day and where at night? When people come, where do they stop spontaneously to talk or to make fire? Where, in particular, do they like to shoot? It took him four years to absorb all this, and the smell of the pastures in the changing seasons, and the feel of each hilltop and each marshy area, and to decide how best to realize his dream.

Everything about this ancient, forgotten skill had to be rediscovered from scratch. The landscape gave him a natural 90-metre course, along which targets would be placed. He acquired a second horse, a poor limping creature he saved from the knacker's yard, and therefore cheap. Over months of tender, loving care, Bella became sleek, gentle and sensitive. With her, Kassai discovered how to accustom a horse to the lunge-rein, the saddle, the peculiar feel of a mounted archer. Bella learned to gallop evenly along the course, then do the same thing without reins, then accept the odd noises and sensations of sticks, ribbons, bags, balls being whirled and thrown above her head, until finally she was ready for the twang of the bow, the zip of the arrow and the feel of a rider firing time after time, with nothing to indicate a turn or a change of pace but small movements of the legs and shifts of bodyweight forward and back.

The first experience of mounted archery was a revelation. His target was a bale of hay, but even galloping right past, no more than 2 or 3 metres away, he could fire only one arrow every pass, and hardly ever hit the mark. In particular, he found it almost impossible to perform the most famous action of the mounted archer, the over-the-shoulder 'Parthian shot', named after the Parthians and then distorted in English into the 'parting shot'. He practised for weeks, doing fifteen to twenty gallops a day. Bella became stronger and stronger; but he – already an expert archer, with numerous wins in competitions – remained as hopeless as ever. There seemed to be no way to overcome the combinations of movements, the forward motion and bounce of the gallop, the shock of hooves, his own leaping body, the arms flailing in automatic response. It seemed quite impossible to aim and then fire accurately, let alone reload.

He almost despaired. There was something he was not getting, something that Attila, that every Hun warrior, every mounted archer from time immemorial, must have learned in late childhood, until it was so much part of them that it was never mentioned to the few outsiders who recorded their ways. He stopped riding, not to abandon his dream, but to search for the essence of the skill he sought, the barbarian artistry hidden away by the obscuring cloud of civilization.

Kassai turned inwards. He would abandon the effort that dominates standard archery, the rational focus on accuracy, the route that has led to the stabilizers and targeting devices of the competitive sport. Technology and reason did not provide the way. He turned instead to Zen archery, which relies on internal harmony, achieving success by trying less. It is, at heart, the same approach with which a child learns to ride a bicycle, or the 'relaxed concentration' by which an athlete in explosive events – javelin-throwing, high jump, pole-vault – produces a seemingly effortless record.

He returned to the basics: horse and rider. He abandoned his saddle to ride bareback. He wanted to feel the body of the horse, the muscles, the sweat, the breathing, become at one with it. Pain became a way of life. He fell constantly. His urine had blood in it for weeks from the battering. He learned this: that pain and suffering are not the same. This was not suffering, because nothing had been imposed on him, and he was free to face more pain, in the certain knowledge that he was making progress. Wounds heal quickly, as he says, and we can continue on our way to meet the next obstacle, always moving in the direction of the greatest resistance. He had chosen this route as monks once chose hair shirts and flagellation, and it filled him with the fierce joy of approaching salvation. Was this obsessive, a little crazy, perhaps? It was, and he welcomed the madness.

For from this madness came renewed sanity, and success. He learned to separate upper from lower body. He imagined the track made through the air by his extended left hand, until, holding a glass of water, he could keep his hand steady while riding bareback at a trot. He acquired more horses, and practised on them all. He explored the worst conditions – rain, mud, snow, frozen ground. He worked in particular at the 'Parthian', the 'parting', the over-the-shoulder shot, keeping the waist forward while the body turned through 180 degrees. He would turn himself into a centaur, the half-horse, half-man invented by the Greeks as a symbol of the Scythian mounted archer.

Meanwhile, he perfected the techniques of firing. A major stumbling block was the need to fire one arrow after another, at speed. This is not something that your average unmounted archer ever does, so even an expert does not have to *feel* the way to reload. An arrow has a nock in its end which slots onto the bow-string, but, as any amateur knows, it takes many seconds and many actions to load an arrow – you lower the bow, turn it flat, reach for the quiver, extract an arrow, turn the arrow to the correct orientation with the 'lead-feather' pointing away from the string, fiddle the slot onto the string, get the tips of three fingers hooked round the string, grip the arrow between first and second fingers to keep it in position against the bow, raise the bow, pull the string, refocus your attention on the distant target, aim, and at last fire. The whole thing takes perhaps half a minute, which is about the time it takes to read the foregoing instructions.

It took Kassai months, and much experimenting, to work out how to fire quickly. For a start, forget the quiver. That's only to store arrows; it is not for the arrows you are about to fire, because it is hopelessly slow to reload by reaching down to your waist or over your shoulder to pull an arrow from your quiver.

This is how it's done: hold a bunch of arrows in the left hand against the bow, making sure they are spread like an array of cards; reach between string and bow; grip an arrow with two fingers bent double so that they form firm supports either side; place the thumb just so; pull the arrow back so that the string slides along the thumb straight into the nock in the arrow; and pull, while raising the bow, all in one smooth set of actions. But these are mere words. To put them into action is to perform crucial gestures as minute and fine as learning Braille (for example, to make sure the nock in the arrow is oriented correctly, you check with your thumb – and without practice you can hardly feel the nock at all, let alone make any correction, let alone do so on a galloping horse). After a year –

*– he could fire three arrows in six seconds.*

Say that out loud, three times, fast: that's how long it takes him to load and fire the three arrows.

Now it was time to apply his new skills. He began loading and drawing at the gallop, aiming in all three directions consecutively, to the front, to the side, to the back. Then, at last, it became reality: a gallop past his bale, firing three arrows – failure after failure, as usual, until one day all three arrows ended up in the bale. It was, of course, a lucky break; but if it could be done once, it could be done again, a thousand times, a hundred thousand times, given perseverance. That was the moment he first truly felt like a horseback archer.

It had taken four years to get that far, and it was only a beginning. New discoveries lay ahead. Standing archers draw the bow to the cheekbone or chin, often kissing the string, and sighting along the arrow. Kassai tried this for months, until forced to admit that, for archery while on a galloping horse, it was hopeless. All that tension, the bow drawn, the muscles of the arms and shoulders rigid, the whole body wracked by different motions – how on earth in these circumstances could the rider choose the right moment to release his missile? At one point, he tried to use technology to help him focus. He attached a small laser to an arrow, and tried to keep the spot of red light on the target as he galloped past. To his astonishment, he failed utterly. He couldn't even get the jiggling spot to remain within a metre of the target, let alone on it. 'The experiment proved that I knew absolutely everything there was to know about horseback archery,' he says wrily, 'with the minor exception of how the arrow manages to hit the centre of the target.'

The answer was first to try drawing the bow, not to the chin, but directly along the line of the outstretched arm, bringing the arrow back to the chest, to the heart, to the seat of the emotions; and second to let the unconscious choose the moment of release. For there is a right moment in the chaos of movement. It comes at that point in the galloping stride when the horse's four feet are all off the ground at once, a split second in which to find peace. In Kassai's words, the moment comes 'at the top of the dead centre of the galloping leap, during the moment we float through the air before the horse's hoof connects with the ground again'. But the brain has no time to bring this moment into conscious awareness. There can be no thinking, no analysis. There is only action.

How do you aim? You don't, you can't, because there's no time. You leave your mind behind, and you respond by pure feeling.

But to do that demands the right experience, the right information for the brain to work with. As with painting and poetry, feeling is nothing without the technical foundation, the years of experiment and pain and failure and despair. There was in Kassai's struggle with this unfolding process something of the medieval mystic wrestling with the long, dark night of the soul.

Then he came through, into a sort of paradise.

At dawn I rode my horse at a gallop on the crystal carpet laid by drops of dew and shot arrows damp with the morning mist at my target. The water thrown off the damp arrow almost drew a line through the air. Then I suddenly noticed the fiery rays of the sun burning my face red, everything around me was crackling with dry heat, and the yellow slope of the hill was reverberating with the noontime bells of the neighbouring village.

I was awake in my dreams, dreaming awake. Time melted like sweet honey in morning tea. How much I had searched for that feeling! I had chased it like a little boy who wants to catch a butterfly in a flowery meadow. The wonderful insect zigzags in flight like a sheet of paper blown by the wind, then lands on a fragrant flower. The child catches up with it, panting with the effort and reaches towards it with a clumsy move to hold it between finger and thumb, but the butterfly flits away, and the boy is running, stumbling after it again.

I had the butterfly in my hand. I enclosed it between my palms, careful not to hurt its fragile wings. The winds of change flowed through me as I awaited the moment when I could turn all my powers towards a new challenge.

The challenge was to be totally serious about mounted archery, which was now life itself – literally: he would, he says, die without it. To fund his obsession, Kassai needed income; so he would have to make his personal mission into a business, which meant inventing a new sport, and all the rules to go with it. His valley gave him the dimensions. A 90-metre course, with three targets, each 90 centimetres across, to be shot at once each – forward, sideways and backward – from a gallop that must take no more than sixteen seconds, with expert riders taking eight or nine seconds. But the first shot cannot be fired until 30 metres into the course, and the final target must be hit as quickly as possible with the 'parting shot' as the rider gallops away. Three shots in six seconds, a shot every two seconds. To establish his new sport, he needed to make a name for himself, using his own expertise to show what could be done.

His next big idea was this: to ride his horses – he now had eleven – in relay, along the course he had set himself, firing continuously for twelve hours. He closed the valley, shut out the curious, 'the unfaithful companions, tenacious enemies, two-faced lovers' – hints here of how difficult it must have been for others to deal with this demanding, uncomfortable zealot – and trained for six months. 'There was not a single day I did not imagine myself to be in a battlefield. Despite being alone, I was not lonely for a minute. My imagination peopled the valley with comrades in arms and deadly enemies.' The challenge opened up new levels of success and freedom. 'I think life tries us all, but the really lucky ones are the people who choose their own trials, and make them as big as they can possibly bear.' This was not all for the sake of spiritual exercise, of course: Kassai's marathon would be used to build up the business side of his operation. It was time to let the world know of the rebirth of mounted archery.

So it happened. The *Guinness Book of Records*, TV and newspapers were informed, helpers and friends called back to hold horses and collect arrows. One June day, at five in the morning, he started, first using the slow horses, firing five arrows in the ten or twelve seconds it took them to gallop the course; then, as the heat built and the hours passed, he switched to the faster horses, which covered the course in less than seven seconds, firing three arrows in each pass. By five in the afternoon, he had galloped 286 laps and fired something over 1,000 arrows. Kassai was catatonic with fatigue, in some altered state of consciousness. Assistants and students tossed him in the air to celebrate his achievement. 'I shall be forever indebted to them for their enthusiasm,' he writes, with heavy irony. 'It took another two hours for me to awaken. Then suddenly, the accumulated fatigue of a decade hit me like molten lead. I showed little sign of activity at the evening dance.'

Fifteen years on, Kassai has honed his performance to something approaching perfection. The sport, using his scoring system, is well established and growing. Since the early 1990s several hundred men and women, more every year, have been practising this gruelling skill, first in Hungary, and now also in Germany and Austria, with a few passionate disciples in the United States. At some point these adepts are going to push for the sport to be included in the Olympics.

Todd Delle, from Arizona, discovered Kassai when he conducted a training session in the United States. Suddenly, a long-term interest in archery and riding acquired a new intensity, because he saw that this was more than just a sport. It was a fusion of body and mind, the two reflecting each other, a foundation for dealing with the successes and failures of life itself, 'for you cannot fully understand success without first understanding failure'. But it's not just about individual achievement; it's also about the group, with everyone encouraging everyone else – a collaborative spirit rare in competitive sport. This is as it should be for a skill that underpinned individual and group survival in battle. There are now others who claim to teach horseback archery. 'Some of these I have met,' Delle explained. 'What makes Kassai different is that what he teaches is not simply the mechanics of how to shoot an arrow from the back of a galloping horse. *What he teaches is the heart and soul of a warrior.*'

There you have it. If Kassai is Attila the archer, he is also Attila the leader, in this respect: he has created a group dedicated to a particular end. In Kassai's case, the work is all positive, with nothing but a creative effect on both individual and group. He speaks of being a warrior, but is well removed from the brutalities of a warrior's life. In Attila's case, there was a whole other dimension. However gruelling the physical hardship, however uplifting the spiritual training, however ecstatic the teamwork, it all led on to conquest, killing, destruction, rape and pillage.

Kassai's valley is now the centre not simply of a sport but of a cult, of a way of life, and of a self-sustaining business.

The sweeping curve of the valley now holds Kassai's house – simple, circular, wooden, with furniture carved from tree-trunks; a barn, sweet with the smell of hay, for the two dozen horses; a covered riding school and an arena; two training runs for mounted archery and two butts for standing archery; and, up on a hillside, a Kazakh yurt, where local children come for lessons in living history. With judicious ditching, the marsh has become a lake. In the nearby town, workshops make bows, arrows and saddles. The whole estate is underpinned by trainees – several hundred of them, mainly Hungarian, but also German and Austrian, with a scattering of English and even a few Americans – and their need for equipment.

You can see him at work on the first Saturday of each month. When I was there, the 35 students ranged from nearmasters down to a six-year-old boy. There were eleven women. The Huns, after all, had women in their ranks, as the Scythians did, and one of his most adept pupils is Pettra Engeländer, who runs courses of her own near Berlin. Kassai masters his world like a sergeant-major teaching a martial art. With a crowd of a hundred watching from the arena's banked sides, the day starts with rigorous drill-work, with three dozen trainees in lines following his actions, stretching arms and necks, moving on to mock-shooting, left leg and arm extended, the other arm pulled to the chest then thrown back in a mock-release to a yell of 'Hö!' from Kassai, and an answering 'Ha!' from his trainees, then a single pace, a 180-degree turn and the same again, left and right reversed.

'It's important to shoot with both hands, to preserve the symmetry. This is not like your English longbow,' he explained later as we walked across the valley. 'We have to be prepared to attack equally well from either direction.'

There follow more variations on the same theme – mock-shots in lines, forward, to the side, backwards, with full squats, now to the tap of a shaman's drum, with Kassai moving up and down the lines – until, after almost an hour, the trainees run to the stable, change into kimono-like warrior robes and reappear with their horses to ride bareback. First they toss bags of hay to each other; then they use the bags to pillow-fight, and staves to slash at posts and spear wooden cut-out figures.

All this is pretty spectacular; but it's Kassai's demonstration that the audience has been waiting for, and it is astonishing. Three men stand along the arena, each holding a pole on which is a circular target 90 centimetres across. Kassai gallops the length of the arena. As he passes, the man starts to run, holding his target aloft a metre or so above his head. Kassai takes six seconds to pass the first running man, during which time he shoots three arrows. Then on past the next – three shots – and the next – another three shots. Eighteen seconds, nine arrows, each released with a Ha!, and all strike true. And then, as an encore, the same gallop, the same men, except this time the men each have two unattached targets. As they run and Kassai gallops past, they throw the targets over their shoulders. Six flying targets, six shots, all within a metre of the runners, and not a single miss. The final runner falls on his knees, as if thanking the gods for his survival, and all line up for a round of applause. Kassai remains as grim as ever.

Later, walking the valley, I saw five trainees firing at targets tossed in the air. I watched for several minutes. Not one of the five scored a single hit. And they weren't even firing at speed, let alone on horseback.

It was Kassai, then, who was able to answer that crucial question: if the Huns were mounted archers, living the same sort of lifestyle as dozens of the other nomadic tribes, why were they so much more successful than their neighbours? It was not all down to Attila. The Huns' conquests started two generations before his, when Alans and Goths fled before them.

The technical key to Hun success – literally, their secret weapon – was the Hun bow. Now, the bow certainly looks different, because it is asymmetrical, like its Xiongnu proto-type; that is, when strung its upper limb is longer than its lower limb. Whether or not the Huns inherited the design from the Xiongnu, the design had been in existence for several centuries; it also spread eastwards, to Japan. Oddly, asymmetry does nothing at all to the power, range or accuracy of the bow; so its purpose remains controversial. Perhaps the length of the bottom limb was reduced to ease handling, as it would when you whip it over the horse's neck to fire to the right (or, if you are a real master, to fire left-handed). Perhaps it was easier to fire when kneeling; but when would you need to kneel? Kassai, playing the mystic, wonders if, when drawn, the bow became a symbol of the Hun tent, or the overarching deity, Heaven above, but it doesn't really add up. I prefer to think of it as a matter of identity, for the details of common objects often contain elements that emerge randomly or for trivial reasons, and endure simply because they become traditional and there is no good reason to change them. Perhaps Hun bows were asymmetrical because they always had been, from the time when a stave newly cut from the tree was more likely to be asymmetrical than symmetrical. Perhaps if you'd dared to ask Attila why Hun bows were bigger at the top, he would have said through his interpreter: That's the way we Huns make bows.

But Hun bows were also different in two other respects, adding up to a third that really did matter: they were bigger; they had a more pronounced recurve; and finally, crucially, their size plus their shape gave them more power. The design evolved in response to the changing environment of steppe warfare. The little Scythian bow served well enough for 2,000 years until, in the third century BC, the Scythians' eastern neighbours, the Sarmatians, developed a defence against Scythian arrows. They covered their warriors and horses with armour and taught them to fight in close formation. There were various possible ways to counter this – with swords, lances, javelins, heavy cavalry. But the most effective was a bow that could punch arrows through armour. This was the bow the Huns brought with them from the east – as we know from those found in Xiongnu graves: a bow with a little 'wing' of horn, some 3 centimetres long, which curved away from the archer. It was this, not the wooden frame of the bow itself, that held the bowstring. The 'wings' provided the weak ends with a rigidity that wood on its own cannot match, as fingernails do things that bare fingers could not. They also extended the length of the bow by a crucial few percentage points; and the extra length increased leverage. This allows the archer to bend a heavier bow with less effort, because the curving ear acts as if it were part of a large-diameter wheel. As the archer draws the bow the ear unrolls, in effect lengthening the bowstring. On release, the ear rolls up again, in effect shortening the bowstring, increasing the acceleration of the arrow without the need for a longer arrow and a longer draw. It was an invention that foreshadowed the system of pulleys used in modern compound bows. In effect, it gave the Hun archer longer arms, allowing him to shoot with slightly more penetration, or a slightly greater range: a few metres only, but a few crucial metres, enabling Hun arrows to be fatal while those of their enemies died.

This beautiful and complex instrument had another advantage. Making one demanded a level of expertise amounting to artistry. This was no Kalashnikov, which could be churned out by some Central Asian bow-factory. Recurved bows of any sort take a year or more to make, but in addition the Hun bowyer had to be a master in carving and applying the horn ears. Each bow was a minor masterpiece, and no other group had the expertise to produce its match.

A superior bow, however, was only one element in the

Huns' dominance. It would be vital for the lone warrior or the small raiding party; but, to an advancing horde, small-scale victories were no more use than no victories at all. The Huns needed to become a machine for massive and overwhelming destruction. One factor in their favour was their nomadic lifestyle, which gave them the ability to fight year-round, unlike western armies, which camped in the winter and fought in the summer. Frozen ground and frozen rivers made good going for strong men on strong horses. Their other major advantage was that they learned to fight as one, and on a large scale. In their sojourn in the wilderness or their drift westwards, they evolved tactics to suit their new weapon. If Scythians could strike like the wind, the Huns learned how to strike like the whirlwind.

It worked like this.

Imagine an army of mounted Huns facing an army of well-armoured cavalrymen – Sarmatians, Goths, Romans; it doesn't matter who for the moment, because all now shared common elements: all had bows, all carried some sort of armour, mostly made of leather, bone or bronze scales. Their horses are similarly protected. The Huns are more lightly clad, perhaps with no armour at all. They will rely on their speed and fire-power. They each carry a bow, a quiver full of 60 arrows and a sword hanging at the waist. Though they can ride bareback, they have saddles and, I think, stirrups made of leather or rope. The front-line Huns are in two regiments, each of, say, 1,000 men (and women as well if need be), while behind them stand dozens of horse-drawn ammunition wagons, loaded with several hundred spare bows and over 100,000 arrows.

A trumpet brays. The horses know the form, and the two regiments – well out of range of the enemy, some 500 metres away – form into two huge masses, circling slowly in opposite directions like gathering storms, raising ominous clouds of dust, soundless but for the dull thump of hooves on grass. Another call, and each of the 2,000 men, using his free hand, picks six, seven, maybe nine arrows from his quiver, depending on skill and experience, and places them in his bow-hand, holding them against the outer edge of the bow.

Another trumpet call. Now the clouds of warriors pick up the pace, trotting in circles 200–300 metres across, waiting for the moment. The horses know what is coming. They sweat as the tension mounts. The attack call sounds. From the outside edge of each swirling mass a line of warriors peels off at the gallop, heading straight at the static line of defenders. The rest follow. The gap narrows: 400 metres, 300 metres. It has been less than half a minute since the last call. Now the two regiments are at full gallop, something like 30–40 kilometres per hour. At 200 metres, a cloud of arrows arises from the enemy, but the range is great, the arrows fired at random. Almost all are wasted. At 150 metres, the first few hundred Huns fire straight ahead, concentrating on a narrow 100-metre section of the enemy lines. At that range, the arrows are aimed low over the heads of those in front. With the added momentum of the gallop, the arrows travel at over 200 kilometres per hour – and these are arrows with small, three-flanged iron tips filed to needle sharpness, with the penetrating power of bullets. At 100 metres, the leaders have already reloaded. Their horses wheel to gallop parallel with the enemy line, the archers turn in their saddles and fire sideways – the arrows flying almost flat – reload, fire again, and again, all within a few seconds, for this is the equivalent of Kassai's 90-metre course in which he can fire six arrows, while behind them the body of the regiment are also raining fire on the same unhappy clump of enemy soldiers. In five seconds 1,000 arrows could hit 200 of the enemy, another 1,000 in the next five. That's a rate of 12,000 shots per minute, equivalent to ten machine-guns. Now, after 100 metres, the leaders wheel again, and gallop directly away from the enemy – but they are still firing, a shot or two each, aiming low over the heads of those behind them.

Around they come again, snatching another handful of arrows from their quivers, slotting them into their bow-hands, feeling for the nocks, twisting each into the correct alignment, swinging around behind the last of the regiment. The whirlwind is in full swing, 100 riders in a rough outer circle, with another ten lines inside, all eager for the best position on the leading edge, all whirling round a 400-metre core of stillness. A whirlwind is exactly what it would seem like on the ground to country folk who would have seen dust-devils sucking dust from sun-scorched steppes. A modern image comes to mind. That first go-around has sliced down men as grass falls to a garden strimmer. In the space of 45 seconds, which is a slow time for a galloping horse to cover 400 metres, the same 200 enemy have taken hits from 5,000 aimed arrows, 25 per man. Most, of course, will be deflected, but some must find a gap between shields, or above a breast-plate, or through an eye-hole, or even straight through a shield, straight through iron armour. From behind, others crowd forward to take the place of the fallen, only to fall themselves.

Let's put this in a wider context. No soldiers had ever delivered such a rate of fire. There would be nothing like them until the French faced English longbowmen in the Hundred Years War; and longbowmen were stationary, lacking the supreme flexibility of the Hun mounted archers. No soldiers would be able to come close to this speed or density of fire until the invention of repeating guns in the latter part of the nineteenth century. Even then, the first bolt-action rifle-men were nothing compared to bowmen: a bowman must learn his craft and his skill from childhood and is a priceless asset; a rifleman is trained in days, and is easily replaced.

This, moreover, is the first lap of ten, with the circling warriors grabbing reloads from the ammunition holders at the rear. In ten minutes, 50,000 arrows have hit a 100-metre front. Now, recall that this is one of two contra-rotating whirls, with one regiment firing right-handed on the left side, the other the opposite. Between them, they are covering 200 metres of battle-front. It only needs one man to fall and a gap opens, into which arrows pour, and the dam breaks apart.

Of course, some enemies were better protected than others. Persians, Sarmatians, Goths and Romans all had cavalry with armour, and armoured infantrymen carrying shields, spears and javelins, backed sometimes by catapults. It might be necessary to break well-armoured ranks by other means; so the Huns had other tactics, in particular the feigned retreat, which would, with luck, draw the opposition forward far enough to break the rigid line of their defence, so that gaps would open, allowing the Huns on yet another go around to ride in with drawn swords to slash open the body of the enemy army. At close quarters they also used lassos, a natural weapon for herders. In Mongolia today, country-dwellers use lassos on the end of long poles to catch sheep and goats. 'While the enemy are guarding against wounds from the sword-thrusts,' wrote Ammianus, 'the Huns throw strips of cloth plaited into nooses over their opponents and so entangle them that they fetter their limbs and take from them the power of riding and walking.'

All this gave the Huns an advantage in open country. The technique was stupendously effective on the steppes as they came up against more static groups of Sarmatians, Alans and Goths. But by the time of Attila's birth, when the Huns were in possession of the grasslands of eastern Hungary, there were no more steppes to be conquered. Traditions based on pastoralism, horsemanship, fast movement and a simple lifestyle had reached their limits. Now the Huns were up against forests, mountains and cities, and would soon face strategic and tactical problems of which they had no inkling.

# II
# THE RIVALS

# 4

# A CONTINENT IN CHAOS

IT IS EARLY IN THE 380S ON HUNGARY'S GREAT PLAIN. THE HUNS
are settling into their new homeland, and finding it less than
ideal. For at least a generation they have been on the move,
living well off the proceeds of warfare. They are hooked on
pillage, not just for luxuries, but for sheer survival. It is all
they know. Now, suddenly, they are hemmed in. To the east
lie highlands – Transylvania and the Carpathians, through
which they came a few years before. There's nothing back
that way for them. To the south and west lies the Danube,
the Roman frontier, with its armies and fortress-towns; to the
north and west, German tribes who may one day be vassals,
but are not exactly rich. It will take a little time to assess
which way to turn. For newly arrived nomads, the future is
full of complexities and unknowns.

After Adrianople the empire struggled, and failed, to remake
the peace within and without. The Balkans remained in
turmoil, with Goth bands raiding freely, until the western

emperor, Gratian, and his eastern co-ruler, Theodosius the Great, made peace with them all individually in 380–2, bribing them with tax exemptions, land grants and employment in the armed forces. It was Theodosius who, at two vital moments, held this tottering enterprise together by sending armies to back Christianity against paganism and his family's claim to the West against rebels. It was he who managed to buy time by converting the Goths into allies, even if their version of Christianity was heretical. It was he who imposed the Nicene version of Christianity empire-wide before his own death in 395. With him fell a bastion against disorder and the infection of barbarism. His heirs were two feeble sons, Arcadius (aged eighteen, ruler of the East) and Honorius (eleven, of the West).

The empire became a cocktail of cultures, interfused, each dependent on others. Some barbarians settled; others kept on the move, notably the Visigoths. A new chief, Alaric, took them raiding across the Balkans so successfully that he was made a provincial governor, but that was just a stepping-stone to a better homeland for his people within the empire. In both parts of the empire, Goths and other barbarians – even individual Huns – became senior officers. In the West, the power behind the throne, Stilicho, a Vandal by descent, was married to a niece of Theodosius. Goths served en masse, as contingents, with the danger that their loyalty was to their own commanders rather than to the emperor. Barbarians were fast becoming the arbiters of imperial destiny. In 401 Alaric led his Visigoths into Italy, forcing the emperor to move his court to Ravenna, where it stayed for a century.

In 405–7 two barbarian armies – ragbags of Goths, Alans, Vandals, Swabians, Alemanni and Burgundians – swept into Gaul and Italy. Stilicho favoured collaboration, provoking an anti-barbarian backlash in which he was purged and executed, with no impact on the advance of the barbarians. In

410 Alaric seized Rome. It was the first time the Eternal City had seen enemies within its walls for 800 years – an event so shocking to Christians that it inspired the North African bishop Augustine of Hippo to write one of the most influential books of the age, *Concerning the City of God*. Alaric died that year, and his rootless army, still in search of a homeland, drifted back to Gaul, then on into Spain, finally swinging round again to settle north of the Pyrenees in what is now Aquitaine. In 418 their new capital, Toulouse, became the centre of a semi-autonomous region, a nation in all but name, supplying troops to the empire in exchange for regular supplies of grain. Barbarian and Roman were intertwined, in geography, arms, society and politics, a process exemplified by the fate of the daughter of Theodosius and sister of Emperor Honorius, the 20-year-old Galla Placidia, who had been dragged off to become the unwilling wife of a barbarian – Alaric's heir, Athaulf.

But fate allowed Galla Placidia a remarkable comeback. When Athaulf died, she was married (against her will, again) back into Roman stock, to a husband befitting her status, the patrician and general Constantius, co-emperor for just seven months in 421. It was this marriage that catapulted her into power, which she preserved through many dramatic twists, turning herself into one of the most formidable women of her age. When Constantius died, she was accused of intrigue against her own brother and fled to Constantinople with her baby daughter Honoria and her four-year-old son Valentinian, heir to the western part of the empire. In Constantinople, the ruler in the East was Arcadius' son, another Theodosius, who in 423 became, briefly, the sole ruler of the entire empire, at the age of 22. Nevertheless, he chose to back Galla Placidia when she demanded the western throne for young Valentinian. As a result, when the same year the court in Ravenna chose to crown a non-family official,

John, Theodosius sent an army to crush the usurper, and placed Valentinian, now six, on the throne (thus returning the boy's mother Placidia to Italy, along with the infant Honoria, who is destined to play a peculiarly dramatic role in our story later).

This, then, was how things stood when Attila was reaching maturity in the 420s: the empire divided, both parts riven by religious and political rivalry, half a dozen barbarian groups as immigrant communities, the northern frontiers in chaos, both armies staffed in part by the very people they opposed. To an ambitious chieftain north of the Danube, it all looked quite promising.

Now retrace the same 40 years to see what the Huns had been doing during that time.

The first Huns appeared in western Europe in 384, when they and their Alan vassals were invited to strengthen the imperial ranks in the civil war against a would-be usurper, Maximus. They helped keep Maximus out of Italy, and would probably have gone on deeper into the empire if they hadn't been bribed to behave themselves and go home. Their good behaviour inspired Theodosius to employ them again four years later in a second intervention to quell rebellion in Italy. 'O memorable thing,' wrote the fourth-century historian Pacatus, 'Goths and Huns and Alans answered the roll-call, changed guards and rarely feared to be reprimanded. There was no tumult, no confusion, no looting in the usual barbarian way.' But this time, after victory, the barbarian contingents refused to go home. John Chrysostom, Bishop of Constantinople, described the result: 'That which has never taken place has now come to pass; the barbarians leaving their own country have overrun an infinite space of our territory, and that many times over, and having set fire to the land, and captured the towns, they are not minded to return home again, but after the manner of men who are keeping holiday rather than making war, they laugh us all to scorn.' These were not troops under centralized control, but small-fry robber barons leading hit-and-run raids. There was no way to beat them in war. It would be like grasping at a fog. Instead, Constantinople offered a deal: the barbarians concerned – mostly Goths, but including groups of Huns – would become allies, *foederati*, bribed into quiescence with land south of the Danube. These Hun clans had no unified leadership, being little more than family groups; but now, for the first time, Huns were officially inside the empire.

To the north, the mainstream Huns, now masters of eastern Hungary and Romania, had at least the rudiments of unity, under Balamber's heirs, named as Basich and Kursich. A cemetery near the present-day village of Csákvár, on the edge of the wooded Vértes Hills between Budapest and Lake Balaton, reveals a culture in mid-change, where former in-habitants, both local tribesmen and Romans, are joined by those who bound their children's heads, buried horses, and wore gold- and silver-plated headbands and silver and bronze earrings. But it was not much of an estate for nomads. The local economy was in tatters. There were few pastures in the wooded valleys of the Carpathians, and those who lived with their herds on the Hungarian *puszta* were probably discover-ing that this was not quite the steppeland of their dreams, for the River Tisza meandering across it flooded in spring, cutting their pastures in two. They had slaves, in the form of defeated Goths and Alans from beyond the Carpathians, and Sarmatians who had been masters in Hungary itself, who all knew how to till the soil. But neither local farms nor imported herds produced enough. The Huns needed food. They could seize it locally – or they could buy it from further afield, if only they had the cash. Gold coins would also be a useful raw material for the gold flake with which their top families decorated their harnesses, weapons and head-dresses.

Where to turn for gold? The Balkans were thoroughly ravaged, and Constantinople was too tough. They looked around for an easier target, one that would yield to, and sufficiently reward, their well-honed tactics.

In 395 they turned to the empire's back door: the eastern provinces, unguarded because the Roman army was bogged down in yet another civil war in Italy. To get there, they had to gallop all the way round the Black Sea, some 1,500 kilometres. But the way there, through the former lands of the Goths and Alans, was now part of their own territory, and it was springtime, with the pastures new-grown. With two or three spare horses each, a nomadic army unencumbered by wagons could cover 160 kilometres a day over the southern Russian steppes, and have the snowy ramparts of the Caucasus in sight within a month. Then another two weeks to wind through the Caucasus, probably through the Darial pass, the main route across the central Caucasus from Chechnya – for the Chechens were there then, and had been for millennia – into Georgia. Christian Armenia, the empire's eastern border, lay ahead, with the rich towns of the Syrian and Phoenician coast another 1,200 kilometres beyond. That summer, villages in central Turkey went up in flames, and Hun bands seized slaves in Syria – 18,000 of them according to one source.

In Bethlehem, Jerome, scholar and future saint, heard news of their coming, and trembled. Jerome had been born in northern Italy and educated in Rome, where he became a Christian. Thereafter he had lived for many years in Antioch, attempting to find a way to resolve the bitter dispute over Arianism, the heresy that denied the divinity of Christ. He had travelled to everywhere that mattered: Rome, Greece, the Holy Land, Egypt; finally – as he thought – he had settled in Bethlehem. Now he judged that his only hope of survival lay in flight to the coast. A year later, when it was all over, he wrote of his experience:

Behold the wolves, not of Arabia, but of the North, were let loose upon us last year from the far-off rocks of the Caucasus, and in a little while overran great provinces. How many monasteries were captured, how many streams were reddened with human blood! . . . Not even if I had a hundred tongues and a hundred mouths, and a voice of iron could I recount the name of every catastrophe . . . They filled the whole earth with slaughter and panic as they flitted hither and thither on their swift horses . . . They were at hand everywhere before they were expected: by their speed they outstripped rumour, and they took pity neither upon religion, nor rank nor age nor wailing childhood. Those who had just begun to live were compelled to die and, in ignorance of their plight, would smile amid the drawn swords of the enemy . . . We ourselves were forced to make ships ready, to wait on the shore, to take precautions against the enemy's arrival, to fear the barbarians more than shipwreck even though the winds were raging.

A Christian priest in Syria, Cyrillonas, found his faith almost shattered by God's apparent withdrawal, and put his reactions into a moving poem:

Every day unrest, every day new reports of misfortunes, every day new blows, nothing but fights. The East has been carried into captivity, and nobody lives in the destroyed cities . . . Dead are the merchants, widowed the women . . . If the Huns will conquer me, O Lord, why have I taken refuge with the holy martyrs? If their swords kill my sons, why did I embrace Thine exalted cross? If Thou willst render to them my cities, where will be the glory of Thy holy church? . . . Not a year has passed since they came and devastated me and took my children prisoners, and lo, now they are threatening again to humiliate our land.

But the Huns did not quite reach Palestine. Jerome returned to his home in Bethlehem. There was no second assault, for a Hun incursion down the Euphrates and Tigris drew the attention of the Persians. It was a Persian army, not a Roman one, that drove them back northwards, seizing back the stolen goods, releasing the 18,000 prisoners. When the Greek civil servant Priscus heard the story of this raid over 50 years later, he was told that, to avoid pursuit, the Huns took a different route, past 'the flame that issues from the rock beneath the sea', which perhaps refers to the oil-rich Caspian shore; Marco Polo refers to the same phenomenon, describing 'a fountain from which oil springs in great abundance . . . This oil is not good to use with food, but 'tis good to burn.'

So the raid was not a complete success; but it was an astounding achievement nevertheless. The Huns may have returned a little short on booty and slaves, but they had greatly extended their geographical knowledge and their military experience. They had never launched a campaign like this before: unprecedented in its speed and ferocity, it remained unequalled for 800 years, until Genghis Khan's Mongols, approaching from the other direction, cut up through the Caucasus on their first raid into Russia. It must have given them tremendous confidence. What might they not achieve if they attacked the eastern empire again, this time taking the direct route south through the Balkans, a mere 800 kilometres from the Hungarian plains, one-fifth of the distance they had just covered?

Nine years passed. All remained quiet on the northern front. Perhaps the Goth slaves were more productive, the Tisza better behaved, the plunder from the Caucasus raid adequate.

Under a new leader, Uldin, the Huns were even able to ingratiate themselves with Constantinople by dealing with one of the eastern empire's more troublesome characters, a Gothic chieftain named Gainas who had betrayed his position as an imperial commander. A short, sharp war ended in the death of Gainas, whose head was sent as a gift to the emperor Arcadius.

Such forays aside, the Huns remained at home, biding their time, until the winter of 404–5, when Uldin led an army across the frozen Danube back into Thrace. This was merely a warm-up exercise: nearly four years later, in 408, he returned at the head of a large-scale invasion. It was a good moment to strike, for the Visigoths were on their way to Rome, there had just been a mass migration of Vandals and other groups across the Rhine, and the eastern empire's army had turned away to strengthen the Persian border. The Hun advance sent shock waves as far as Jerusalem, where Jerome concluded that God's punishment had descended again on the immoral Roman world in the form of savage tribes 'who display womanly and deeply cut faces, and who pierce the backs of bearded men as they flee'.

There was no stopping the Huns by force; so an unnamed Roman general arranged peace talks to offer cash. Early one summer morning, the two leaders met somewhere on the borders of Thrace. Uldin was not impressed. Pointing to the rising sun, he said he could take every land it lit, if the Romans did not pay enough. Unluckily for him, some of his officers were eager to accept the offer, and seceded, allowing the Romans to mop up Uldin's loyal forces and cart them off to Constantinople in chains. The major source for this anecdote, Sozomen, a church historian writing in Constantinople in the mid-fifth century, reported seeing many of these men later working on farms near Mount Olympus. Uldin, his authority much undermined, made a hair's-breadth escape back over the Danube, being kept in his place there-after by imperial patrol ships hastily sent to reinforce the Danube fleet.

Uldin's demands are revealing: he was not interested in land, or the right to settle, as the Goths had been 40 years before. New territory colonized by Huns would have scattered his people and diluted his power. He wanted cash, because pastoral nomadism, even when bolstered by slave land-workers, was no longer enough. What he needed to maintain his rule was national unity; and that could be achieved only if he had the money to buy loyalty; and the obvious source of wealth was Rome and Constantinople; and to get his hands on it he needed a powerful army. Authority, unity, control of vassals, leverage over Rome and Constantinople, cash – all to maintain authority and unity: already the Huns were trapped in a cycle of conquest, from which retreat meant failure, ignominy, poverty and collapse.

The Huns had their new homeland more or less to them-selves; but Uldin's authority was weakened by the 408 campaign, and vassals were slipping away. So too were bands of his own people. Ignoring him, small groups of Huns took off on their own, some to join the Goths in their march against Rome, some to join the Roman contingents defending it.

What did Uldin do about all this? Nothing that made any impact on the world beyond the Danube. Instead, he con-solidated power locally, in particular over a small group known as Gepids, who lived on the grasslands east of the Tisza, as archaeologists know from about 100 sites, many of which contain examples of the eagle-headed silver buckle that was the defining Gepid decoration. From then on, Gepids became part of the Hun federation. Otherwise, what the Huns were up to in the first two decades of the fifth century is a blank. One historian, Olympiodorus of Thebes in Egypt,

## ATTILA REBORN

The Hungarian Lajos Kassai has made mounted archery his life's work (see chapter 3). Having singlehandedly reinvented this long-vanished skill, he now teaches and gives exhibitions at his estate near Kaposvar. Here, controlling his horse with movements of leg and body, he uses the last of nine arrows in a backward 'Parthian' shot.

A gryphon attacking a reindeer, from a Xiongnu tapestry in Ulaanbaatar's Museum of Mongolian History.

One of Kozlov's team of archaeologists, S. A. Teplouchov, poses with Mongolian workers in an excavated Noyan Uul grave, 1925.

That's me beside a shaft into one of the mounds, all of which are now overgrown and almost invisible from a few yards away.

**IN NORTHERN MONGOLIA, POSSIBLE ECHOES OF THE HUNS' ANCESTORS**
Scholars have long suspected that the Huns originated from the Xiongnu (Hunnu in Mongolian). If so, finds in the Xiongnu graves of Noyan Uul (see map pp. 36–7) and several other sites suggest that they lost the memory of their origins, because the Xiongnu were a sophisticated people, with several towns and traditions of fine artistry (like the ones pictured here, which date from *c.* 200 BC – AD 200).

Xiongnu iron stirrups, dated prior to the second century. If the Huns were Xiongnu, they may have used iron stirrups on their migration westward, though no evidence has been found.

An earring of a Xiongnu noblewoman. The reindeer design is similar to the reindeer in the tapestry (*top left*).

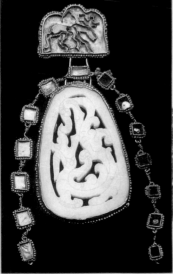

Needlepoint portrait on a scrap of textile.

The 'Devil's Ditch', a recreated Sarmatian defence near Debrecen, eastern Hungary.

## WESTWARDS

As the Huns emerged from their dreamtime in Central Asia, they crossed
the Dnieper (*main picture*), entering the territory of the Alans (a sub-group
of Sarmatians), then that of the Ostrogoths and Visigoths, who dominated
remnants of other Sarmatians. These were tribes with few fixed borders,
but in eastern Hungary archaeologists have reconstructed some Sarmatian
defences, which the Huns overran on their move westward. As they
travelled, the Huns brought with them traditions (like cranial deformation)
and artistic skills (like jewellery-making and iron-working).

An elongated skull, created by binding
in childhood.

A cauldron: big ones like this weighed
about 40 kilos.

This view of the Dnieper in 1881 by Arkhip Kuindzhi
portrays the river before the Ukrainian grasslands were
colonized. It must have looked much like this when the
Huns crossed it in about 375.

In a Roman bas-relief, a legionary battles with a barbarian. Perhaps he's a Hun – the round house in the background is built of saplings, but it is in the style of a Central Asian yurt, the type of tent probably used by the Huns when they first arrived in Europe.

## FIGHTING CONSTANTINOPLE

Though Attila's Huns plundered many Balkan cities, they had no chance
against Constantinople itself. Its walls, built by Theodosius II in the early
fifth century, were just too massive, as today's surviving sections suggest
(*main picture*). The Theodosian walls were damaged by an earthquake in
447, possibly giving Attila a chance to attack. If so, he was too slow: they
were quickly repaired.

Medals portraying the Byzantine emperors Valens (*top*) and Gratian (*left*), and one
of Theodosius II's coins (*right*). Valens, Emperor of the East, was killed at the
battle of Adrianople in 378, when some Huns joined the Goths to fight and defeat
the Romans. Valens died partly because his nephew Gratian, Emperor of the West,
failed to reach him in time. Theodosius (after whom the walls above are named)
tried to buy the Huns off. Gold coins like this would have been familiar to Attila.

# HUN TREASURES REVEALED

Hun artefacts, often plated with gold and inlaid with semi-precious stones, have been found in several hundred sites from Hungary to southern Russia. Among them is the 'treasure' unearthed near the monastery of Pannonhalma, Hungary, in 1979.

Golden clasp in the form of a cicada.

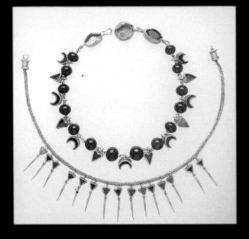

Golden necklaces inlaid with garnets.

Bits of gold and two corroded swords (*left*) were part of the Pannonhalma Treasure. Peter Tomka, the cheery director of Györ's János Xánthus Museum (*right*), concluded they were offerings buried separately from their owner's body.

Diadems like this were buried with rich Hun women. About twenty have been found. This one, of gold-plated bronze set with garnets, came from a grave near Kerch, Crimea, in the early twentieth century. It was on the head of a woman with an artificially deformed skull.

wrote a rich and detailed account of his visit to a certain King Charaton of the Huns in about 412. We know this because others mention it. But of the original, or indeed of his whole 22-volume *History*, there is no trace, and Charaton remains nothing more than a name.

It seems likely that differences arose in the Huns' relations with the eastern and western empires. Two eastern laws of 419 and 420 cast tiny lights in the gloom, suggesting that Charaton's ambitions were directed at the east. The first law decrees the death penalty for anyone betraying to the barbarians the art of shipbuilding; the other bans the export by sea of certain goods. These odd details suggest that the Huns, impoverished but still unified, had ambitions to build a seaborne trading empire, and that the eastern Romans stopped them. If so, then perhaps it was imperial opposition that caused the Huns to look once again at ways of earning a living by pillage.

And pillage they did, apparently. That is one conclusion to be drawn from a surviving edict concerning the defences of Constantinople, in particular the new walls, begun in 413 in response to the Hunnish threat. The walls are named after the emperor, Theodosius II, but he was only a child when construction got under way. The work was actually conceived and carried forward by the regent, the praetorian prefect Anthemius, who had already done much to guard the eastern empire. As well as ordering the new naval patrols on the Danube, he had signed a peace treaty with Persia and worked for better relations with Rome. Now there were to be new walls; for on the landward side the city had outgrown Constantine's old defences, spilling over onto the plain beyond – a clear risk in time of war. The new ramparts would extend for 5 kilometres, running from the Sea of Marmara to the Golden Horn inlet, with nine gates and dozens of towers. The towers were large enough for the authorities to engage in a little private enterprise, allowing the original owners of the land to use the lower floors, freed of the usual restriction that public buildings should be available for the use of troops when necessary. Nine years later, the wall was in place and power in the hands not of the fifteen-year-old Theodosius, but of his ambitious elder sister, Pulcheria. So it was probably her idea to issue a controversial edict to those living in the new towers. From now on, 'the ground-floor rooms of each tower of the New Wall' would be made available to soldiers preparing for or returning from war. 'Landholders shall not be offended' at this change of use, said whoever drafted the law, knowing well enough what protests it would cause. 'Even private homeowners customarily furnish one third of their space for this purpose.'

Why was this necessary? One terse comment by a sixth-century chronicler, Marcellinus Comes, tells us: 'The Huns devastate Thrace.' He gives no further details. For the moment, this was thunder too distant for comment.

Relations with the western empire took a rather different course. In that direction, all seemed set fair. Some Hun groups were signed up as *foederati*, being offered land around the eastern end of Lake Balaton; Huns formed contingents in the regular army; and locally Huns and Romans seem to have lived cheek by jowl in mutual tolerance, even under the gaze of Roman soldiers, who continued to man the great fortress of Valcum, guarding the roads that led round the western end of Lake Balaton through the area known to Romans as Valeria. From its ruins by the present-day village of Fenékpuszta, this huge quadrangle – 350 × 350 metres square, with 44 towers and 4 gates, one facing each compass-point – was as much town as fortress, with a command centre, civil offices, a church and a 100-metre-long building that may have been a trade hall. A surviving plough and other farm tools show that the town relied on its surrounding countryside for supplies. An 82-kilo anvil suggests industrial capabilities. Valcum had its blacksmiths, masons, potters, leather-workers, weavers and goldsmiths (who, judging from the remains found in the workshop, did not produce their own gold, but only refashioned and repaired existing items). Hundreds must have lived there, thousands looked to it for trade – even, it seems, the local Huns.

It was in these propitious circumstances, probably towards 410, that a Roman teenager, Flavius Aetius, came for a time as a hostage to the Huns: a small event that would have momentous consequences for all of Europe. 'Hostage' is the word usually used, but it is not quite right. The young man would have been sent officially for two reasons: as proof of honourable intent – in exchange, of course, for an equally eminent Hun – and as a sort of youthful ambassador, an equivalent of a VSO or Peace Corps volunteer, whose job would have been to ensure good relations and a flow of information. Like any ambassador, he would have been in effect a spy by another name. He had already played the same role among Alaric's Goths, remaining with them for three years. His experiences made Aetius uniquely qualified both to broker peace and, if necessary, to act as military adviser. He spoke Gothic, Hunnish, Latin and Greek. He had friends everywhere. He would use his knowledge and contacts to preserve peace with the Huns for the next 30 years, an achievement that helped him rise to become the empire's greatest general.

Aetius' experience was soon put to good use. In 423 the empire was torn by war between Rome and Constantinople – civil war, to those who still saw the empire as one – when the usurper John (Johannes), a mere civil servant, was made emperor in Ravenna and an eastern army set out to depose him. John needed help, and Aetius, now in his twenties, could be relied upon to provide it in the form of his Hun friends. In 425 Aetius went back to the Huns, carrying chests of gold. This, of course, would have been merely a down-payment, with more to follow once the easterners were vanquished. A huge army of Huns – later reports spoke of 60,000, but scholars accept that almost all reports were wildly exaggerated, perhaps tenfold – rode towards Italy and attacked the eastern army from the rear just after they reached Ravenna. They were too late: three days earlier, John had been executed. The Huns fought anyway, until Aetius saw there was no point, and made peace – in exchange, of course, for additional gold for his avaricious army. There was no ideology or loyalty involved. These Huns would fight for whoever paid them, and would have been happy to stay on serving the empire. But the new rulers in Ravenna were keen for a wider peace. Aetius, now a *comes* (count), was sent to sort out the unruly northern frontier in Gaul, where he remained for the next seven years, and the Huns returned home, to Pannonia and Valeria, where, in gratitude for their help, they were apparently allowed to take over estates and fortresses with no sign of opposition.

It was thanks to Aetius and the western empire, therefore, that the Huns were able to consolidate their hold on what is now Hungary, a firm base for leaders with wider ambitions. (It was not the last time that westerners would back barbarians in the hope of peace, only to see their protégés turn nasty.) The leaders in question were two brothers, Octar and Ruga. Where they came from no-one knows. Perhaps they were descendants of Balamber, Basich, Kursich, Uldin and/or the shadowy Charaton; or perhaps they were scions of some new, upstart clan. They have inspired all sorts of academic argument about the nature of 'dual kingship', and the reasons for it. Probably there was no great mystery, because it had happened before among the Huns and it happened again later, twice. Most likely the two simply ruled different bits of territory, Ruga in the east, Octar in the west. What can be said is that dual kingships were unstable (witness what happened between Rome and Constantinople). To reach such heights, both men had to be ambitious and ruthless. Rivalry was virtually inevitable.

Their first campaign did not turn out well. Fenced in by the empire on land and sea, they rounded on the only available victims: the German peoples along the Rhine, to the north-west. Among them were the remnants of a tribe known as the Burgundians or Nibelungs (after a former chief, Niflung), most of whose relatives had crossed the Rhine some fifteen years before. Those Burgundians who remained were no threat to anyone. They were the dregs left behind by the *Völkerwanderung*, the Migration of the Tribes, and were happy to live in peace, working mainly as carpenters in the valley of the Main. Their tale is told by an ecclesiastical historian, Socrates, writing a few years later. Now, suddenly, come the Huns, and devastation. Distraught, the Burgundians decide to seek help from Rome, and do so by sending a delegation across the Rhine and asking for a bishop to make them Christians. It works. Conversion leads to a revival of spirit. When the Huns come again, 3,000 Burgundians kill 10,000 Huns – among them the co-ruler Octar – and this small branch of the tribe is saved. The figures are exaggerated, no doubt, but there is probably some truth in the story, because the Burgundians' conversion is also mentioned in a world history by a fifth-century Spanish writer, Orosius. However many the Huns lost, it must have taught them about the difficulties of operating in the forests of southern Germany.

In 432, then, with Octar's death, Ruga emerged as sole leader; and it was he who was responsible for strengthening the link with the Huns' old friend Aetius, who had become the victim of some vicious infighting in Rome. Having been fired by the regent, Galla Placidia, he fled across the Adriatic to Dalmatia, then north across the no-man's-land where Romans, Germans, Goths, Sarmatians and Huns lived in interfused confusion, across the Danube into the Hun heartland. Here Ruga provided his old ally Aetius with a band of mercenaries, who gave him the military clout he needed to return home and regain his position from the regent-empress Placidia.[1] The same year, he was made consul (the first of his three consulships), appointed commander-in-chief of the army of the West, and sent off once again to secure the Rhine frontier against the Franks.

Ruga was the man who, it seems, gave the Hun kingdom a firm foundation. He had an army formidable enough to launch successful raids against the eastern Romans, and envoys smart enough to negotiate an annual tribute of 350 pounds of gold from them, along with yet another promise to return Hun refugees. Not a huge victory, not a huge sum; but a good start on both counts. The cash was paid to him directly, which means he had the authority to distribute it and thus preserve the loyalty of his chiefs. If some objected – and some did, several whole clans – they fled, seeking refuge over the border as illegal immigrants. Ruga could not tolerate this if he was to maintain and extend his authority. He would clamp down on his less willing clans and demand the return of the outlaws from Rome.

At which point, in the mid-430s, Ruga died – unless we are to believe the melodramatic account of the church historian Socrates, who said that God rewarded the emperor

---

[1] Easily said; but, like many a background statement, this one conceals epics. Aetius was up against a certain Bonifatius, or Boniface, once the warlord ruler of North Africa, contender for power in Italy, and thus opponent of the regent Galla Placidia. Back from North Africa, reconciled to Galla Placidia, he had become her champion against Aetius. It was Boniface that Aetius defeated to regain his position – in single combat, according to legend.

Theodosius for his meekness and devoutness by striking Ruga dead with a thunderbolt, following up with plague and heavenly fire that decimated Ruga's subordinates. Socrates did not explain, however, why God missed Ruga's two remaining brothers, named Mundzuk and Aybars (Oebarsius in its Latin form).[2] Mundzuk, the elder, had two sons, and this pair now move to centre stage, in another double king-ship, with the task of keeping their unruly subjects united and ensuring a flow of funds and goods from the Romans, both eastern and western. One was called Bleda; his brother, Attila.

---

[2] For those eager for evidence of links between the western Huns and the Xiongnu, the name Mundzuk survives in the small, newly independent state of Tuva, between Mongolia and Siberia. Maxim Munzuk played the hunter in Kurosawa's award-winning film *Dersu Uzala* (1975).

# 5

# FIRST STEPS TO EMPIRE

NESTORIUS, THE EX-BISHOP OF CONSTANTINOPLE, WAS A BITTER and angry man. He had wrestled with the central problem that divided Christianity in its early days – Was Christ god, or man, or a bit of both? – and discovered what he considered – no, *knew* – to be the truth: that, although Christ had been both god and man, he possessed two distinct persons, because quite obviously the *god* part of him could never have been a *human* baby. Therefore Mary could not have been the Mother of God, since that would suggest that a mortal woman could produce a god, which was a contradiction. Therefore, he, Nestorius, was right, and all Christians who disagreed with him – namely, those who accepted the tenets laid down at the Council of Nicaea in 325 and all other, anti-Nicaean, heretics – were wrong.

The world had not appreciated his insight. His great rival, Cyril of Alexandria, had had him condemned and banished to Oasis, in the southern reaches of Egypt. There, as the 430s wore on, he railed against the injustice done to him. He would be revenged upon the lot of them – or, rather, God would on his behalf. Indeed, divine vengeance had already started. How else to explain the rise of the Huns? Once they were divided among themselves, and were no more than robbers. Now, suddenly, they were united, and likely to rival Rome itself. This was surely the Christian world's punishment for its 'transgression against the true faith'.

Nestorius might have been shaky on the causes, but he was right in the grand sweep of the problem. The Huns had indeed risen. Petty pillagers no longer, by the late 430s they had become pillagers on a grand scale. In fact, this had nothing to do with God backing Nestorius, and everything to do with the rise of our hero and anti-hero, Attila.

For a decade after Ruga's death in about 435, Attila's hands were tied by joint rule with his elder brother Bleda. For those ten years the two would work together to consolidate their kingdom, with Attila the junior, and increasingly resentful, partner.

How and why they came to power is a mystery. Of their childhood in the early years of the fifth century nothing is known, and their names, both fairly common in Germanic, are not much help. Bleda is a shortened version of something like Bladardus/Blatgildus. Attila derives from *atta*, 'father' in both Turkish and Gothic, plus a diminutive *-ila*; it means 'Little Father'. The name even spread across the Channel, into Anglo-Saxon. A Bishop of Dorchester bore it, and so did the local bigwig recalled by the villages of Attleborough and Attlebridge in Norfolk. It may not even have been our Attila's original name at all, but a term of affection and respect con-ferred on his accession, a Hun version of the pseudo-cosy *dedyshka* ('Granddad') by which Russians once referred to Lenin and Stalin.

At first all seemed set fair for the two princes. They were at peace with western Rome, and settled down to bind in local groups and focus on bleeding the East. Not that all was sweetness. Ruga's death must have unleashed some nasty squabbling between the brothers, who for the moment divided the kingdom between them, Attila taking the down-river area in today's Romania, while Bleda governed in Hungary, the forward territory with easier access to the rich west. Both must have demanded commitment from their relatives and subsidiary chiefs, and done so with menaces, because two royal cousins fled south, rejecting their own people to seek refuge among their supposed enemies.

The year of Ruga's death, Attila and Bleda together completed the peace agreed between their uncle and the empire, riding south to the border fortress of Constantia, opposite Margus, guarding the mouth of the Morava river where it joins the Danube 50 kilometres east of Belgrade, just inside today's Romanian border. Here they were met by Constantinople's ambassador, Plintha – a good choice, according to Priscus, for Plintha was himself a 'Scythian', a term that was used for any barbarian or, as in this case, ex-barbarian. Plintha and his number two, Epigenes, chosen for his experience and wisdom, no doubt came prepared with a few wagons loaded with tents and scribes and cooks and a lavish banquet, ready to flatter with formality. The Huns, rough and ready and proud of it, were disdainful. As Priscus writes, 'The barbarians do not think it proper to confer dismounted, so that the Romans [i.e. those from the New Rome, Constantinople], mindful of their own dignity, chose to meet the Scythians [i.e. Huns] in the same fashion.'

There was no doubt who was in control. Attila and Bleda dictated the agenda; Plintha's scribes took down the terms. All Hun fugitives would be sent back north of the Danube, including the two treacherous princes. All Roman prisoners who had escaped were to be returned, unless each were ransomed for 8 *solidi*, one-ninth of a pound of gold (given that a Byzantine pound was slightly less than a modern one, this was about $600 in 2004 gold prices), payable to the captors – a good way of ensuring a direct flow of funds to the top Huns. Trade would be opened, and the annual trade fair held on the Danube made safe for all. The sum due to the Huns to keep the peace was doubled, from 350 to 700 pounds of gold per year (about $4.5 million in current terms), the peace to last as long as the Romans kept up payments.

As proof of their good faith, the eastern Romans later handed over the two royal refugees, Mamas and Atakam ('Father Shaman'). The manner of their reception suggests both the vicious rivalry seething beneath the surface of Attila's co-operation with his brother and the brutality of the times. The princes were delivered on the lower Danube, at a place called Carsium (today the Romanian town of Hârşova in the Danube delta), straight into Attila's hands. There was no hope, apparently, of winning their loyalty. To punish and make an example of them, he had them killed in the manner made infamous 1,000 years later by Vlad the Impaler, the original Dracula, who was ruler of the same region.

This was a peculiarly terrible death.[1] First, the executioners cut a wooden stake about 3 metres long, quite thin at one end, this end being finely sharpened and well greased with lard. The other end was thicker, to act as a secure base. The legs of the victim were spread-eagled by men hauling on ropes, the clothing cut, and the stake hammered into the anus with exquisite care and frequent pauses to avoid damaging the internal organs. The advancing stake pushed aside the intestines, colon, stomach, liver and lungs, until it reached

---

[1] These details are taken from *The Bridge over the Drina* (1945) by the Nobel Prize-winning Serb writer Ivo Andrić (trans. Lovett Edwards, London, 1959/1994).

the shoulder, emerging with the help of a knife through the skin of the upper back, to one side of the spine. The victim was skewered, 'as a lamb on the spit' – except that the heart and lungs were still working. Then the legs were bound to the stake at the ankles to prevent slippage in what was to follow. The stake with its burden was raised upright, and set very gently, in order not to jolt the body, into a firm holder of stones or wood, where it was held in place with struts. If everything had been done in the correct manner, the public agony that followed would last a couple of days. The Romans watching from the far bank, and any Huns who might have considered siding with Bleda, would have heard the slow, steady hammer blows and the screams, learned that Attila commanded some people well practised in the arts of ruth-lessness – for impaling was a skill that demanded experience and a clinical hand – and taken note.

It is clear from the terms imposed by the Huns what they were after. Though they liked to melt down gold coins for jewellery, they were also developing a cash economy based on Roman currency, and there was no easier way to get the cash than by extortion. They could offer horses, furs and slaves at the trade fair on the Danube, but that would not bring real wealth – not enough to acquire the silks and wines that would make life pleasant, or to pay for foreign artisans who could construct the heavy-duty weapons upon which their long-term security would depend. Besides, it was only by matching Roman wealth that they could avoid being ripped off. According to St Ambrose, it was perfectly OK for Christians to bleed barbarians dry with loans: 'On him whom you can-not easily conquer in war, you can quickly take vengeance with the hundredth [i.e. a percentage]. Where there is the right of war, there is also the right of usury.' When Attila and Bleda returned to their own domains, they had what they wanted in the short term – some gold, some breathing-space;

but peace did not serve their long-term interests. They needed war, and events elsewhere soon gave them opportunity.

During this decade, disaster loomed on several fronts for both parts of the empire. Aetius was fire-fighting in Gaul, quelling the Franks in 432, then the Bacaudae (435–7), an obscure and disorderly band who fought a guerrilla war from their forest bases, and finally the Goths, who almost took Narbonne in 437. In 439 Carthage itself, the old capital of Rome's North African estates, fell to the Vandal chief Gaiseric. After 40 years of wandering – over the Rhine, across France and Spain, over the Straits of Gibraltar – the Vandals had seized present-day Libya only fourteen years previously. Carthage, with its aqueduct, temples and theatres (one of which, named the Odeon, served as a venue for concerts), was vandalized, in every sense. The invaders found their new homeland, though fertile enough, rather a tight fit between the Sahara and the Mediterranean, and quickly learned a new skill: shipbuilding. Carthage was wonderfully located to dominate the 200-kilometre channel dividing Africa from Sicily, and became a base for piracy, and then for a navy. In 440 Gaiseric prepared an invasion fleet, landed in Sicily, did some vandalizing, and crossed to the Italian mainland, intending no-one knew what. From the East, Theodosius II sent an army to help repel the invaders, but he was too late: the Vandals had headed home with their spoils before the easterners arrived.

Attila and Bleda took advantage of these desperate times. In the West they had a wonderful opportunity for pillage, thanks to their alliance with Aetius, who needed them to bolster his campaign against those unruly barbarians inside Gaul. There were Huns helping to fight the Franks, and the Bacaudae, and most memorably the Burgundians/Nibelungs. This was the tribe that had crossed the Rhine almost en masse 30 years before, leaving behind a remnant that successfully resisted the Hun attack. They had settled, with Rome's unwilling agreement, on the Roman side of the middle Rhine, taking over several towns, with Worms as their capital. Under their king, Gundahar, better known to history and folklore as Gunther, they remained a restless bunch, trying to take more land. An invasion westwards through the Ardennes in 435 drew the attention of Aetius and his mercenary Huns, who had a score of their own to settle after their defeat a few years previously. The results were devastating, though no details of the assault survive. Thousands of Burgundians died (though probably not the 20,000 mentioned in one source), Gunther among them, in a slaughter that would be transformed into folklore, notably in the great medieval epic the *Nibelungenlied* and in more recent times by Wagner in his Ring cycle. Along the way, folk memory made the assumption that Attila himself was behind the destruction of the Burgundians. That doesn't fit. He had his hands full back home. But there is an underlying truth to the legend, for there could have been no slaughter without an understanding between Aetius and the Huns. Now they had their reward: vengeance, and booty. The few surviving Burgundians were chased on west and south, their name clinging to the area around Lyon and its vineyards long after the tribe itself and the later kingdom had vanished.

Already, Attila and Bleda needed more, if not from other barbarians, then from the eastern empire. They had their pretexts ready. Tribute had not been paid. Refugees who had fled across the Danube had not been returned. And, to cap it all, the Bishop of Margus had sent men across the river to plunder royal tombs. (Priscus says they were Hun graves, but the Huns made no burial mounds; they must have been ancient *kurgans*, which had always been ransacked as if they were little mountains to be mined at will.) The bishop should at once be surrendered, came the order, or there would be war.

No bishop was handed over, and Attila and Bleda made their move. Some time around 440, at the trade fair in Constantia, Huns suddenly turned on the Roman merchants and troops, and killed a number. Then, crossing the Danube, a Hun army attacked Viminacium, Margus' immediate neighbour to the east, subjecting the town to an appalling fate. No-one recorded why it was so vulnerable, but the townspeople seemed to know what was in store, because its officials had time to bury the contents of their treasury, over 100,000 coins which were found by archaeologists in the 1930s. The survivors were led away into captivity, among them an unnamed businessman whom we shall meet again in rather different and much improved circumstances. The city was then flattened, and not rebuilt for a century. It is now the village of Kostolac.

Then the Huns turned on Margus itself. The grave-robbing bishop, terrified that he would be handed over by his own people to ensure their safety, slipped out of the city, crossed the Danube, and told the Huns that he would arrange for the gates of his town to be opened for them if they promised to treat him well. Promises were made, hands shaken. The Huns gathered by night on the far bank of the Danube, while somehow the bishop persuaded those on watch to open the gates for him. Right behind were the Huns, and Margus too fell, and burned. It was never rebuilt.

What happened then is unclear. Sources and interpretations vary so dramatically that no-one is certain whether there was one war or two, or how long it, or they, lasted, estimates varying from two to five years. Two or three seems to fit best. It was all mixed up with the Vandals invading Sicily and the eastern army being sent to help the West. There was much destruction in the Belgrade region. In any event, the Huns were now in possession of Margus and its sister town, Constantia, on the Danube's northern bank, and could dominate the Morava valley, along which ran the main road into Thrace. Two other cities fell, Singidunum (Belgrade) and Sirmium (now the village of Sremska Mitrovica, 60 kilometres west of Belgrade up the River Sava), where the bishop handed over some golden bowls that would, a few years later, become the cause of a nasty dispute.

Then something seems to have stopped the Huns in their tracks – trouble at home, perhaps, or a rapid offer of gold from Theodosius. Attila and Bleda pulled their troops out, leaving the borderland of Pannonia and Moesia in smoking ruins. There was another peace treaty, agreed by Anatolius, commander-in-chief of the eastern empire's army and friend of the emperor.

It was perhaps as part of this renewed peace that the Huns picked up another item of booty: a black dwarf from Libya who adds a bizarre element to our story. Zercon was already a living legend. He owed his presence in Hun lands to one of the greatest of Roman generals, Aspar, who was in command of the Danube frontier for a few years until 431, when he was sent to North Africa in a vain attempt to quell the Vandals. It was Aspar who captured Zercon and took him back to Thrace. Here he was either seized by the Huns or perhaps handed over by Aspar. Zercon was not a prepossessing sight. He hobbled on deformed feet, had a nose so flat it looked as if it wasn't there at all, just two holes where a nose should be, and he stuttered and lisped. He had had the sense to turn these deficiencies into assets, and became a great court jester, specializing in parodies of Latin and Hunnish. Attila couldn't stand him, so he became his brother's property. Bleda thought Zercon was hilarious – The way he moved! His lisp! His stutter! – and treated him like a pet monster, providing him with a suit of armour and taking him along on campaigns.

Zercon, however, did not fully appreciate Bleda's sadistic sense of humour, and escaped with some Roman prisoners. Bleda was so furious that he ordered those sent in pursuit to ignore all the fugitives but Zercon and to bring him back in chains. So it was. At the sight of him, Bleda asked why he had fled from such a kindly master. Zercon, speaking in his appalling mixture of Latin and newly learned Hunnish, apologized profusely, but protested that his master should understand there was a good reason for his flight: he had not been given a wife. At this, Bleda became helpless with laughter, and allocated him a poor girl who had once been an attendant on his own senior wife. Zercon will reappear, and his story continue, later.

For a couple of years the Danube front remained quiet, Attila having discovered the benefits of diplomatic exchanges. As Priscus tells it, Attila sends letters to Theodosius – letters which must have been in Greek or Latin; the illiterate Attila must already have had at least one scribe and translator, if not a small secretariat. He demands the fugitives who have not been delivered and the tribute which has not been paid. He puts a diplomatic gloss on what is little more than a gangster's threat. He is a patient man. He is willing to receive envoys to discuss terms. He also portrays himself as a man with a problem, namely his impatient chiefs. If there is a hint of a delay or any sign that Constantinople is preparing for war, he will not be able to hold back his hordes.

It seems that Attila did indeed have a problem with some of his own people. Since peace was cheaper than war, and ambassadors cheaper than armies, Theodosius sent an envoy, an ex-consul named Senator. The land route was apparently too dangerous, for Thrace was still a prey to freebooting Huns who had not yet been brought under Attila's control, the 'fugitives' he wanted returned by the terms of the Treaty of Margus. So Senator opted to make the first part of his journey by ship, sailing up the coast of the Black Sea to Varna, where a Roman contingent was able to provide him with an escort inland. Senator duly arrived, impressing Attila, who would later cite him as a model envoy, but nothing else seems to have been achieved.

Perhaps something was promised, for Attila rather took to the idea of exchanging envoys. His reason for sending embassies had nothing to do with diplomacy and fugitives. This was a gravy train for his top people, and a way to win time. It was not the issue that was the issue, but the generous reception his ambassadors received, which was something along these lines: My dear chaps, how wonderful to see you! Fugitives? Tribute? All in good time. We'll talk after supper. Let us show you to your rooms. Yes, the carpets and the silks are nice, aren't they – nothing but the best. A glass of wine, perhaps? You like the glass? It's yours. Oh, and after supper, there are the dancing girls. You've had a long journey. These girls are chosen specially to restore the spirits of great warriors such as your good selves. Priscus noted all this in rather staider terms: 'The barbarian [Attila] seeing clearly the Romans' liberality, which they exercised through caution lest the treaty be broken, sent to them those of his retinue he wished to benefit.' Four times in the mid-440s this happened, and each time a retinue returned happy, with trinkets and cash as diplomatic gifts.

Neither side believed in the peace. Constantinople was nervous – or so scholars surmise on the scanty evidence of two laws rushed into effect in the summer and autumn of 444. Landowners had long been required to supply recruits from their tenantry, or pay cash in lieu. But senior officials, most of them also landowners, were exempt; that was a perk of their high office. Now, by one of the new laws, they too had to provide troops, or pay a fine. The second law was a 4 per cent tax on all sales. Clearly, the city needed more men in arms and the money to pay them. And, according to one of Theodosius' edicts, the Danube fleet was being reinforced and the bases along the river being rebuilt.

The emperor was in fact quite right to expect trouble, because he was about to give the Huns cause for complaint. He had no intention of losing more money to the barbarians. In the succinct words of Otto Maenchen-Helfen, one of the greatest of experts on the Huns, 'To get rid of the savages, Theodosius paid them off. Once they were back, he tore up the peace treaty,' and simply cut the payments dead.

Perhaps it was this crisis that inspired Attila to make his move for absolute power. He would by now have had his own power base, in the form of an elite referred to by Greek writers as *logades* (we will meet half a dozen of them in person later, in the company of the Greek diplomat Priscus), and the inner circle would already have been in place, or Attila would not have been able to grab supreme power. Among them were his deputy, Onegesius; Onegesius' brother Scottas; some relatives (we know of two uncles, Aybars and Laudaric); and Edika, the leader of a tribe immediately to the north, the Skirians, now in alliance with Attila's Huns, whose foot soldiers would henceforth form the heart of the Hun infantry. They were all bound to Attila by something more than fear of his brutality, for they must have equalled him in that. This was the man who would best serve their interests, and those of the Huns as a whole. They were a substantial group, these *logades*. Historians have debated whether they are best seen as local governors, policemen, tribute collectors, priests, wise men, shamans, military commanders, clan leaders, nobles or diplomats. Probably, each played several roles. The implication is there in Liddell and Scott's *Greek–English Lexicon*: *logades* is the plural of *logas*, 'picked, chosen'. *Logades* means 'picked men': the elite. As

Maenchen-Helfen concludes: 'There is no evidence that these prominent people of the Huns had anything in common but prominence' – something like Hunnish SS officers, if you regard Attila as a Hitler figure.

And the rest of the Huns? All that can be said is that there was a tribe or people, subdivided into clans, across which cut a hierarchy consisting, at the very least, of slaves at the bottom, then common people made up of herders and house-holders, then an aristocracy, which may have been both of birth and of merit, and at the head a supreme leader, who was now ready for a coup.

It would have been sudden, brief, and bloody. Bleda vanished from history. Attila assumed power over the whole estate, from the Black Sea to Budapest, a kingdom 800 kilo-metres across and 400 deep. The *putsch* must have been over almost as soon as begun, because no word of civil war reached the outside world, and Attila had the confidence to spare at least one, presumably the most senior, of Bleda's wives: we shall come across her again later, apparently in good heart, living not far from the headquarters the victor now snatched from his brother's dead hands.

We can infer something of the flow of goods and the brief panic unleashed by Attila's fratricide thanks to some Hungarian turkeys. This story is set just outside a little town 18 kilometres north-east of Szeged. I hesitate to tell you the name of the town, because it obeys the First Law of Hungarian Linguistics, which states that the smaller the town, the more impossible it is for outsiders to pronounce. It's Hódmőzávárhely, which for Hungarians is no problem at all: it means 'beaver-field-market-place', this whole low-lying area having once been frequently flooded by the nearby Tisza, with little lakes where beavers thrived (in fact there is still a 'Channel-of-the-Beaver-Lake' near the village). The land, now drained, runs flat to a straight horizon. In 1963 a middle-aged farmer's wife named Józó Erzsébet – Elizabeth Józó – was tending her turkeys when she saw that they had scratched up something glittery from the subsoil. She stooped down, scratched a little more, and found a mass of gold coins: 1,440 to be exact, together weighing 64 kilos. Her son cannily took one of them to the National Museum in Budapest and offered to sell it. They gave him 1,500 *forints*, the equivalent of about two months' wages. Next day, he turned up again with another two coins. At this point the museum curators realized that Mrs Józó's turkeys needed expert attention. The treasure was whisked off to the museum, pictures were taken of Mrs Józó in her headscarf and the shallow pit – the picture is still there in the Szeged museum – and the family was left richer by 70,000 *forints*, enough to buy two houses.

The coins are Byzantine, minted by Theodosius II, and a good proportion of them are dated 443, right when Attila and Bleda started sending their ambassadors on their gravy-train missions to Constantinople. Finds like this are an invitation to imagine. Why would someone bury coins like this in a field, with no other goods? Here is a possible scenario. Attila has just made his move. Bleda is dead. He too had his *logades*. Most of them are also dead now, but one has escaped. Like the unfortunate royal cousins whose skeletons for years graced the sharpened stakes downriver, he thinks his chances will be better if he flees across the Danube. He gathers his share of the latest payment to arrive from Constantinople and heads south. But then, all of a sudden, he sees horsemen ahead of him, and behind. He's surrounded. He doesn't give much for his chances if he's caught with the cash on him. Hastily, he buries it. He will take shelter with peasants, and hope to fade into the landscape until things calm down, when he will retrieve his loot and build himself a better life somewhere else. Does he survive? I doubt it, because he never returns, and the hoard lies hidden for 1,500 years, until scratched up by Mrs Józó's turkeys.

As leaders often do, Attila boosted his natural self-confidence by rewriting tradition so that it supported his rise to power. This he did by hijacking the ancient cult of sword-worship. Many tribes worshipped, venerated or swore by their swords, sometimes seeing in one particular sword a symbol of divine support. There is perhaps a recollection of this practice in the Arthurian legend of the 'sword in the stone', which may recall the respect conferred upon the metalworkers who knew how to abstract iron from rock, in effect drawing swords from stones. The Xiongnu, the Avars and the Bulgars all had their sword-cults. So did the Huns. Shortly after Attila came to power he made the cult his own. This is the story as heard by Priscus, our main source for the court of King Attila, whose adventures are the subject of the next chapter. Some of his work was lost, though some of the lost bit was saved at second hand, quoted by the Gothic historian Jordanes over a century later. It seems that one particular sword – Latinized as the Sword of Mars – had always been esteemed by the Hun kings, but had been lost. This is how it was rediscovered, according to the story as it must have been approved by Attila:

A certain herdsman saw one of his heifers limping. Unable to find a cause for such a wound, he anxiously followed the trail of blood and at length came to a sword the beast had unwittingly trampled while grazing. He dug it up and straight away took it to Attila. He rejoiced at this gift and being of great courage he decided he had been appointed to be ruler of the whole world and that, thanks to the Sword of Mars, he had been granted the power to win wars.

Attila had both the power and the incentive to wage war on

the empire of Theodosius. What he lacked for the moment was focus. He faced a threat from a tribe or clan named as Acatiri or Akatziri – they have various spellings and much disputed etymologies, which Maenchen-Helfen takes ten pages to summarize. In brief, they were probably steppe-dwellers living on the shores of the Black Sea, somewhere over towards the Don. Trouble of some kind was brewing there. It would eventually be sorted out with one of the Acatiri tribal leaders retaining his independence by an ingenious and outrageous piece of flattery. Offered gold by Attila along with an invitation to visit, he suspected a trap, and sent a message saying he couldn't possibly come because, as a man could not look at the sun, so he could not look upon a god – small evidence that Attila was beginning to be seen as selected by Heaven above for conquest. Attila decided to settle for control rather than conquest, sending his elder son Ellac to assert Hun rule.

Aetius himself arrived from Rome to negotiate another peace. No-one left an account of his visit, but it is deduced from a Latin verse by an eminent Gaulish poet, Sidonius, who will become a significant source later in this story. The poem was a panegyric in praise of Aetius, probably written to commemorate his third term as consul, which began in 447. As one line put it, 'he returned with peace from the Danube and stripped the Don of its rage'. Aetius was certainly the man for the job, confident that his old hosts would give him a good welcome. If Attila and Aetius had not met as children – Aetius was some ten years the elder, quite the patriarch now at fifty-something – they surely met now, and saw in each other matching qualities of leadership. They could do business together, and serve each other's interests.

This would have been the first time a high-ranking outsider had been to Attila's headquarters since he had assumed sole leadership. It is a good time to ponder where he lived, how he lived and what he was like. To do so, I must get a little ahead of myself, because I have to draw upon the description set down by Priscus, whose visit took place a couple of years later.

First comes the much-disputed position of Attila's headquarters. Historians have taken a great interest in the course Priscus took on his journey north from Constantinople, because if they could pin that down they would know where Attila lived, and then they could excavate and open many windows on Attila and Hun life. But all we have are strong hints, like a treasure-hunt with half the clues missing. Priscus crossed three large rivers, which he names Drecon, Tigas and Tiphesas; but Jordanes, in quoting him, distorts the names and the order into Tisia, Tibisia and Dricca. Or perhaps Jordanes got them right and Priscus wrong, or both were trying to record local usages now forgotten. This uncertainty has inspired many an academic footnote. The names can be paired, but the three pairs can be made to yield only two known rivers (and even these are disputed):

Tiphesas/Tibisia = Tibiscus (Latin)/Tamiš (Serbian), Timiş or
    Timişul (Romanian);
Tigas/Tisia = Tisza (Hungarian)/Theiss (German);
Dricca/Drecon = unknown, but possibly today's Begei.

The Tamiš joins the Danube just north of Belgrade, close to where the Begei flows into the Tisza. But there are several other rivers, and names have changed as peoples and languages have changed. The identification that makes most sense is that of the Tigas/Tisia with the long, broad, meandering and variable Tisza/Theiss, which dominates the central Hungarian plain, and did so to a far greater extent before it was tamed in the nineteenth century by Count István Szécheny, who practically reinvented his country politically and physically (he regulated the Danube as well). The Tisza/ Theiss had scores of different spellings over the centuries (and still has quite a few in this multi-lingual part of Europe). Unfortunately, not a single one has a *g* in the middle. Still, it is inconceivable that a scholar like Priscus would not have known of the Tisza, and it is widely accepted that this was the river Priscus meant. If he crossed it, it means Attila was based on the other side i.e. the west. This makes sense, because Attila needed his army to have rapid access west as well as south, and the Tisza could, in spring, spread out for miles, a barrier best avoided by basing himself on the western side.

Estimating the distance Priscus travelled brings us up the west bank of the Tisza to the flat lands near present-day Szeged, in southern Hungary. Szeged itself is right on the river, and even with the embankments is still subject to flooding. It was almost wiped out in 1879, and swamped again in 1970 and 2000. If Attila was based west of the river, he would have settled 20–30 kilometres west, safely away from the flood plain, with its bogs and slow streams, out on the *puszta*, with open ground on which the Hun cavalry could operate and manoeuvre.

But this was no military camp. It was a regular little town, with wooden buildings, plus a couple with stone bases, and one entirely of stone – of which more in the next chapter. It was not much in modern terms, but it is still an expression of Attila's imperial outreach. There were no trees and no quarries in the area, so every log and stone had to be brought in on wagons and rafts. Despite a vast amount of academic wrangling over the possibility that the village was some sort of fort, with a surrounding palisade, no such thing is mentioned by Priscus. Inside the village there were indeed palisades, encircling collections of wooden buildings. One, for instance, belonged to Attila's deputy, Onegesius; another to his senior wife, Erekan. But these served no military purpose, for their gates were unguarded and unlocked. They indicated status. There was plenty of space between these enclosures for tents to be pitched.

You can see little towns like this today in Mongolia, put up by people in the process of abandoning their herds for urban life. In the north, where the mountains and forests roll down from Siberia, it has always been easy for those who wish to build in wood. Here are villages of spruce and pine planks, the single-storey houses set in compounds to keep thieves out and dogs in, separated by spider's webs of tracks, punctuated by the occasional round felt tent and horses tethered next to a motorbike. Even in the Gobi, you may be driving over an infinity of gravel plain and see, shimmering on the horizon, a little town, the centre of local administration. The houses are more likely to be brick and concrete, and there will be a telephone line and poles at odd angles, but they have similar compounds of wooden planks. If pastoral nomads have to settle, this is how they do it. They are, in effect, Hun villages.

I imagine Aetius' first view of Attila's new palace must have been much the same as Priscus'. 'Wooden walls made of smoothly planed boards', whose joints – the addition is from Jordanes – 'so counterfeited solidity that they could scarce be distinguished by close scrutiny . . . a courtyard bounded by so vast a circuit that its very size showed it was the royal palace'. This was a place designed to impress, not only by its size but also by the quality of its workmanship: fine wood and excellent carpentry, possibly the work of captured Goths or Burgundians, both of whom had traditions of building in wood.

Now for the man himself. Priscus described him, in Jordanes' Latin version:

He was a man born to shake the races of the earth, a terror to all lands, destined I know not how to frighten everyone as terrifying reports spread about him. His gait was haughty, his eyes darting here and there, so that his power and pride was apparent as he moved. Yes, he was a lover of war, but he knew how to restrain himself. He was excellent in council, sympathetic to supplicants, gracious to those received into his protection. He was short of stature, broad-chested, with a large head, small eyes, thin beard flecked with grey, snub nose, and the repulsive complexion of his forefathers.[2] His nature was such that he always had great confidence.

Having dealt successfully with this new king, Aetius duly returned with peace from the Danube, sealing the renewed bond by sending his son Carpilio, perhaps on a second embassy, perhaps as a hostage, as he had himself been sent in his youth. This is confirmed by a letter written in the first half of the sixth century, a hundred years after the events, by the historian Cassiodorus, who wrote a history of the Goths. In the letter he described how his grandfather had been sent to Attila along with Carpilio. This must therefore have been the second group of outsiders to meet Attila as sole leader. Naturally, Cassiodorus is keen to show his grandfather in a good light, and the Huns as the evil conquerors of his own Goths, but his account backs up Priscus' portrait. Cassiodorus writes that his grandfather

> looked undaunted at the man before whom the Empire quailed. Calm in his conscious strength, he despised all those terrible wrathful faces that scowled around him. He did not

---

[2] The word translated as 'repulsive' is *teter,* a variant of *taeter*, 'foul, hideous, noisome, repulsive'. Inexplicably, this appeared as 'swarthy' or 'dark' in some translations, a mistake much copied. The 'complexion of his forefathers' is *originis suae signa restituens*, literally 'restoring the signs of his origin'. This odd phrase recalls Ammianus Marcellinus' prejudiced descriptions of the Huns, but I think Jordanes is referring to a family trait.

hesitate to meet the full force of the invectives of a man, who, driven by some fury, seemed to strive for the domination of the world. He found the king insolent; he left him pacified; and so ably did he argue down all his slanderous pretexts for dispute that though the Hun's interest was to quarrel with the richest empire in the world, he nevertheless condescended to seek its favour . . . Thus did he bring back the peace which men had despaired of.

Together Cassiodorus and Priscus give us a portrait of an ugly little man of extreme contradictions, mercurial in his moodiness and adept at putting on the appearance of moods, suspicious of all but his most trusted lieutenants, often brutal, tough as a bare-knuckle fighter. He had killed men, might actually have killed his brother with his own hands. It was impossible to know what he really felt or guess what he would do next. Stalin and Hitler had that same talent of keeping even the closest aides on tenterhooks, absolutely dependent on their every whim. Like them, he and only he held the secret of victory, and not even he could say what that secret was. Part of the mystique of leadership was his self-confidence, part his austerity – and part his generosity, in which his chosen ones and honoured guests basked as if in sunlight. I think he had a sudden smile that could melt rocks. To be in his presence would have been to feel charisma in its original, theological sense, the power that flows as a divine gift and turns an ordinary man into a leader.

A few dribs and drabs of tribute, the odd diplomatic gift – it was simply not enough to keep a restless people happy. To retain power, Attila had to seize the initiative, fast. And so, in 447, he went on the warpath. His aims were threefold: one, to get as much loot as he could as quickly as possible; two, to ensure he could do this again in the future; and three, at the same time to deny the eastern empire any chance of retaliation. This meant occupying the whole Danube frontier region, taking over the river with its fleet, and occupying the cities that acted as the empire's outposts. Previously, when the Huns were consolidating, they had avoided territorial gain; but Attila's new ambitions demanded expansion. For the first time, Attila was seeking territory, en route to empire.

Of the 447 campaign itself there are few details. Two things seem certain: that the Huns reached but could not take Constantinople; and that they destroyed many cities in the Balkans. How events unfolded exactly is not recorded, so the following sequence is my conjecture, the reason for which I will explain later.

Consider what this ex-nomad was up against. He could advance whenever he liked, but with what war aims? Surely not simply to ravage and pillage an already ravaged and pillaged countryside. Wealth lay in towns, of which there were several. But they were well defended, with thick, high walls against which mounted archers would be useless. There is only one way for nomads to take cities, and that is to besiege them so thoroughly that the inhabitants are starved out, always assuming that no heavily armoured reinforcements arrive. That means a siege of several months, during which a hungry army grows restless for lack of loot. No, this time, the Huns would have to take cities.

What of the greatest prize of all, Constantinople? Attila had never been that far south, but he would have known what awaited him if he got there. It was quite a march. From the Hungarian plains you would follow the Tisza for 160 kilometres to Belgrade, then the Morava for a further 180 kilometres down to well-defended Naissus (Niš as it is today). Another 120 kilometres would take you through the narrow valley of the Nišava, where the railway runs now, to Sofia; picking up the Maritsa for the ancient road across southern Bulgaria, where the mountains give way at last to flatter ground and the Turkish town of Adrianople (now Edirne, 220 kilometres), after the final 160 kilometres, making in all a march of 840 kilometres, you would see before you the totally impregnable walls of Constantinople.

The city was now defended by the new Theodosian Walls built by Anthemius after 413. The walls endure to this day, the russet brickwork looming up from the plain. They are much eroded now, but in 445 they were one of the world's wonders, running from river to sea for 5 kilometres, lined with hewn stone at their bases, mounting like a stairway. An attacker first faced a moat, 20 metres wide, 10 metres deep, partitioned by locks, each section having its own pipes that could flood it and also carry water to the defenders. Then came a parapet – a *peribolo*, as it was known – some 20 metres wide, which would of course be manned by defenders. Once they were cleared, invaders came up against the outer wall, some 10 metres high, with a roadway along the top, and punctuated with guard towers. Beyond this another parapet, 15 metres wide, and finally the inner wall, up to 20 metres high, wide enough at the top for soldiers to parade. Every 50 metres along its whole length rose a tower. Each of its 10 gates had a drawbridge that was removed entirely in time of siege.

If facts and figures do not impress, listen to the awed words of Edwin Grosvenor, Professor of History at Amherst College, Massachusetts, one-time history professor in Constantinople, in his 1895 account of the city:[3]

In days when the cannon was unknown, the most dauntless commander and the mightiest army might well shrink back in terror at the sight of such tremendous works. Like a broad,

---

[3] The introduction is by his friend Lew Wallace, author of *Ben Hur*.

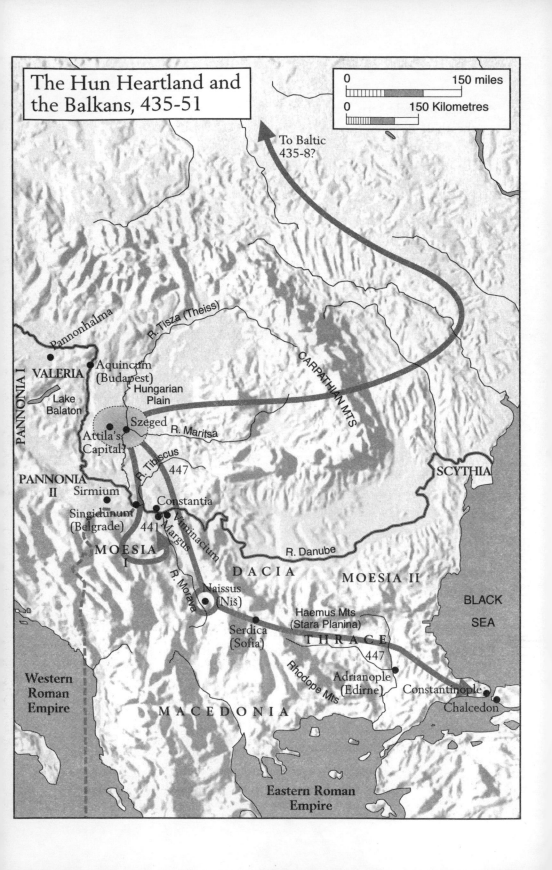

The Hun Heartland and the Balkans, 435-51

0          150 miles

0          150 Kilometres

To Baltic 435-8?

Pannonhalma

R. Tisza (Theiss)

CARPATHIAN MTS

VALERIA

PANNONIA I

Aquincum (Budapest)

Hungarian Plain

Lake Balaton

Szeged

R. Maritsa

Attila's Capital?

SCYTHIA

R. Tibiscus

447

PANNONIA II

Sirmium

Constantia

Singidunum (Belgrade)

441

Viminacium

Margus

MOESIA I

R. Danube

DACIA

MOESIA II

R. Morava

Naissus (Niš)

Haemus Mts (Stara Planina)

BLACK SEA

Serdica (Sofia)

THRACE

447

Rhodope Mts

Adrianople (Edirne)

Constantinople

Chalcedon

Western Roman Empire

MACEDONIA

Eastern Roman Empire

deep, bridgeless river stretched the moat in its precipitous sheath of stone. Even were it crossed and its smooth, high face of rock surmounted, there rose beyond the formidable front of the outer wall and towers, defended on the vantage ground of the *peribolos* by phalanxes of fighting men. And if those bastions were carried, and their defenders driven back in rout inside the city, there loomed beyond, mocking the ladder and the battering-ram, the adamantine, overawing inner wall. Along its embrasured top the besieged might stroll, and laugh to scorn the impotent assault of hitherto successful but now baffled foes.

No enemy ever managed to breach this barrier until the Turks took the city in 1453, and they managed it because they deployed an 8.5-metre bombard that was hauled by 60 oxen and could lob half-tonne balls from a kilometre away. Attila would not have dreamed of making the attempt.

But he was granted a chance for easy victory, a heaven-sent chance it must have seemed, for at the end of January 447 the city was struck by a terrible earthquake that turned whole sections of the new wall to rubble. The emperor led a congregation of 10,000, barefoot in deference to God's will, through the rubble-strewn streets to a special service of prayer. But there would be no deliverance from the barbarian menace without hard, fast labour. The work was taken in hand by the praetorian prefect Cyrus, poet, philosopher, art lover and architect, who had already been responsible for more public buildings than anyone since the time of Constantine.

It could well have been that this was the very moment Attila was preparing to head south. One interpretation of the sources is that, upon hearing news of the earthquake and the collapse of the walls, he rushed together an army and led it on a hard march through the Balkans to Constantinople. If there is anything in this conjecture, then the city would have been in a complete panic at his approach. There is one hint that this is how it might have been. Callinicus, a monk living near Chalcedon (modern Kadıköy), across the Hellespont from Constantinople, recalled the horrors 20 years later:

> The barbarian people of the Huns, the ones in Thrace, became so strong that they captured more than 100 cities, and almost brought Constantinople into danger, and most men fled from it. Even the monks wanted to run away to Jerusalem. There was so much killing and blood-letting that no one could number the dead. They pillaged the churches and monasteries, and slew the monks and virgins . . . They so devastated Thrace that it will never rise again.

According to the fifth-century Syrian writer Isaac of Antioch, the city was saved only by an epidemic among the would-be invaders. Addressing the city, he says, 'By means of sickness he [God] conquered the tyrant who was threatening to come and take thee away captive.' In fact, Isaac makes the same point again and again. 'Against the stone of sickness they stumbled . . . with the feeble rod of sickness [God] smote mighty men . . . the sinners drew the bow and put their arrows on the string, then sickness blew through [the host] and hurled it into wilderness.' It is all very vague; but perhaps it is significant that there is no mention of an assault, and certainly no siege engines.

That was because Cyrus had been an answer to the city's prayers. The walls were repaired in double-quick time. Inscriptions in Greek and Latin, still visible to Grosvenor when he was gathering material for his book in the 1880s, praised the achievement of the prefect, who had 'bound wall to wall' in 60 days: 'Pallas herself could hardly have erected so stable a fortification in so short a time.' Attila would have been confronted not by enticing gaps in a ruined wall, but by the whole restored and impregnable edifice. A wasted journey, then; though he may have drawn a tiny consolation that a decision already taken had now to be followed through.

That decision, I suggest, was to adopt a whole new type of warfare, which owed little to the Huns' nomadic past. The most vivid record of the 447 Balkan campaign is Priscus' description of the siege of Naissus, the consequences of which he saw for himself two years later. The Huns, not being city people, would not have been good at sieges. Yet over the last few years they had learned much from their Roman enemies to east and west, and now they put their research and development to good use in a massive, mechanized assault. Naissus lies on the river now called the Nišava. The Huns decided to cross by building a bridge, which would have been not of the usual design but a quickly built pontoon of planks on boats. Across this came 'beams mounted on wheels' – siege towers of some kind, perhaps tree-trunks fixed to a four-wheeled frame. With the details given by Priscus, it is possible to guess how they worked. Above the frame was a platform protected by screens made of woven willow and rawhide, thick and heavy enough to stop arrows, spears, stones and even fire-arrows, but with slits through which the attackers could fire. How many bowmen on the platform? Shall we say four? Below, well protected, were another team of four (or perhaps eight) who pedalled the wheels. There could have been a third team behind, steering the contraption with a long lever. There were 'a large number' of these siege towers, which, when in place, delivered such a hail of arrows that the defenders fled from the walls. But the towers were not high enough to reach the ramparts, not up to the standards of classical siege towers like the *helepolis* ('city-taker') used by Philip of Macedon when he tried to take Byzantium in

340 BC, or other towers that were supposedly up to 50 metres high (an extraordinary size: even half that height would be astonishing). Nor is there any mention of drawbridges, vital if the assault were to be carried through, which had been used in siege towers since the time of Alexander the Great 800 years previously. The Huns were learning, but they had a way to go yet.

Now the Huns brought up their next devices: iron-pointed battering-rams slung on chains from the point where four beams came together, like the edges of a pyramid. These too were screened by willow and leather armour, protecting teams who used ropes to swing the rams. These were, says Priscus, very large machines. They needed to be, because their job was to batter down not only the gates but also the walls themselves. The defenders, returning to the ramparts, had been waiting for this moment. They released wagon-sized boulders, each of which could smash a ram like a sledge-hammer blow on a tortoise. But how many giant boulders could have been stored on the battlements, and how many men were ready to risk the hails of arrows to drop them? And how many siege towers and how many rams did it take to assure victory – 20, 30, 50 of each? Priscus gives no details. Whatever the actual numbers, these tactics would have demanded a huge investment of time, energy, expertise and experience – armies of carpenters and blacksmiths, months of preparations, wagonloads of equipment. Attila's army was not yet something to rival the best that Rome and Constantinople could muster; but it was too much for Naissus. With the walls kept clear by a steady rain of arrows, the rams ate away at the stone even as the Huns finished off their assault by deploying scaling ladders, and the city fell.

Naissus was wrecked. When Priscus travelled past it two years later, the bones of the slain still littered the riverbank and the hostels were almost empty (but at least there *were* hostels, and people: devastation was never total, and there were always survivors to make a go of reconstruction).

How are we to put these events together? Some historians assume that Attila took Thrace town by town, working his way down to Constantinople. If so, what happened to the siege machinery which would have been vital to take the city? Actually, it wouldn't have been good enough to tackle Anthemius' new walls, and he would have known that; so why even bother to get it there? My feeling is that he raced to the capital in the hope of finding its walls still in ruins from the earthquake, found them intact, retreated, and met up with his advancing siege machines to take out easier targets like Naissus. In this way he could hold the eastern empire to ransom anyway, get piles of booty, and gain vital experience in siege warfare that would stand him in good stead down the line, especially if and when he wanted to move against Constantinople at some later date.

Theodosius sued for peace, and was given it – on Attila's terms.[4] Fugitives were handed over, the ransom for Roman captives raised from 8 to 12 *solidi*, the arrears – 6,000 pounds of gold – paid, the annual tribute tripled to 2,100 pounds. To the Huns, this was real money: $38 million down, with $13.5 million to follow every year, a river of gold for pastoral nomads. Roman sources claim that Constantinople was being bled dry. When the tax collectors came to collect, rich easterners had to sell their furniture, even their wives' jewels, to raise the money. Some were said to have committed suicide.

In fact, it wasn't that bad. In 408, Alaric was paid off with 9,000 pounds (4,000 from Constantinople, 5,000 from

---

[4] Many scholars place these events and the one-sided treaty in 442, when Bleda was still alive. 'This is certainly not correct,' comments Maenchen-Helfen, relying on Priscus to back him up. 'Attila is the sole ruler of the Huns. *He* sends letters to the emperor, *he* is ready to receive the Roman envoys, *he* demands the tribute money. There are no more "kings of the Huns". Bleda is dead.'

Rome). Other enemy leaders were bribed with annual subsidies of 1,000–3,000 pounds. In 540–61 the Persians received four payments amounting to 12,600 pounds, or just over 1,000 pounds per year. These were sums matched occasionally by a ransom paid for an eminent captive or an emperor's celebratory games or the building of a church. According to one estimate, the revenue of the eastern empire averaged 270,000 pounds of gold annually. So Attila managed to extort about 2.2 per cent of the treasury's income as a down-payment, with less than 1 per cent per year thereafter: well within the amount a prudent chancellor would allow in his budget under the heading of 'bribes and miscellaneous'. Anyway, it lasted at most for three years. Attila guessed that there was more to be had, and must surely have been planning his next move.

The key element in his strategy was his acquisition of the huge swathe of land south of the Danube, stretching 500 kilometres west to east from Pannonia to Novae (today's Šistova), and 'five days' journey' – say, 160 kilometres – north to south: 80,000 square kilometres, an area the size of Scotland or Maine. Now there were no walled cities and campsites for Roman troops, no Danube fleet, and the way through the Balkans to Constantinople was wide open. The site of the annual trade fair shifted south, from the banks of the Danube to ruined Naissus, which would henceforth be the main frontier town. Thrace was at Attila's mercy. When the campaign opened, his authority over outlying areas had been shaky. Now, with all the cash he needed, his people well heeled with loot and ransom-money, all the Hun clans brought to heel, and his authority imposed over those who had fled, he was perfectly positioned to set his bounds yet wider.

Attila's empire was already something that this part of Europe had never seen before, something Europe as a whole had not

seen since the growth of Rome. There had once been a kingdom centred on Dacia, built by a certain Burebesta in 60 BC,
which stretched from the Black Sea west to Hungary and
north into Slovakia, but it had lasted only ten years, then
vanished almost without trace. Attila already exercised influence over a much larger area, across to the Caspian in the
east, to the Baltic in the north-east, northwards to the North
Sea. The evidence for a Hunnish presence comes from
scattered references across this area. As we have seen, the two
princes handed over for impaling after the Treaty of Margus
were delivered at Carsium, today's Hârşova, on the Danube
only 60 kilometres from the Black Sea. Archaeologists have
found hundreds of Hun objects from Austria (bits of a
recurved bow and a deformed skull in Vienna) to the Volga
(pots and swords in Ukraine). Priscus makes a vague reference to Hun rule over the 'islands in the ocean', which most
scholars understand to be islands in the Baltic, off the coast
of Denmark and Germany (a much debated point, this; but it
makes sense, because Attila had inherited control of
Ermanaric's Ostrogothic federation, which had fallen to the
Huns in the 370s). This huge estate embraced all of central
and eastern Europe from the Rhine eastwards, including a
dozen of today's nations, together with bits of southern
Russia, the Balkans and Bulgaria – some 5 million square
kilometres, an area almost half the size of the United States.
Not that it was a unified empire, all under Attila's direct
control; not that every tribe would do as he said; but at least
none would march against him, and most would back him
with troops if asked. By the late 440s he was the *barbaricum*'s
top Alpha Male, who could virtually guarantee the booty that
justified an offensive war.

It was an empire largely hidden from those who might have
recorded it, since it reached eastwards and northwards,
and did not therefore seem to leaders in Constantinople and

Rome to be an imminent threat to all Christendom (not yet; not for another year or so). As a result its nature is unclear. Different experts have different views, and argue mightily, sometimes quite rudely. 'Thompson views the Huns as a howling mass of savages,' writes Maenchen-Helfen. 'He even mistranslates the text.' Marxists have seen Attila as the epitome of the last stage of barbarism, on the verge of a military democracy, destined in the Marxist scheme of things to break down the slave-owning society of Rome in preparation for feudalism, capitalism, socialism and heaven on earth. None of this can be supported by facts, because so little is known about how the new society worked.

What, for example, was Attila's position? All sorts of terms have been bandied about – *basileus* (the term for the Roman emperors), *rex, monarchos, hegemon, archon, phylarchos*. All of these terms are Greek or Roman, and all are ambiguous. Was he, perhaps, more – a god to his people? It has been suggested, and it sounds plausible, given that Roman emperors were accorded divine status, as Augustus deified Caesar and Caligula deified himself and Constantine graciously allowed a hint of deification to attach to himself. But this madness was never part of nomadic culture. A ruler might at best claim to be chosen by Heaven, as Genghis later felt himself to be selected for world dominion by the Blue or Eternal Sky, and as Chinese emperors claimed the Mandate of Heaven. But this was not the same as claiming divinity. It was apparently OK to flatter by mentioning the Leader in the same breath as Heaven, God or a god. That was what sparked a row on Priscus' journey (as we shall see in the next chapter), and that was the basis of the Akatziri chief's specious excuse for not coming to kow-tow to Attila in person. But he didn't really mean it. Attila was no Sun King, whose every expression was a command. Respect was given to the man, not to a god.

*

The Huns were now on their way up, with growing wealth, an expanded territory, and a multi-ethnic elite eager for more of both. Hard evidence for all this emerged in 1979 in northern Hungary, as I learned on a visit to Győr.

I was there to meet Peter Tomka, Hun expert, one of Hungary's top archaeologists, and head of the János Xánthus museum. I was new to my subject and would have been a little nervous, except that it was a glorious summer's day, the town's eighteenth-century centre was pastel-pretty, I had Andi Szegedi to interpret and I knew I had a little something in common with Tomka. We both knew Mongolia. People who know Mongolia are a freemasonry. It would help break the ice, and I was glad of it, for this was to be an important interview. Tomka had supervised the recovery of one of the greatest of Hun treasures. I would like to say Mongolia did the trick, but actually there was no ice to break. Tomka was every child's idea of a big, friendly bear. Solidly built, white-bearded, tousled, clad in baggy shorts, Tomka welcomed me to his den of books, papers and iron shelves with a Mongolian greeting, 'Sain bain uu!', a huge, infectious laugh, and a story.

It starts in mid-May 1979, in a field in the lee of the massive, white hilltop monastery of Pannonhalma. Farm workers were making a new vineyard. One of them was digging the footing for a concrete post in the soft, sandy soil when, almost a metre down, his spade struck something hard. It was iron – a long piece of iron. He dug, and found more iron, and levered, and up came two swords. By the time his supervisor had managed to get through to the museum, the labourer had found more objects, mostly little flakes of gold. Hours later, safely boxed, they were all driven to the museum. That was when Tomka first saw the Pannonhalma Treasure.

'Oh yes, it was very exciting. The experience of a lifetime!'

He threw back his head and roared with laughter at the memory. 'They were typical Hun things, with shell-shaped ornaments, a horse decoration the shape of an omega, the bits of gold foil which had been on the swords' wooden scabbards. So I went out to the field, and did some more digging and hunting around with my metal detector, but found nothing but a few flecks of gold. There was no sign of a grave, no ashes, no bones. So I was very certain that this was an *Opferfund* [sacrificial trove].' He spoke excellent German, which made things easier, because Hungarian was Greek to me.

The site lies off a farm track in the middle of a maize field. When I went there, I stood amid silent fields and scattered trees, the scene made significant not by the long-gone treasure but by the mass of the 1,000-year-old monastery presiding over the surrounding farmland from its hill a couple of kilometres to the south. The same hills would have been there 1,500 years ago. This was Hun land, just, but right on the edge of the Roman territory, because the Romans never left Aquincum, the town on which Budapest now stands, 100 kilometres to the east. And this part of Pannonia was under Hun rule for only 20 years, from 433 to 454. What were they doing, these rich Huns, burying these valuables in an unmarked hole?

These were things valued by those who hid them: iron horse-bits, two-edged swords about a metre long and a bow, both weapons adapted for decorative or ritual purposes with little 3- or 4-centimetre rectangles and clover-shaped pieces of wafer-thin gold foil, worked with circular and oval patterns. Similar gold pieces were also used to decorate reins. They were attached with bronze tacks, the points of which were neatly folded over. In his paper on the finds, published in 1986, Tomka pointed out that some of these are stylistically identical to others found in the Rhineland and near the Sea of

Azov, which for Tomka is proof of the extent of the Hun empire. 'The two groups, separated by many thousands of kilometres [about 2,000], are linked geographically and chronologically by the Pannonhalma find.'

There is meaning, too, in what was not there. No arrowheads; no coins; no buckles (such as are common in other finds). So this is neither a time capsule of everyday objects nor a proper treasure trove of real wealth or loot. They were things loaded with emotional significance, but useless in any practical sense.

'The really exciting things were the bow-decorations,' Tomka said, leaning forward urgently. Other finds contained similar horn ears, but not little bits of gold like this, with net-like and fir-tree-like patterning. 'No parallels! Unique! The golden bow of the Huns!' He gave another delighted laugh.

'A bow that was actually used?'

'Good question. There was no bow, of course, just the decorations. After all, these things were just lying in the earth. There must have been a wooden box once, because the nails were there, but all the wood had rotted away, like the sword-scabbards. I believe that with such a bow, decorated with very fine gold leaf, you would not be able to shoot, because the decorations would fall off. It must have been a symbol of power, a status symbol. I like to joke – but also I'm serious – that it must have been the status symbol of Attila himself. Perhaps the original had the fingerprints of Attila.'

Well, the likely location of Attila's HQ was almost 200 kilometres to the south-east. But a status symbol makes sense. Tomka speaks of a ceremony, recorded during Hun times and extremely widespread among steppe people, in which the funeral involved a feast, during which special items like horse harnesses and weapons would be placed on show. The dead man's soul would not yet have risen to Heaven, and he would need his familiar objects around him on earth – not his real wealth, of course, because that would be shared among his heirs, but his cult objects. Then, when the time came for the final farewell, which might be months or even a year later, an effigy of the departed would be burned, along with – often, but not always – his cult objects, the remains of which were then buried nearby. Over 100 such sacrificial repositories have been found, and in none were there any human bones. 'And so', concludes Tomka, 'we can no longer doubt that the Pannonhalma find is the buried remains of a funeral sacrifice.'

But Pannonhalma is 100 kilometres west of Aquincum, Roman Budapest. Some important Hun had established himself well inside what had until recently been Roman territory, up in rolling hills and woodlands which are not as well suited to herds as the open *puszta*. Attila's new empire is reaching westwards and northwards; and men like this and his surviving family would need slaves, and possessions, and cash, and land if their way of life were to be maintained, and their loyalty assured.

# 6

# IN THE COURT OF KING ATTILA

ATTILA LIVES AND BREATHES TODAY BECAUSE OF ONE MAN, A CIVIL servant, scholar and writer: Priscus, the only person to have met Attila and to have left a detailed record of him. It is largely from Priscus that we get a sense of his true character – less the beastly barbarian, more the revered leader with mixed qualities: ruthless, ambitious, manipulative, swift to anger, even swifter to pretend it, acquisitive for his people but personally austere, terrifying in opposition, generous in friendship. It is the portrait of a man who almost has it in him to change the course of Europe's history.

For Priscus, a bookish 35-year-old with a flair for writing, this was an absolute gift of a story – a visit to the empire's greatest challenger, court intrigues, an assassination plot, a journey full of incident and tension, deception and life-threatening revelation. These bits of Priscus' *Byzantine History* – eight volumes originally, most of it lost – would make a good thriller, which is why his account was quoted so thoroughly by others and has survived. Priscus slips easily from history into narrative. He lacks a flair for the details of daily life, military matters and geography, because they did not loom large in the literary tradition of his classical models, but he has a novelist's feel for relationships, because diplomacy was his main interest. His point of view is not all-seeing, not quite eye-of-God, because he does not enter minds, even concealing his own emotional responses. He is good on structure, though. He reveals up front what he could not have known at the time, but learned later. As a result, *we* know of the assassination plot, although *he* doesn't until the very end. His whole journey is undertaken in ignorance, which injects a modern undertow of tension. Who knows what, exactly? When will all be revealed? How is he going to survive?

What follows is a version of Priscus' account. The narrative technique is modernized by putting much of Priscus' indirect speech into the form of direct quotation. I have added some details from other sources and brought others forward when it seems we should know them sooner. But the structure, the characters and many of the direct quotes are in his words, taken from the 1981–3 translation by R. C. Blockley (for details see the bibliography). Quotations from Priscus and other original sources appear in *this different typeface* to distinguish them from my own words.

The story starts with the arrival of Attila's envoys at the court of Theodosius II in Constantinople in the spring of 449. The eminent team is led by Edika, the ex-Skirian leader and now Attila's loyal ally, *who has performed outstanding deeds of war*. Orestes, a Roman from the strip of land south of the Danube now under Hun control, is the second senior member of the party, with a small retinue of his own, perhaps two or three assistants. Orestes, though rich and influential, is one of Attila's team of administrators. He is always being sidelined by Edika and resents it. They are in the audience room of the

Emperor Theodosius, in the Great Palace built at the behest of Constantine himself just over a century before, and they are open-mouthed with awe.

The Great Palace, the Mega Palation, is a sort of Byzantine Kremlin, a maze of residences, churches, porticoes, offices, barracks, baths and gardens, all surrounded by its own wall: a vast conglomeration of habitation, devotion and defence. Edwin Grosvenor, in his 1895 portrait of Constantinople, recalls its vanished glories: 'In all the endless succession of those vast chambers and halls, all glittering with gold, mosaic and rarest marble, it seemed as if human resource and invention could achieve nothing more in overpowering gorgeousness and splendor.' It was at this time still on the lower slopes of splendour, its peak lying 1,000 years in the future, but it already rivalled anything in Rome. Theodosius held court in Constantine's core structure of the God-guarded palace, a mass of apartments and state rooms known as the Daphne, named after a diviner's column brought from a grove in Greece.

Orestes reads the letters he took at Attila's dictation, and Vigilas, the court interpreter, translates. In summary, Attila tells the emperor what he should do to secure peace. He should cease harbouring Hun refugees, who are cultivating the no-man's-land that he, Attila, now owns. Envoys should be sent, and not just ordinary men, but officials of the highest rank, as befits Attila's status. If they are nervous, the King of the Huns will even cross the Danube to meet them.

A tense silence, no doubt, as an official takes the papyrus rolls. That is half the business done. Now responses must be considered, replies drafted. The delegation will be official guests for the next few days. Edika, Orestes and the assistants are ushered into a suite of rooms belonging to the chamberlain, Chrysaphius. They are nervous, for Chrysaphius is the most powerful official in the land, as was his much admired and famously incorruptible predecessor, the praetorian prefect Cyrus, the poet, philosopher and art lover who sponsored numerous beautiful buildings, developed Constantine's university, rebuilt the walls damaged by the 447 earthquake, and was the first to publish decrees in Greek rather than in Latin. Chrysaphius is very different: a baby-faced eunuch, as venal as Cyrus was honest, whose power derives from schemes and plots. It was he who had engineered Cyrus' fall from grace, and soon (in the words of another historian, John of Antioch) 'controlled everything, plundering the possessions of all and hated by all'. He now holds the compliant emperor in the palm of his hand, and it is he who will decide the best way of dealing with Attila. Chrysaphius joins them just as Edika is muttering his amazement at the lavish furnishings, thick carpets and gold-leaf ceiling.

Vigilas covers Edika's embarrassment: 'He was just praising the palace *and congratulating the Romans on their wealth.*' He refers to his bosses and himself as Romans, although the 'New Rome' is becoming more Greek by the year.

No doubt there is an exchange of courtesies (I'm guessing: Priscus was not present to record such minor details and probably wouldn't have done so anyway); then Chrysaphius picks up Edika's comment with a hint at what he has in mind, speaking through Vigilas, who becomes a shadow: 'You too, Edika, *would become the owner of wealth and of rooms with golden ceilings* if you should ever decide to work for the Romans.' Chrysaphius has his eye on Edika, for he knows that Edika was once master of his own tribe, and must surely be resentful of his new overlord.

Edika is wary. *'It is not right for the servant of another master to do this without his lord's permission.'*

Chrysaphius probes delicately. So Edika is that close to Attila? Does he, for example, have unrestricted access?

'I am one of Attila's closest attendants, responsible for guarding him.'

'You alone?'

'There are several of us. We take turns, a day each.'

'H'm.' Chrysaphius pauses. 'There is something I would like to discuss with you, which I think may be to your advantage. It would be better to do so at leisure, in private, over dinner, at my place. Without the others.' A glance across the room at Orestes and his entourage. 'But I will need your assurance that it will remain between us.'

So there are just the three at dinner that evening, except for the slaves waiting at table. With Vigilas whispering his interpretations, Chrysaphius and Edika clasp right hands and exchange oaths, the one swearing he will speak not to Edika's harm but to his *great advantage*, the other promising total discretion, even if he should feel unable to comply with whatever it is his host is about to suggest.

This is the proposal:

Edika will go home, kill Attila, then return to Constantinople, and *to a life of happiness and very great wealth.*

Edika does not react outwardly, but there would surely have been a stunned silence while he absorbed the implications of this astonishing suggestion. Vigilas waits, the image of professional composure.

Then, quite simply, Edika agrees. It will take money, of course. He will have to pay off the guards under his command. Not much, he says casually; 50 pounds of gold (3,600 gold coins, or *solidi*;[1] $320,000 today) should be enough. It certainly should: enough to set up all his underlings for life.

---

[1] A *solidus* weighed 4.54 grams/0.22 oz. A fifth-century gold *solidus* today fetches up to $600.

Mere pocket money for such a man as the chamberlain. Edika can have the money immediately.

Well, not so fast. Edika lays out the practicalities. When he returns to Attila to report on the mission, Orestes and the others will be in the party. 'Attila always wants to know all the details of gifts and who the donors are. He'll question everyone. There is no way we could hide fifty pounds of gold. But Vigilas will have to return to Constantinople with instructions on what to do with the fugitives. He will tell you how to send the gold.'

This seems sensible to the chamberlain. Vigilas is a good man. After dinner, Edika goes to his room while Chrysaphius seeks an audience with the emperor, who summons his Master of the Offices, Martialis, the man in charge of messengers, interpreters (which includes Vigilas) and imperial bodyguards. The plot thickens. The three of them decide that Vigilas, despite previous experience on embassies, is not after all the right person to carry the emperor's reply to Attila's demands. He is told he is now under the authority of Edika (fair enough, considering that these two are the plotters, but putting a Roman under a Hun will be a potential source of tension). Besides, there is another delicate matter to be resolved, which involves negotiating the ransom of a number of Roman prisoners held by Attila. This should all be in the hands of an imperial ambassador. The man they have in mind is Maximinus, a man of illustrious lineage and an imperial confidant, just the sort of high-level envoy Attila had demanded. Although Priscus does not say so, there must surely be a hidden agenda too: they wish to have a senior man on hand when Attila is assassinated.

They brief Maximinus, without telling him about the plot. He is to point out that there is no need for Attila to stage a meeting across the Danube, which would obviously be a way of showing that he could enter Roman territory at will. If he wants a meeting, he can send his deputy, Onegesius (about whom we shall hear more later). Moreover, the letter from the emperor states categorically: *'In addition to those already handed over, I have sent you seventeen fugitives, since there are no more.'* The fugitives are to be picked up from a military base on the new frontier, near Naissus, the town sacked by the Huns two years before.

This is where Priscus enters. Maximinus knows him, and of his skill with words. Possibly, Priscus is one of those who has been busy over the last ten years drafting the Theodosian Code of imperial laws. He certainly knows his Herodotus and his Thucydides well enough to lend his own writings authority by echoing their style and phraseology. He is good at writing speeches, too. He will be ideal for keeping an account of this important mission: scrupulous, a bit of a civil service fuddy-duddy, but with a fine turn of phrase. Unadventurous by nature, though; it takes more than a little persuasion to get him on board.

So they prepare to set out. The seven officials have been joined by a businessman, Rusticius, who has dealings with one of Attila's several secretaries. And this connection reminds us that nothing is as simple as it seems in this barbarian-versus-Roman rivalry, for this secretary of Attila's is an Italian named Constantius, sent to him by Aetius – Aetius, the great Roman general, who is happy to help Attila with his international contacts. Rusticius, with his friends inside Attila's court, also has the advantage of speaking Hunnish, which will prove useful when the time comes.

Eight official appointees, then, plus Edika's attendants to pitch the tents and prepare the meals, all on horseback: per- haps fifteen horses in all, with a large tent, some smaller ones for the slaves, cooking utensils – silver, as befits an embassy – and peppers, dates and dried fruits to tide them over in case fresh food is in short supply.

\*

Over 300 kilometres and almost two uneventful weeks later they are in Serdica (Sofia). There, approaching the borders of Attila's new territory, some of the hidden tensions begin to emerge. They break the journey for a day or two. Having slaughtered some locally bought sheep and cattle, the Romans offer their Hun travelling companions hospitality. Wine flows. There are toasts: To the emperor! To Attila!

It is Vigilas who starts the trouble. Vigilas, remember, is in on the plot. Priscus isn't, and has no idea of the tension Vigilas must be under. Vigilas has a sudden thought that perhaps he had better show himself loyal to his emperor, and mutters to Priscus, 'It is *not proper to compare a god and a man.*'

'What did you say?' That's Orestes, who knows Greek.

'I said,' slurs Vigilas, 'it is not proper to compare a god to a man.'

'Right. Attila *is* a god. Good to hear it from a Greek.'

'No. Theodosius is the god, Attila the man.'

'Attila a mere man?' The Huns are up in arms at Vigilas. After what he has achieved? Doesn't Vigilas know Attila's authority comes from the sword of Mars himself? How could he do what he did if he were not a god? And so on, with every sign of coming violence, until Maximinus and Priscus *turned the conversation to other matters and by their friendly manner calmed their anger* with post-prandial gifts of silk and pearls.

But tensions remain. Orestes (not in on the plot) is still resentful at being left out of the supper with Edika, Vigilas and Chrysaphius back in Constantinople. He complains to Maximinus, who takes the matter up with Vigilas, who tells Edika, who is appalled that things have come to such a pass. Edika is cross with Vigilas, and Orestes is cross with Edika, and now the Huns and the Romans are cross with each other. Vigilas knows Edika plans to kill Attila, Edika has his own plans that he has told no-one. And the senior Romans,

Maximinus and Rusticius, don't know the half of it yet. Where will it all end?

The sight of Naissus brings them all up short. It's a wreck, pretty much as the Huns left it two years before: the walls half rubble, hardly anyone around, the Christian hostels acting as hospitals for the sick. Between the tumbledown walls and the river, where the Huns built the pontoon bridge for their siege machines, is a litter of bones. Aghast at the desolation, they ride on in silence.

Not far beyond is a military camp where they spend the night. Here the Hun fugitives are being held – but not the seventeen promised in the emperor's letter; only five.

Next day they depart for the Danube, with the fugitives in tow, literally – all tied together. They are heading on north-west, aiming to cross the river at Margus, 120 kilometres and at least four, maybe five days' journey away. The road is unfamiliar to Priscus. All day they plod on, through forests, up and down hills, and on and on as darkness falls. They find themselves *in a thickly shaded place, where the path takes many twists and turns and detours.* There's nothing for it but to struggle on by flickering torchlight, hoping they are still going north-west. But then, saddle-sore, footsore and exhausted, they see the sky lightening straight ahead of them. The sun, a Roman shouts from the shadows – it's rising in the wrong place! It's a portent! You can imagine the response from the front. That's the *east*, you idiot. It's just this winding road. We'll be fine.

On then through a forested plain, always north-west on the single road, until by chance they come across a contingent of Huns. The Huns have just crossed the Danube to prepare the way for Attila himself, who is going to come hunting in his newly acquired forests, not just for fun and for meat, but as a means of training his troops in unfamiliar territory. Not far beyond is the river, and a mass of Huns with dug-out canoes who have been acting as ferrymen for their soldiers, probably with rafts for horses and wagons.

On the other side, they travel on for another couple of hours before being told by their Hun guides to wait while Edika's attendants go to Attila to announce the new arrivals. Late that evening, while they are dining in their tents, the Hun attendants gallop back with the news that all is ready. Next day, late in the afternoon, they arrive at Attila's camp – wagons and circular tents by the score, line upon line flowing across the billowing, open pasture of what is today the Serbian province of Vojvodina. Maximinus wants to pitch his own tent on the hillside, but that is forbidden, because it would place the Romans' tents higher than Attila's.

With the tents erected in a suitably low and submissive spot, a delegation of senior Huns led by Orestes and Scottas come to ask what the Romans want exactly. Consternation and an exchange of glances between the Romans. 'The emperor has ordered us to speak to Attila, and to no-one else,' Maximinus tells them.

Scottas, brother of Attila's second-in-command Onegesius, and number three in the Hun hierarchy, speaks up (Onegesius himself being away among the Akatziri, imposing Attila's elder son, Ellac, as their new king). The Romans had better understand that it's Attila himself who is asking. No Hun would make such a demand on his own account.

Maximinus stands upon protocol, with which, as he points out, the Huns should be familiar, having come on so many embassies to Constantinople. *'It is not the rule for ambassadors that they should wrangle through others over the purpose of their mission. We deserve equal treatment. If we do not receive it, we will not tell the purpose of the embassy.'*

An unnerving pause. The Huns leave with Edika, and return again without him, to thumb their noses at Maximinus by announcing that Edika has just told Attila the Romans' purpose (at least, their *official* purpose; the unofficial purpose is still a secret known only to Edika and Vigilas). And Attila is not interested in anything more they have to say. So there. Now the Romans can go home.

There's nothing to be done. The despondent Romans are packing up when Vigilas, who must see that his hidden mission has suddenly become impossible, becomes desperate. He is the key to the assassination plot; it'll be up to him to fetch the gold, and he stands to lose a substantial reward if it fails. They can't just leave, without achieving anything, he blurts out. Better to lie, say we've got other things to discuss, and stay rather than tell the truth and go! *'If I had been able to speak to Attila, I should easily have persuaded him to set aside his differences with the Romans. I became friendly with him on Anatolius' embassy.'*

Meanwhile, what of Edika? He is keeping a low profile, embarrassed at his minor betrayal of the Romans, and in a bind. He has divulged the official purpose of the visit, but that's not the half of it. He also knows its real purpose, and is afraid that Orestes will tell Attila that he and Vigilas dined alone with the dreadful and duplicitous Chrysaphius, and what would Attila make of that? Especially as he, Edika, is a foreigner, and dispensable. He spends the night in an agony of indecision – to tell or not to tell? To betray or to remain loyal? – fearing that, whatever he does, he's doomed.

Next morning, the tents are packed, the horses already moving off, when Priscus sees how depressed Maximinus is. The sight goads Priscus into making one more try. He beckons Rusticius, the Hun-speaking businessman, who must be equally depressed at the imminent failure of his commercial plans, and leads him over to Scottas. 'Tell him that he will receive many presents if he can get Maximinus an interview with Attila.' Rusticius passes this on. 'And another thing – tell him he will also benefit his brother Onegesius, because if he ever comes to settle outstanding matters with us, he too will receive great gifts. I'm sure he will be very grateful.' Scottas is listening carefully. Priscus looks him in the eye. 'We hear you too have influence with Attila. Perhaps you would like to prove it?'

'Be assured', says Scottas, 'that I speak and act on *an equal basis with my brother*.' He mounts, and gallops off to Attila's tent.

Priscus returns to his two colleagues, who are lying down-cast on the grass, and jolts them with his news. Get up! Get the pack animals back here! Prepare gifts! Work out your speeches! In seconds, despair turns to shouts of joy and thanks to Priscus, their saviour. Then a flurry of anxiety: how will they address Attila? How exactly will they present him with their gifts?

Priscus is not aware of anything that's going on back at Attila's tent, so we must guess. Perhaps it is Scottas' arrival that precipitates the crisis. Perhaps Edika sees Scottas gallop up, and his imagination works overtime. Attila guesses some-thing – Vigilas is going to be tortured to reveal all – he, Edika, will appear as a traitor, unless— He can't afford to wait, he must move now to prove his loyalty. As Scottas leaves with the news that Attila will, after all, see the Romans, Edika begs an audience . . . and tells Attila all about the plot as proposed by the eunuch Chrysaphius, confessing that he himself is supposed to be the assassin, to be financed with the gold that Vigilas is supposed to collect.

Meanwhile, Scottas has arrived back at the Roman tents, where the Romans are ready.

They thread their way through the lines uphill to the grand tent surrounded by guards.

The door is opened (for no doubt the king's tent has a wooden door, as Mongol *gers* do today).

They enter.

What is it like in there? Priscus does not say anything about a richly carpeted floor, a central brazier, a table crowded with little shamanic figures, the crowd of guards, attendants and secretaries, because his attention is wholly taken with the sight of Attila himself, the unsmiling, scary little man sitting on a *wooden chair*, which is also a *throne*, which implies solid, carved arms and a high back.

This is their first view of the man who has so devastated the Balkans and terrified the rulers of the eastern empire these last ten years. It is at this point that Priscus describes him in the words that survive second-hand in the account left by the Gothic historian Jordanes, the words quoted in the previous chapter painting a portrait of the little man with the haughty gait, the small eyes darting here and there, the broad chest, the large head, the thin beard flecked with grey, the snub nose, the bad complexion, and in behaviour that surprising combination of self-restraint, graciousness and supreme self-confidence.

He certainly has every reason for confidence at this moment, because he now knows about the plot, and can afford to play cat-and-mouse with the Romans.

Maximinus steps forward and hands Attila the emperor's scroll. 'The Emperor', he says, through Vigilas, 'prays *that Your Majesty and his followers are safe and well.*'

'You will have what you wish for me,' Attila replies coldly. Then he turns to Vigilas as interpreter and tears into him. How dare he, the shameless beast, appear at all – a moment to savour, this, because Attila might have accused him then and there of planning regicide – when, according to the last treaty, *no ambassadors should come to him before all the fugitives had been surrendered*!

Vigilas stutters that all the fugitives *have* been surrendered. There are no others . . .

'Silence! Shameless effrontery! I would have you impaled

and fed to the birds, if it did not infringe the rights of ambassadors. There are many fugitives among the Romans! Secretaries: the names!'

And so, their bowels turning to water, Vigilas, Priscus and the rest must listen as scrolls are selected and unrolled, the grim silence broken by the rustle of papyrus. Then come the names. 'Seventeen' the emperor had mentioned; five were picked up outside Naissus; and here, scroll after scroll, are listed all those known to have fled across the border over past years – since the time Aetius' son, Carpilio, was a hostage – traitors all, carefully noted by the secretariat – scores, hundreds perhaps, who knows how many? Who was counting? Certainly not the Romans.

Silence at last, and Attila speaks.

He will have the fugitives, if only because he could not have Huns fighting with the Romans in the event of war. Not that they are any use to the Romans, of course. *For what city or fortress had been saved by them after he had set out to capture it?* Not one. Vigilas would leave immediately with a Hun, Eslas, to demand the lot of them. Only then, Priscus implies, would it be possible to discuss the ransom to be paid for the Roman prisoners held by Attila. If the Romans would not comply, it would be war.

Maximinus could remain to draft letters, and as for the rest of you – hand over the presents, and get out.

Back at their tents, the Romans worked over what had happened.

'I can't understand it,' says Vigilas. 'Last time, he was so calm and mild.'

Priscus sighs. 'Perhaps he had heard about you calling Theodosius a god and him a man.'

Maximinus nods. That must be it.

Vigilas remains perplexed. He's sure he's in the clear. The

Huns would be too scared to report that loose talk at supper (and, he must have thought, Edika would never divulge the assassination plot, and condemn himself as a traitor).

Just then Edika himself comes in. He beckons Vigilas aside and mutters something. As Priscus learns later, Edika tells Vigilas to make arrangements to go and get the gold for the conspirators.

This is the only time Edika has appeared since he told Attila the purpose of the embassy. He can only have come at the behest of Attila himself, who must therefore have decided Edika is not a traitor after all. Edika's gamble has worked.

So now there are two plots – the planned assassination and Attila's revenge – in both of which Edika is central. He has compromised the first, and has now kick-started the second.

What was that about? someone asks as Edika leaves. Oh, nothing much – Vigilas waves an arm dismissively – just that Attila is still angry over the fugitives and the rank of the ambassadors, that's all. Fair enough; everyone knows that Edika was given authority over Vigilas before they set out from Constantinople.

He is saved from further questions by a bevy of attendants from Attila, bringing new orders. None of the Romans is to buy anything – no Roman prisoners, slaves, horses, nothing except food – until all disputes are settled. Vigilas is to go back to Constantinople with Eslas and sort out the fugitive question. Everyone else stays. Onegesius, on his way back from overseeing Attila's son crowned King of the Akatziri, is the next designated ambassador to Rome, and he will certainly wish to pick up the presents he's owed.

Now Attila has everyone where he wants them. The Romans are virtually under arrest, while Vigilas – as Attila very well knows – is off to fetch the gold for Attila's assassination. On his return, the trap will spring.

*

The day after Vigilas leaves, Attila orders everyone back to his main HQ. There will be no hunting south of the Danube after all, for there are more important matters to attend to. A chaos of folding up tents, packing and spanning wagons, and saddling horses gives way to ordered columns – wagons, out-riders, bowyers and grooms and cooks all trailing deferentially after Attila's entourage, all winding north over the grassland of what is now northern Serbia.

After a while, the column splits: Attila is sidetracking to a village where he is to pick up yet another wife, the daughter of one of the local *logades*. The rest continue over a plain and across three large rivers and several smaller ones. Sometimes there are locals with dug-outs, sometimes, while the rank and file swim with their horses, the VIPs cross with the wagons on the rafts carried for just this purpose. Along the way, villagers supply millet, mead and barley-beer. (Note that these people are villagers: no longer pastoral nomads, but making their living as settled farmers living in huts of wattle, daub and thatched reeds.)

After a hard day's travel, they camp near a small lake. In the middle of the night they are awoken from their exhausted sleep by one of those summer storms that sweep the Hungarian *puszta*, one so violent it flattens the tent and blows the spare clothing and blankets into the pond. This is a Roman tent, not designed for wilderness living; not like the round Hunnish yurts, which remain snug in the coldest weather and can shoulder a hurricane. Blinded by rain, deafened by thunderclaps, the Romans find their way by lightning flashes to the village, yelling for help. Villagers waken, light reed tapers and lead them inside to the welcome warmth of reed fires.

It turns out that the village has a matriarch. Even more surprising, she is a widow – one of several – of Bleda, the brother Attila killed. Apparently she has been allowed to keep her own enclave on Bleda's territory, where she is still in effect queen. Although it's the middle of the night, she arranges for food to be sent. Then, when they are dry and fed, there troop in a number of attractive young women, who, Priscus is told, are *for intercourse, which is a mark of honour among the Huns*. 'Attractive women', Priscus calls them: what has happened to those racist opinions that the Huns were so revolting in their looks and behaviour that they were scarcely human? Wiped out by the reality of being confronted by hospitality and beauty. A bit embarrassing, this, for Christians, civil servants and diplomats, especially as the women had been chosen for their looks. Polite reserve was the answer. '*We plied the women generously with the foods placed before us, but refused intercourse with them.*'

The next day is fine and hot. The Romans retrieve their sodden baggage, dry it in the sun, pay a courtesy call on the village matriarch to thank her with a gift of three silver bowls and some dried fruit, and are on their way.

So it goes, for a week and probably something over 200 kilometres. They come to another village. Here there is something of a traffic jam. Everyone has to wait because Attila is to rejoin the convoy, and he has to lead. And here, too, by an astonishing coincidence, is another embassy, this one from the western empire, from Rome, with some familiar and eminent faces: a general and a governor; a returning envoy, Constantius, the secretary originally sent by Aetius to Attila; a count named Romulus and his son-in-law, who is none other than the father of Orestes. It seems that being part of embassies to Attila is a family business.

The western envoys have their own story, which centres on the golden bowls of Sirmium. These had once belonged to the bishop who, when the city was besieged by the Huns in the early 440s, gave them to one of Attila's other secretaries for safe keeping, thinking the gift might come in handy if he were captured. That made the bowls Attila's. But the secretary pawned the bowls to a banker in Rome. When Attila learned of this, he had the man crucified. Now he wants either the bowls or the banker. Here was a whole embassy come to tell Attila that, since the banker had received the bowls in good faith, they were not stolen goods and the Hun leader cannot now claim either them or the innocent banker.

At last Attila turns up, and the swollen columns proceed across an open plain until they reach a *very large village* – Attila's capital, which, as suggested in the previous chapter, is probably some 20 kilometres west of present-day Szeged, well away from the meandering and flood-prone Tisza.

As the royal procession winds between the wooden buildings, women give a ritual welcome, lines of them holding up long strips of white linen that form a canopy under which walk a procession of young girls, all singing. They lead the way between the compounds, and then straight into Onegesius' enclosure.

Second only to Attila's, Onegesius' compound contains a surprise – a bath-house made of stones brought all the way from Pannonia, 150 kilometres to the south. It was built by a Roman architect taken prisoner in Sirmium. Priscus does not mention the furnace and hot water, *sine qua non* for a bath-house, nor does he explain how the water got to the bath – there was no aqueduct, of course, because this was a mere village in Roman terms; a ditch, perhaps, or just pot-carrying Roman prisoners trooping back and forth to the river at bath-time. In any event, in this barbaric setting the bath is a terrific status symbol for Onegesius, for baths were temples to civilization, bathwater its very essence. He would have approved a poem by one of the greatest poets of the age, Sidonius, who wrote in praise of his own baths in southern

Gaul, baths of which we shall hear more praise later, and of which Attila himself might hear rumours in two years' time:

> Enter the chill waves after the steaming baths,
> That the water by its coldness may brace your heated skin.

Priscus makes no mention of Attila taking a bath, but it is inconceivable that the work would have gone forward without his permission, even encouragement. The unnamed Roman architect had no doubt provided Onegesius with *tepidarium*, *calidarium*, hypocaust and perhaps even *laconium*, a sweat-room, complete of course with furnace. Not much point in a bath-house, he would have argued, if you freeze in winter. He hoped it would win him his freedom. No such luck: as Priscus notes, he is the bath attendant.

In the enclosure, overseen by Onegesius' wife – his senior wife, perhaps – servants from many households offer the horsemen food and wine from silver plates and goblets. Attila deigns to take a delicacy here, a sip there, and the servants hold up the plate and cup to boast of the honour to the surrounding throng. Then onwards, out of Onegesius' compound by its other entrance, up a rise to the palace.

This is the Romans' first view of their destination, though all they can see for the moment are the wooden walls made of smoothly planed boards so well set by the Gothic or Burgundian carpenters that the joints are hardly visible. Only the size of the walls shows it to be the royal palace. Attila vanishes inside, into instant audience with Onegesius on the subject of the Akatziri and their new young ruler. In fact, it is quite urgent: Attila's son has fallen and broken his right arm. No doubt a healer must be called to set it, with the correct rituals.

Meanwhile, after dinner provided by Onegesius' long-suffering wife, the Romans set up camp between the two compounds, ready for their summons into the royal presence next day. They wait. No-one comes. Maximinus sends Priscus down to Onegesius' place, with servants carrying the presents both for the king and for his right-hand man. The doors are still closed. It's going to be another long wait.

As Priscus wanders about outside the stockade, a Hun approaches, dressed, as Huns usually are, in jerkin and felt trousers. To Priscus' amazement, the Hun hails him in Greek: *Khaire!* The Huns are a mixed bunch, both Hunnish and Gothic being spoken routinely, while those used to dealing with westerners – like Onegesius himself – also have reasonable Latin. But not Greek. The only Greek-speakers around are prisoners taken in the recent wars, the ones the Romans want to ransom. You can tell them at a glance, oppressed and tousled down-and-outs. This man, in his forties I imagine, is smartly dressed, with his hair neatly clipped in the Hunnish style, confident, relaxed.

'Khaire!' replies Priscus, and fires off a string of questions. Who is he? Where does he come from? How is it that he's adopted barbarian ways?

'Why do you want to know?'

'You speak Greek! Of course I'm curious!'

The man laughs, and must surely have introduced himself, though Priscus avoids giving us his name, for reasons that will become clear. Yes, he's Greek, a businessman who had set up in Viminacium, had married a rich wife and was doing well when the Huns attacked eight years before and burned the place to the ground. He had been among those led away into captivity. The business was ruined, of course, but because of his wealth Onegesius had chosen him as a prime hostage. It turned out well for both. He had shown valour in fighting the Romans and the Akatziri, which probably means he had supplied and commanded his own troops. In whatever way, he had acquired enough booty to buy his freedom. Now he is part of Onegesius' entourage, with a new Hun wife and children, and once again doing very well.

In fact, life is better here than it was in Viminacium. He should know; he is in a unique position to compare the two cultures. In the empire, he says, ordinary people rely on their leaders, so have lost their fighting spirit. But the generals are useless cowards, so we're bound to lose wars. In peace, we're at the mercy of taxmen and criminals. There's no such thing as justice any more. The rich bribe the judges, the poor languish in gaol until they die. Faced with incompetence, insecurity, corruption and oppression, no wonder it's better here.

Priscus, remember, is a civil servant, writing an official report. His ears are open to criticism, because no-one can deny that the empire is going to the dogs for just the reasons given by this Greek-turned-Hun. But it would not look good officially to let this sort of thing go unchallenged. So he writes himself a prim reply. The men who framed the Roman constitution were good and wise. They ordained that there should be soldiers, good military training, fair taxation, fair-minded judges, independent lawyers to defend the rights of the common people. If trials last a long time, it is only because the judges want to make sure they come to the right conclusion. How unlike the barbarians are the Romans, who treat their slaves as fathers do *and punish them, like their own children, if they do wrong, so that they are restrained from improper behaviour.* Even in death, a Roman can provide for increased freedom, because wills are legally binding. Why, even the emperor himself is subject to the law. It is a very long speech, which would all be in direct quotes if ancient Greek had direct quotes. It has them in Blockley's translation. And what was the result of this peroration?

*'My acquaintance wept and said that the laws were fair and the Roman polity good.'*

Well, really. Have you ever heard anything so unlikely? This unnamed man, who had had a wife, a business, a home, and lost the lot and lived through four wars and started again in a foreign land and rebuilt himself from scratch – he hears prim and pious phrases that come straight from some civil service handbook on how to sound like Socrates, and *he weeps*?

Many have remarked on Priscus' presumed deficiencies here. A feeble and prolix declamation, says Gibbon. Indefensible ... throws a sinister light on his recording abilities, says Thompson. But I think he knows exactly what he's up to. It's a common device of the scholar or civil servant who wishes to criticize: This is just a hypothesis or the opinion of others, which of course I do not support, so it's not my fault if my readers take it seriously. Galileo later used this ploy in his *Dialogue* proposing a sun-centred solar-system; so did Luther in his 'Ninety-five Theses' condemning the pope and setting off the Reformation. In a minor way, this is what Priscus is doing – using a chance meeting to sneak in a sharp critique of Roman society, then making it even more persuasive by countering it with no more than tight-lipped and tedious pedantry. This is why the man remains anonymous: Priscus blows the incident up out of proportion, and would not wish either to embarrass his source or to risk a rebuttal. His protest is to be taken not with tears, but with a knowing nod and many grains of salt.

The doors open. A message is passed, and answered. Onegesius emerges, receives gifts, and comes to see Maximinus, who urges him to visit Rome as an ambassador and work out a new peace treaty. Onegesius is aloof. He will do only what Attila wants – '*or do the Romans think that they will bring so much pressure on me that I will betray my master?*' Service to Attila, he says, is better than wealth among the Romans! Better for him to stay at home.

Next day, it falls to Priscus as go-between to make direct contact with Attila. He approaches the palace's wooden wall, and is let in. Now he sees the true size of Attila's compound, which contains a palace, a separate dining-hall and a large cluster of other buildings, some of planks ornamented with carvings, others of planks merely stripped of bark, planed and fitted, some – belonging to Attila's senior wife, Erekan – of planks rising from stone foundations. Now known to Hun officials, Priscus makes his way through a milling crowd of guards, servants, envoys from other barbarian tribes and ordinary Huns anxious to have Attila judge their complaints. Voices babble in Hunnish, Gothic, and Latin. Somewhere in the crowd are the members of the other Roman embassy, the ones who have come to settle the dispute of the golden bowls. Priscus enters the queen's house, probably removing his sandals to walk over the felt rugs, and finds the queen reclining on a couch, Roman-style, surrounded by servant girls embroidering linen cloaks. There's no interpreter to hand, so Priscus presents gifts, and takes his leave again.

He is in the crowd outside Attila's palace when Attila and Onegesius come out. Attila has a habit of glancing around him (a trick of leadership taught to politicians and public speakers nowadays to help them grasp the attention of all and give an impression of authority). As petitioners make their appeals and receive judgement, members of the other Roman embassy come up to find out what's going on. Priscus asks about the golden bowls affair. It's not good news. Attila is adamant: it's the bowls, or war. One of the team, Romulus, with long experience as an envoy, explains why. No previous ruler has ever achieved so much in so short a time. Power has made him arrogant. He's ambitious for more, too. Wants to attack Persia. *Persia?* comes an astonished voice from the crowd, which prompts Romulus to tell the story of the war of

395, when the Huns raided through the Caucasus and returned past the flaming rocks of the Caspian shore. Yes, it would soon be the Persians' turn again.

'Better the Persians than us.'

'Yes, but what then?' This is one of the senior western officials, from the bit of Pannonia now under Hun rule. Attila will return as master, he says. Now we call him an honorary general, so that our tributes look like regular payments. But if he defeats the Persians he won't be interested in Roman gold. He'll want to be addressed as king and make the Romans his servants. Already, he says, Hun generals are as good as Roman ones, and—

At this point Onegesius comes out. A flurry of questions ends with Maximinus being summoned to see Attila.

Inside, as he reports later, he gets short shrift. Attila wants ambassadors he knows, high-rankers like Nomus, Anatolius or Senator, men who have been before. When Maximinus says it might make the emperor suspect treachery if Attila prefers them, Attila says: Do as I say, unless you want war.

Back at the tent, as he is pondering what to do, a dinner invitation arrives for the Romans. This is their first opportunity to see Attila relaxing, if he ever does. When the time comes, the Romans walk up to the dining-hall, where waiters offer a cup of wine so that guests can make a prayer before being seated.

Note the wine. Traditionally the Huns drank *kumiss*, fermented mare's milk, and barley beer. Wine was a new addition to the Hun diet, an important trade item, and a welcome part of formal feasts like this one.

There's Attila, in everyday clothing, even his bootlaces free of the usual Hun adornments, sword at his side, sitting on a Roman-style couch, with young Ellac sitting deferentially on the end, his broken right arm presumably bound up. He's a king in his own right now, but he doesn't look like it, his eyes downcast in awe of his father. His brother Ernak, Attila's favourite, sits on a chair beside him. Actually, Priscus now sees, this dining-hall is also Attila's official bedroom. Behind Attila is a second couch, and behind that a few steps lead up to a bed screened off by ornate and colourful hangings of linen and silk.

The chairs line the walls, each chair with its waiter. Priscus does not count the number, but I imagine 30 or 40, as befits a state banquet with Roman embassies from both eastern and western capitals. Onegesius is on Attila's right, the side of honour, with other Hun notables ranging away along the same wall. The Romans are seated on the left. Waiters offer gold and silver goblets. A waiter gives Attila wine in a wooden cup. The king formally greets everyone in turn, his cup being passed to each guest, who takes a sip and returns it, at which point everyone sips from his own cup. Priscus has a hard time explaining exactly how this long introduction is done, but it sounds like a cross between a Roman drinking session and a Christian communion service. Then tables are carried in, one for each group of three or four, so that everyone can eat without leaving his place. Now comes the food: meat of various kinds and bread, on silver platters – for everyone except Attila, who makes a show of his simple, honest nomad roots by using a wooden plate and his wooden cup.

The first course ends, and all must stand, drain their cups, toast Attila and wish him good health. Now comes another course. Priscus does not record what exactly is served: he is not interested in food, and besides, his gaze is getting blurry, the impressions running together. It's just a different lot of cooked dishes. End of second course. Everyone stands. Another toast, once again the whole cup to be drained. It's got dark. Here come pine torches, and it's time for entertainment. Two bards chant songs of their own composition in praise of Attila's victories and his courage. This is very affecting. Around the hall young men recall the battles with nods and smiles, old men become tearful. Now it's the turn of a comedian. For a Roman, it is hard to imagine anything worse than a Hunnish comedian, and of course his act goes entirely over Roman heads. Priscus dismisses the man as deranged, *uttering outlandish, unintelligible and altogether crazy words*. But to the Huns he is a hoot. They fall about with laughter.

And the best is still to come. This is the moment they've all been waiting for. It's Zercon, the hobbling, noseless, hunchback dwarf captured in Libya who had been Bleda's jester. Everyone knows the story of how he ran away, was recaptured and received a wife from among his master's entourage. When a year or two later Bleda was murdered, Attila parted Zercon from his wife and gave him to Aetius, who gave him back to Aspar, his original master. What a strange life Zercon has had, snatched from beggary in Libya and then passed between patricians, generals and chiefs from Romans to Huns to Romans, and now back at last to the Huns. It was the Skirian chief, Edika, with his international contacts, who had somehow brought him back to Attila's court, having persuaded him that he had a right to reclaim his lost wife. Attila was not happy to see this reminder of Bleda, and the lost wife remained lost.

Now Zercon enters. He is not a dimwit; he knows his fate depends on his entertainment value; so he probably has an act, a speech of some kind, uttered with his usual lisp, and a deliberate mixture of Hunnish, Gothic and Latin. To modern sensibilities, it is a dreadful idea. Unfortunately, sensibility to deformity is quite modern. Most audiences until the early twentieth century would have loved it, as they loved bearded ladies and midgets and the Elephant Man. To get an idea of just how low this act is, imagine a black dwarf with crippled feet performing a music-hall song in a pastiche

Franco-German accent, and with a lisp and a stutter. The onlookers fall about, point, slap their thighs, and laugh until the tears run.

All except Attila, who sits stony-faced and unmoving. After all, he has had Zercon on and off for the last seven years. Enough is enough. He responds only when young Ernak comes and stands by him. Ernak is special. As a Latin-speaking Hun whispers to Priscus, the shamans had told Attila that the Huns would fall, but their fortunes would be restored by Ernak. Attila draws his son closer with a soft hand on his cheek, and smiles gently, while Zercon brings his bizarre performance to a close.

Official business takes another five days: letters written for the emperor, a Roman woman prisoner ransomed for 500 *solidi*, another meal arranged by Attila's senior wife Erekan; and a final supper with Attila. They will leave with one matter to be resolved, concerning Constantius, the secretary sent to Attila by Aetius. Aetius had promised Constantius a wealthy wife. The emperor had found just the woman, but the arrangement had been scuppered by court politics. As part of the Roman–Hun interplay of bellicosity and diplomacy, Attila insists that his secretary shall have the promised wife. That is what has been agreed. Let it be so!

Then the embassy sets out on its journey home. It is not a happy one. They see a spy impaled – a grim reminder of Attila's ruthlessness and the awful skills of his executioners – and two slaves dying a slow death for murder, hanging by their necks from V-shaped branches. Their main Hun companion turns nasty halfway, reclaiming the horse he had given as a gift.

And on the road from Constantinople, for there is only one, they meet Vigilas, returning with his Hun minder, Eslas, and the (carefully concealed) 50 pounds of gold which he is planning to give to Edika to fund the assassination of Attila. Since he was sent off to discuss fugitives and prisoners, his return is no big secret. He has no Hun fugitives with him, but he does presumably carry another letter from the emperor on the subject. He is at the head of a mini-embassy of slaves and horses, and blithely unaware that he is walking into a trap. He cannot, of course, learn the truth, because it is known only to Edika and Attila, and Edika has not been seen or heard of since his muttered briefing to Vigilas just after he spilled the beans to Attila. It does not seem to occur to him that one of the main struts of the plot – that there should be a high-level Roman delegation in Hun lands when Attila is assassinated, ostensibly by his own officers – has been cut away. So confident is Vigilas that he has brought along his son as a companion.

Priscus will learn later what happens. When Vigilas crosses into Hun lands, Attila's men are waiting. An escort would be in order, a pleasant surprise. It turns into a nasty shock. He is arrested, searched, relieved of his bag of gold and dragged with his son before Attila.

So what exactly is all this gold for? asks Attila, as if he didn't know.

For me, for the others – Attila allows Vigilas to stumble on, miring himself in a swamp of deceit and pompous words – so that we might not fail to achieve the object of the embassy through lack of supplies. Or, he struggles, or . . . through the inadequacy of the horses and baggage animals. In case they became exhausted on the long journey, and more had to be bought. (In which case, what need of the gold in Hun lands, now that the Romans have left?) And to purchase captives. So many in Roman territory had begged him to ransom their relatives.

What Vigilas might have done, had he been truly sure of himself, was to come back at Attila with outrage at such treatment – an ambassador arrested and robbed! Unheard of! The emperor will hear of this, etc., etc. Instead, he stands condemned by his own mealy-mouthed words.

'*Worthless beast!*' yells Attila, who does anger very effectively. These are his words as Priscus reports them: '*You will escape justice no longer with your tricks! Your excuses cannot save you from punishment!*' Vigilas is being treated as a mere criminal, and a Hun criminal at that, not the Roman that he is, let alone a diplomat. Attila is very sure of his ground, and rants on. The money is much more than any delegation needs for provisions, horses, baggage animals and captives. And, anyway, Vigilas must surely recall that Attila refused to ransom captives when he first came with Maximinus.

At this point, Attila nods to the guards holding Vigilas' son. A sword is drawn. One word from me, says Attila, and the boy dies. Now tell me the truth.

This is the moment Attila has been waiting for since he first learned of the scheme some six weeks ago. A Roman ambassador caught in an assassination plot, and such a stupid one. Could anything better reveal the duplicity of the Romans and the superiority of the Huns?

Vigilas breaks down, bursts into tears, and calls upon Attila, in the name of justice, to let the sword fall upon him, not on the innocent lad, who knows nothing.

The truth, then.

So it all comes out: the truth, as Attila has known it all along. Chrysaphius, Edika, the meetings in the palace in Constantinople, the emperor's agreement, the gold, everything.

It was enough to save lives. If Attila can do anger, he can also do magnanimity. But there is more to be squeezed out of this. Vigilas is put in chains, and becomes a hostage. He, who said he had come to ransom others, will himself be ransomed. The son is to be sent back with the news, and will return with another 50 pounds of gold. There is something poetic in the way this works out. Fifty pounds was the amount suggested to fund the assassination of a king. Now Attila demands the same sum for a mere ambassador. The emperor will lose twice what he committed, and will gain nothing but humiliation. For anyone with a sense of drama, and Attila has that in abundance, this revenge is exquisite.

But there is no point unless he can ensure the humiliation is public, for both the emperor and the dreadful eunuch Chrysaphius. He sends Orestes and Eslas, both of proven honesty, along with the boy. Their job is to rub salt into the emperor's wound.

When they have their audience with Theodosius in Constantinople, Orestes wears around his neck the bag in which Vigilas had hidden the gold. Chrysaphius is present, of course. The words in this scene are Attila's, given to Eslas to speak:

Do the emperor and Chrysaphius recognize the bag? A significant pause for explanation and recognition, then Attila's message:

'Theodosius is the son of a nobly born father. So am I, Attila, the son of my father the King of the Huns, Mundzuk. I have preserved my noble lineage, but Theodosius has not. Who now is the barbarian, and who the more civilized?'

The answer is obvious: the bag proves the point. Theodosius, by plotting the assassination of Attila, his superior, his master, has acted like a rebellious slave. *As a result, Attila declared, he would not absolve Theodosius from blame unless he handed over the eunuch for punishment.*

There is something else to be resolved as well: the matter of Constantius' wife. His intended has been married off to some-one else, taking her dowry with her. But Theodosius surely knew about this, in which case he had better get her back. Or was he not in control of his own servants? In which case,

Attila would be happy to make the man an offer he would be unlikely to refuse.

There is only one way to get out of this mess and save the life of Chrysaphius: find a lady even richer and better connected than the one promised to Constantius, and then pay, and pay, and pay. An embassy is prepared, headed by men even more eminent than Maximinus. In exchange for cash on a scale never seen before, all is resolved. Attila withdraws from the lands south of the Danube, lands he would have struggled to keep anyway. Constantius gets his rich wife (she is the daughter-in-law of the general and consul Plinthas whose son has died). Vigilas is ransomed, Chrysaphius saved to scheme again, the Roman prisoners of war released, the fugitive Huns conveniently forgotten.

And Attila is free to turn his attention to a softer target than Constantinople – the decaying empire of Rome itself.

# 7

# THE BARBARIAN AND THE PRINCESS

IN 450 ATTILA'S SOUTHERN FRONTIER ALONG THE DANUBE WAS AT peace. His advance across the Danube, the disputes over prisoners and fugitives, and now the easterners playing into his hands with their foolish plot: all of this had given him the money and security he needed to raise him from robber baron to empire-builder. He might have taken the road to consolidation and stability.

But that was not his nature. For a robber baron there can never be money and security enough. It would not do to trust Constantinople to honour its new commitments for long. His eyes turned westward. Of course, there had been fifteen years of peace with Rome, rooted in the Hun–Roman alliance underpinned by the Huns' long-term friend Aetius. But Attila was not one to let friendship stand in the way of booty. Within the year his vassals, possibly even his own *logades*, would be restless. Something had to be done.

Rome itself was too tough a nut to challenge head-on – yet – but its northern province, Gaul, was a softer target.

Poor tattered Gaul had been a playground for barbarians for almost 50 years. Britons had fled their troubled isle for the north-west, the area that would become Brittany. Vandals, Alans and Suevi had crossed the Rhine in 406, streaming south-west into Spain; the Burgundians, having been chased out of the Main area by a combined Roman and Hun army in 435–7, had settled in Savoy; and the Visigoths had wandered via Rome and Spain to Aquitaine, where in 439 Rome recognized their independence. Wandering bands of brigands, the Bacaudae, terrorized the north. There were Alans living near Valence, more near Orléans.

Historians like to deal with discrete entities such as tribes and nation-states, but in fifth-century Gaul individuals, armies and tribes flow and scatter and combine and part so continuously that it is hard to define the fundamental units, let alone weave them into a narrative. No rules of geography or politics stand up for long. Barbarian tribes tended to drift from east to west, except when they didn't or when they settled; they were Rome's enemies, except when they weren't; they preserved their own identities, except when they didn't.

One undeniable truth was that Gaul was now well frayed at its edges, offering Attila some interesting openings.

On its north-eastern edge, the Franks retained a sturdy independence. Having mopped up the intervening tribes along the Rhine, the Huns had easy access to them.

In the north-west, a huge area centred on Brittany, the Bacaudae were as restless as ever. Attila knew of them because a wealthy Greek doctor, Eudoxius by name, who had been living among them, had got into some sort of trouble and had had to make a run for it. A turncoat in Roman eyes, he could not go to Rome. He fled instead to the Huns.

In the far south-west, today's Aquitaine, the Visigoths had settled after their long migration through Spain. The Visigoths were old enemies of both the Romans and the Huns. It was a

Hun army, under Aetius' principal lieutenant, Litorius, that had driven the Visigoths from Narbonne in 437, and then been virtually wiped out near the Visigothic capital, Toulouse, the following year.

Yet Gaul's heart went on beating, for Gallo-Roman provincials in the secure central and southern parts looked to Rome for their protection and culture. In 418 it acquired its own local administration, the Council of the Seven Provinces, asserting Roman-ness and Christianity from its new capital, Arles (still today a city rich in Roman remains), dominating the Rhône delta. It was here that Aetius had based himself as Gaul's defender from 424 onwards, standing as firmly as possible first against the Visigoths, but also against the Germans on the Rhine frontier. Of course, to do so he employed some of the very barbarians he was opposing – as he also did in his own cause: when Aetius, the defender of Gaul against Franks and Huns, was fired by the regent Galla Placidia in 432, he led a rebellious army of Frank and Hun mercenaries to force his reinstatement. In 450 Aetius was still playing the same role, his power spreading along Rome's network of roads to garrison towns like Trier guarding the Moselle valley, and Orléans, holding the Loire against Visigoths to the south, and the wild Britons and Bacaudae of the north-west. This was, however, a province on the retreat, guarding its core. The Rhine, the old frontier, had its line of forts, but they were beyond the Ardennes, and hard to reinforce in an emergency.

Military force and Aetius formed only half the equation. For the other half, the cultural bit, we may turn to Avitus, statesman, art lover and future emperor. He was to be found 15 kilometres south-west of Clermont-Ferrand, in the steep volcanic hills of the Massif Central, beside a lake formed when a prehistoric lava flow blocked a little river. Romans called the lake Aidacum. Today, it is Lake Aydat, 2 kilometres across, smaller than it was in Roman times, but still edged with trees and open fields. It was here that Avitus built a villa to administer Avitacum, as he called it. It was described in a letter by his son-in-law, Sidonius, one of the best-known poets of his age, who made sure of his fame by writing obsequious homilies to the rich and powerful.[1] The panegyric in question was written not long after these events to mark Avitus' brief reign as emperor in 455–6, just before his death, when Sidonius was in his mid-twenties. In poems and letters full of floweriness and orotundities (he would have liked that word) he paints a portrait of what it meant to be a provincial Roman just before the Hun invasion. It is like looking back to the long Edwardian weekend just before 1914, or the life of privileged Anglo-Indians in the 1930s, or the old American South of *Gone With The Wind* just before the Civil War. There's an empire going to pot all around, yet the provincial rich go on with their house-parties and baths and dinners and sports and pretentious discussions of literature, as if nothing will ever change.

Avitus, one of the most eminent men of his age, was in 450 virtually Gaul's equivalent of royalty. He was the province's anchor in turbulent times. The head of a rich and influential family, he had been a military commander under Aetius, and his service had been rewarded with the senior posts in Gaul, both military and civilian. In 439, after many envoys had failed, he persuaded the Visigothic king, Theodoric, to sign a peace treaty. By 450 Avitus was a noted patron of the arts, a lavish host, an impassioned collector of manuscripts, admired across the empire for his diplomatic skills.

Sidonius' letter takes us on a guided tour of Avitus' palatial

---

[1] Letter II, ii, to a friend, Domitius, an academic who (he writes elsewhere) was so severe that 'even the man who, they say, laughed only once in his life was not as critical as he'. Perhaps the description of Avitacum was intended to lighten his friend's grim temper.

## A LOST SKILL REDISCOVERED

Lajos Kassai, the acknowledged master of mounted archery (*main picture and inset*) has some 250 pupils who gather at his estate near Kaposvar. Several now teach the sport themselves. One is Kassai's star female protégée, Pettra Engeländer (*below*), who runs courses in Gut Seeburg, near Berlin, living proof that Hun women could fight as effectively as men.

Trier's Black Gate was one of several of the city's military blockhouses that failed to stop the Hun advance.

Honoria, the emperor's sister, appealed to Attila for help – which he took as an offer of marriage, demanding half the empire as her dowry.

Aetius, portrayed in this fifth-century ivory panel, got to know the Huns in his teens, and may have known Attila personally. As Rome's greatest general, he organized the empire's defence against Attila.

## THE INVASION OF WESTERN EUROPE
In 451 Attila used Princess Honoria's plea for rescue as his excuse to invade. He led his army from Hungary across Germany, up the Moselle valley, past Trier and Metz, and into France. He attacked several cities, including Reims and Troyes. Turned back at Orléans, his invasion was finally defeated by the Roman general Aetius on the Catalaunian Plains north of Troyes.

In Reims cathedral, a portal commemorates the martyrdom of Bishop Nicasius at the hands of mail-clad Huns. He prepares for execution (*right*), his severed head (*left*) guaranteeing him a sainthood.

An infantryman of the Franks, a confederacy of Germanic tribes on the lower Rhine. The Franks, allies of Rome, were attacked by the Huns during the invasion of western Europe.

There is no firm evidence, but some like to believe that the Pouan treasures, on show in Troyes' museum, are the grave-goods of Theodoric, the Visigothic king killed by Attila's forces and given a hasty battlefield burial.

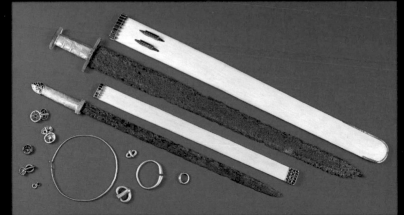

hundert dusent ludes ver gode konig

koning ezele vor dammen to langbarden

driv iar. vn do he se nicht gewinnen ne mo

nen varen. wan vat he sach vat de storke ere

ezele                                    vorden. var van k

stormve de stat vn

ve se al. vammen v

e paues leo qua t

var he ves landes genave havve var loved

paues dat he vat von wolve

Ezele      leo

## THE ITALIAN CAMPAIGN, IN FACT AND FICTION

When Attila invaded Italy in 452 he took Aquileia – but was he really inspired in his decision by the flight of a mother-stork (*left*)? He never advanced south of the Po – but was he really deterred by Pope Leo I in person (*above*)? This incident quickly became the stuff of legend. A thousand years later, Raphael honoured the earlier pope's namesake, Leo X, by painting him as Leo I. *The Meeting of Leo the Great with Attila* (1511–14) in the Vatican's papal suite has its own story. Only the pope and his attendants are by Raphael; the rest, including the panic-stricken Attila (*centre*), was done by his assistants. Leo I originally bore the features of Julius II, who commissioned the work. When Julius died, Raphael painted Leo I as Julius's successor Leo X, who had been one of Julius's attendants. So Leo X appears twice, as pope and an attendant.

An illustration in the *Saxon Chronicle of the World* shows Attila pointing out that storks abandoning Aquileia presage the city's imminent fall.

## 'THE BEASTLY HUN'

Attila and the Huns lived on as symbols of barbarity, acquiring a new and spurious significance in modern times. In 1870s France, the Huns came to stand for the Germans, newly united under Prussian military leadership, a comparison that the Germans themselves encouraged. English-speakers then adopted 'the Hun' as a derogatory term for 'German', as exemplified in First World War propaganda and newspaper headlines. Today, it survives only as a self-consciously blimpish archaism.

A French stained-glass window of 1883 turns Attila into a Wagnerian warrior.

A US government First World War poster urges its citizens to buy war bonds.

In Fritz Lang's two-part epic *Die Nibelungen* (1924), Attila seems the very essence of evil. This is from Part II, *Kriemhild's Revenge*, with Rudolf Klein-Rogge as a fearsome Attila. Hitler loved the films, as did his architect Albert Speer, who was inspired by its haunting lighting effects when he staged the Nuremberg Rallies.

**A BLOODY DEATH**
A haemorrhage during his wedding night with his new wife Ildico was
a suitably dramatic end to Attila's astonishing life. Later authors and
illustrators retold the incident in their own ways. Almost a millennium
after the event, the anonymous author of the fourteenth-century
*Saxon Chronicle of the World* portrayed Attila as a medieval king.

home. To the west rises a steep hill, with ridges that run north and south of the villa and its 2-acre garden. The lake is to the east. Avitacum is more of a village than a villa in the modern sense, encompassing separate accommodation for estate administrators, tenant farmers and slaves. One important set of buildings, the central statement of wealth, culture and identity, are the baths, hugging the base of steep woodland, from which, when the tree-cutters get to work, the logs 'slide in falling heaps almost by themselves into the mouth of the furnace'. By the furnace is the hot bath, supplied with steaming water through a labyrinth of lead piping. Off the hot room are the anointing room, where masseurs work their magic with perfumed oils, and the *frigidarium*. All these rooms are topped with a conical roof and enclosed by plain white concrete walls, decorated not with the usual murals but austerely and tastefully with a few lines of verse. Three arches with porphyry columns lead out to a 20-metre-long swimming-pool, its water, taken from a stream running down the hill, gushing through six lion-headed pipes with a roar that drowns conversation. Adjacent are the ladies' dining-room, the main store-room and the weaving-room. Facing the lake is a grand portico, from which a corridor leads to an open area where slaves and their families gather for meals.

Somewhere nearby – the layout is becoming hard to follow – are the winter dining-room, with a vaulted fireplace, and the summer dining-room, with a short flight of stairs leading up to a veranda overlooking the lake. Here guests enjoy watching the fishermen cast their nets or set lines dangling from cork floats to catch trout overnight. If it gets too hot, you can always recline in the north-facing drawing-room, a good place to be lulled by the midday chirp of the cicadas. Nature has other choruses, too: frogs at twilight, geese in the evening, cocks before dawn, prophetic rooks at sunrise, nightingales in the bushes, swallows in the rafters. A walk down the grassy slope to the lake brings you to a grove, over-shadowed by two huge limes, where the family play ball or dice with guests. You can take a boat-ride, if you like. Avoiding the marshy western end, with its vulgar and disorderly bulrushes, you row along the forested and sinuous southern bank, circling the small island, turning at a post dented by the oars of rowers frantic with sweat and laughter during one of the annual races. And over all this Avitus watches, because the library overlooks the baths and the lawn and the lake, and, while dictating his letters and conferring with managers, he likes to make sure his guests are enjoying this Roman Arcadia.

And what might the guests be up to, besides boating, bathing and eating? Sidonius tells us in another letter describing country-house activities (on two estates near Nîmes, actually, but such things were common upper-crust pastimes). In the morning, there might be a sort of pig-in-the-middle ball-game, in which a circle of players toss the ball while one of them tries to intercept it. Inside, others play at dice. To one side lie piles of manuscripts, as it were the Sunday news-papers, *Country Life* and a few of the latest hardbacks: some of a devotional nature for the ladies, and literature noted for its eloquence and stylistic grandeur for the men. Then, while the men discuss the latest Latin version of some eminent Greek writer, a butler announces lunch, it being the fifth hour by the water-clock – a range of roast and stewed meats and wine, enjoyed while listening to a reading of a short story. Afterwards, a light walk to work up an appetite is followed by a sauna. In those estates unlucky enough to lack a steam-bath, servants dig a trench, fill it with heated stones and build a roof of branches covered with rugs. While guests crowd in, servants throw water onto the stones.

Here we whiled away the hours with no lack of witty and humorous conversation, in the course of which we became wrapped and choked in the breath of the hissing mist, which drew forth a wholesome perspiration. When this had poured out sufficiently to please us, we plunged into the hot water. Its kindly warmth relaxed us and cleared our clogged digestions; and then we braced ourselves in turn with the cold water of the spring and the well or in the full flow of the river.

Remember as we wander the estate that although this was the grandest of provincial villas, the very pinnacle of refinement, elegance and wealth, there were hundreds of other lesser villas, all the product of Gaul's 100 or so towns, some of them sizeable regional capitals like Narbonne and Lyons, even the meanest outshining Attila's village on the Hungarian grasslands. It is just possible that one of Attila's Roman secretaries had heard of Avitacum, and told his master of its delights. Such people, with their corrupting luxuries, would be easy prey.

And then, would not this be a wonderful spot for a conqueror to take his ease from the affairs of state – a country retreat, a Berchtesgaden or Chequers or Camp David, where some high-class Roman beauty could be allowed to play at culture, and entertain, and await the occasional gracious visit from her lord and master?

How to proceed? The main problem was to manoeuvre without seeming to threaten Gaul directly, and thus threaten Rome, and thus risk losing the friendship with Aetius, Gaul's guardian. The Visigoths seemed to be the key, because they were traditionally enemies of both Romans and Huns. Attila tried to play the diplomat, at which, to be frank, he was a novice. To Rome, Attila made a specious argument about the Visigoths being vassals who had fled from their Hun overlord, and had to be brought back into the fold. He could give himself some diplomatic cover by claiming that, since the Visigoths were the enemies of Rome, he would be acting 'as guardians of the Romans' friendship', in the words of a contemporary chronicler, Prosper of Aquitaine. Such a move might even win friends among Romans in Aquitaine, where landowners would be happy to retake estates seized by the Visigoths only a generation before.

But of course the Visigoths would not take kindly to Attila's arrival. They too had to be neutralized. To Theodoric, Attila sent a message with an altogether different argument, urging him to recall who his real enemies were – i.e. the Romans – and in so many words offering assistance. As Jordanes comments, 'Beneath his great ferocity he was a subtle man.' Not very subtle, though. Was Attila really naïve enough to think that his enemies might not see where the greatest danger lay? I rather think he was.

His ambitions were encouraged from afar by another new barbarian kingdom, that of the Vandals in North Africa. Jordanes explains why in a striking anecdote. A Visigothic princess, Theodoric's daughter, had married a Vandal prince, Huneric by name, son of the king, Gaiseric. At first, all went well. There were children. Then Huneric turned brutal, and paranoid. 'He was cruel, even to his own children, and because of the mere suspicion that she was attempting to poison him, he had [his wife's] nostrils and nose cut off, thus despoiling her natural beauty, and sent her back to her father in Gaul, where this wretched girl was an ever-present unsightly ruin. The act of cruelty, which affected even strangers, spurred her father powerfully to take revenge.' So Gaiseric had cause to be nervous about what Theodoric might do. A pre-emptive strike by Attila would come in very handy.

What a prospect for Attila if he achieved his aim! With the

Visigoths beaten, Attila would rule from the Caspian to the Atlantic, a sweep as wide as both parts of the Roman empire put together, with a supply line across Gaul cutting between the unruly Bacaudae of the north and the Roman legions to the south. It would surely then be possible either to crush the Bacaudae or simply ignore them and go for Gaul itself. Attila would rule all of northern Europe, a new, dynamic empire balancing, and then dominating, and eventually – why not? – conquering the decaying, corrupt and divided imperium to the south.

The long-term strategy is a guess, but there is some evidence that he had at least started on this road. He sent a note to Valentinian III in Rome stating his intention to attack the Visigoths and assuring him that he had no quarrel with the western empire. This was in the spring of 450, just the time to prepare for the long march westward. The campaign might well have gone according to plan – but for two events that changed everything, tempting Attila to reach far beyond his grasp, and thus assure his downfall.

The Emperor Valentinian III, still only in his early thirties, had a sister, Honoria, the two of them being the children of the formidable Galla Placidia, twice-widowed daughter of Theodosius the Great. Her own story had been a drama: carried off from Rome by the Gothic chieftain Athaulf, handed back to the Romans after Athaulf was assassinated, and then married to Athaulf's Roman opposite number, Constantius (another Constantius, not to be confused with Attila's secretary). What follows now is melodrama: the story of her daughter, the princess Honoria, of her wounded pride and how she changed the course of history.

The imperial family had been in the current capital, Ravenna, for the last 25 years, since the defeat of the usurper John (or Johannes). Honoria had from her girlhood been raised in a position of power and privilege, having been given the honorary title 'Augusta' far too young for her own good. She had her own residence in the palace, an establishment run by a steward named Eugenius. Like her mother, she was an ambitious woman; unlike her mother, she had plans to rule in her own right; and unlike her dim and feeble brother, the Emperor Valentinian, she had the wit to do so. All that she lacked was opportunity, which might have come her way had her brother not produced heirs, threatening to consign her to obscurity. But dreams of power remained, to achieve which she needed a consort. Eugenius was to hand, first as conspirator, and then as rather more, a story well milked by Gibbon: 'The fair Honoria had no sooner attained the sixteenth year of her age than she detested the importunate greatness which must for ever exclude her from the comforts of honourable love: in the midst of vain and unsatisfactory pomp Honoria sighed, yielded to the impulse of nature and threw herself into the arms of her chamberlain Eugenius.'

It slightly spoils the story to know that she was actually no dizzy teenager but a scheming thirty-something when this happened. Gibbon says she became pregnant, and was shuffled off to remote exile in Constantinople. No-one else mentions pregnancy or an exile in Constantinople, and Gibbon does not provide his source, but in any event the affair and plot were discovered, Eugenius was put to death and Honoria betrothed to a rich and safe consul with no whiff of intrigue about him.

Driven into paroxysms of rage by the loss of her lover, the failure of her plans and the prospect of a boring husband, Honoria planned a dreadful revenge and a new life that would give her the power she longed for. As she knew from his recent note to her brother, Attila, already Europe's most powerful monarch outside the empire, was planning to extend his rule to the land of the Visigoths and would perhaps end up as ruler of all Gaul.

This was how she would have her revenge on her brother: she would become Attila's consort. She would reign, if not as empress of Rome, then as empress of Gaul.

Gibbon's account of her plan is pure Hollywood, with a classic swing and a good dose of xenophobia:

> Her impatience of long and hopeless celibacy urged her to embrace a strange and desperate resolution . . . In the pursuit of love, or rather of revenge, the daughter of Placidia sacrificed every duty and every prejudice, and offered to deliver her person into the arms of a barbarian of whose language she was ignorant, whose figure was scarcely human and whose religion and manners she abhorred.

There is enough in other sources for us to have faith in the main lines of the story. Among her entourage was a loyal eunuch, Hyacinthus, to whom she entrusted her extra-ordinary mission. Giving him a ring to hand to the Hun ruler as proof of her good faith, she sent Hyacinthus off to Attila with a plea for help. In exchange for a certain sum of money, he was to come at once and rescue her from a marriage that was hateful to her. Her ring carried the implication that in return for her rescue she would become his wife.

Valentinian had his spies, but Hyacinthus was long gone before he knew what was up. News of this scandalous business swept through the top ranks of society, and thus to the ears of Theodosius in Constantinople. Theodosius, who had just finished appeasing Attila after the collapse of the assassination plot, did not want either him or the newly made peace upset. His advice to Valentinian was to hand over Honoria at once. She could be sent off across the Danube, and good riddance. But Valentinian was not going to take this challenge to his authority. How Hyacinthus accomplished his mission was not recorded, of course, there being no official historian at Attila's HQ to record it. I have a feeling that Onegesius would have been initially inclined not to bother his master with this envoy and his batty offer – but then had second thoughts. Perhaps the two of them heard Hyancinthus out after all, because Attila stored up the idea until it suited him to recall it. All this would have taken a few weeks. When Hyacinthus returned to his mistress to report the success of his mission, Valentinian had him arrested, tortured for the details, and then beheaded.

He must have been tempted to get rid of his troublesome sister as well, but was prevented by their ever-formidable mother, Galla Placidia, who demanded the care of her errant daughter. Valentinian duly handed her over; later that same year Placidia died, at which point Honoria vanished from history into her dull marriage, where her husband kept her from wreaking any more damage.

But the consequences of her actions lived on, boosted by the second unexpected event of 450. Honoria having made her extraordinary offer in the spring, on 28 July Theodosius, emperor of the East, fell from his horse and broke his back. Two days later he was dead, at the age of 50, leaving two daughters, no male heir, and a problem. Having come to the throne as a child 43 years before, he had never been a strong emperor. The power behind the throne had been his elder sister, Pulcheria, and she was not about to give up this power simply because her brother had died. Within three weeks she had married a Thracian senator named Marcian, revealing to a surprised but compliant court that he had been named successor by Theodosius on his deathbed. Marcian, like Pulcheria, was no appeaser. Now was a good moment to show some resolve and staunch the northward flow of gold, for Attila, in the midst of planning his move westward, would have neither the time nor the inclination to change tack. One of Marcian's first acts was therefore to repudiate the payments to Attila agreed by Theodosius.

Attila was already gathering an army such as the Romans had never seen before, drawing on all the tribes of his empire, a list that grew ever larger with the passing years, until chroniclers bolstered the force with tribes drawn from myth and spoke glibly of half a million men. Well, it could hardly rival the combined might of Rome, but it might have numbered tens of thousands. Among them were Gepids from the Transylvanian hills, under their king Ardaric, much admired (Jordanes says) for his loyalty and wisdom; three Ostrogothic contingents from their new homeland south of the Danube, now returned to the care of Constantinople, but providing men for both sides, these ones being commanded by Valamir – tight-lipped, smooth-tongued, wily – with his lieutenants Theodomir and Vidimir; the Rugians, perhaps originally from northern Poland, soon to resettle in the hills north of Vienna; Skirians, whose foot soldiers had formed the backbone of Hun infantry units since the days of Ruga and whose ex-king, Edika, was very much in Attila's good books, having proved his loyalty in the assassination fiasco; Akatziri and Herulians from the Sea of Azov, near the Huns' homeland; those renowned lancers the Alans, some of whom had been absorbed in the early days of the conquest; from the Rhineland, contingents of Thuringians, and remnants of those Burgundians who had remained when the rest of the tribe migrated westward; and, from Moravia, Langobards ('Long-Beards'), who had once lived on the Elbe and would later migrate to Italy as the Lombards, giving their name to their final homeland around Milan.

Attila was now in a bind. He had a campaign ready to roll, an army numbering tens of thousands to feed, no more funds from Constantinople, and the very real possibility that his long-term plans – first the Visigoths, then Gaul, then the empire itself – would be scuppered by Marcian's army. There was no time to waste. But which way to turn first?

Perhaps Marcian was a paper tiger, who would crumple at the first firm touch? Far from it. A Hun embassy requesting aid received short shrift. As one account put it, Marcian replied that gold was for his friends, iron for his enemies. The most Attila could expect were 'gifts' if he kept the peace. And if he threatened war, he could rest assured that he would meet a force more than equal to his own. Hope flickered back to life when, in late 450, Marcian sent his own ambassador, Apollonius; but, on learning that he was not bringing tribute money, Attila furiously refused to see him, sending a message that he could leave whatever gifts he had and go, or be put to death. Apollonius, a general and one of the most senior envoys Marcian could have chosen, was not a man to be intimidated. It was not right, he replied, for Attila to make such a demand. He had the power to steal and kill, of course; and that's just what he would have to do, if he wanted the Romans' gifts without negotiation. Or he could act the diplomat, and have the gifts. A bold response, and well judged. Attila still refused to negotiate, but let Apollonius go, taking his goodwill gifts with him.

There was one chance that Attila could get what he wanted with hardly a battle – a remote chance, but still worth exploring. He had in his hand Honoria's ring, and her words as reported by Hyacinthus. Thus did the crazy act of a woman wild with grief and frustration inspire an equally crazy response. The emperor's own sister had begged for rescue, had surely – with her ring – offered herself to him in marriage; and just as surely a wife came with a dowry – in this case, a dowry limited only by Attila's dreams. There were just two problems: first, she had to be freed; then she had to achieve what she had always wanted, which was to be co-ruler with Valentinian. As her betrothed, he assumed the right to make all this happen.

Priscus takes up the tale: 'He sent envoys to declare that Honoria should not be wronged at all, and that if she did not receive the sceptre of sovereignty, he would avenge her ... The Romans replied that Honoria could not come to him in marriage since she had been given to another and that she had no right to the sceptre since the rule of the Roman state belonged not to females but to males.'

It was mad. Attila must have seemed to Valentinian's officials as removed from reality as did Idi Amin, Uganda's buffoon-dictator in the 1970s, to Whitehall when he proclaimed himself Conqueror of the British Empire. When the inevitable reply came, Attila's mind was made up. Westward it would be, as fast as possible to forestall action from Marcian in Constantinople. He would forget the Visigoths, and go for Gaul right away. With victory there, all northern Europe would be under his control, and even a united empire would quail.

First, though, there was the matter of getting there. This demanded a campaign such as Attila had never previously attempted. He was about to cross mountains and rivers and forests, which he had done when advancing into the Balkans, but never when simultaneously tackling such a great distance – indeed, he had never faced so great a distance at all. And speed was of the essence. What was needed was an equivalent of a *Blitzkrieg*: a fast thrust up the Moselle, then a cross-country dash that would outwit and outmanoeuvre the opposition and establish a bridgehead on the Atlantic. For this he needed his cavalry, with the infantry mopping up behind him. Better to do without the mangonels and trebuchets and siege towers with which he had taken Naissus. Such things could grind along at only 15 kilometres a day, and needed firm going. He would have to cover the entire width of France – over 700 kilometres – in a month.

But this could not be. He was trapped in paradox. He needed the speed; but there were towns that had to be neutralized. Fast-moving mounted archers were good in open country against infantry and the slower, heavily armed Roman cavalry, but it was no use galloping right past fortress-towns like Trier and Metz, leaving their battalions untouched to retaliate at their leisure. He had to have some siege gear after all, which meant wagons. There would be some wagons anyway, of course, to keep the archers supplied with arrows; but the heavy machinery required solid ones, which meant teams of oxen, and fodder, and outriders, who would also need feeding. It was possible to combine mounted archers and siege warfare near home, but not if you were moving steadily away from it.

It was a fearful risk. He would have liked, if possible, to avoid a conflict that was bound to be a tough one. He returned once again to the matter of Honoria. By now – with his army right on the imperial frontier, as committed to war as the German army in 1914 – he seems to have convinced himself that he actually had a strong case. Back went the envoys, with yet higher demands. Honoria was his by rights – they had the ring with them as proof – and so was everything that was hers, because she had received it from her father and been deprived of it only by her brother's greed.

And what was it exactly that was hers, and which was now his? Priscus states Attila's case: 'Valentinian should resign to him *half of his empire*.'

It was an outrageous claim: all Gaul. Again came the inevitable rejection. Back went a final, uncompromising demand from Attila, who must by now have been on his way westward through the German forests to the Rhine. His ambassador told Valentinian: 'Attila my master and your master has ordered you, through me, to prepare your palace for him.'

At last Rome got the message. No more self-deception about the target being Visigoths, no more reliance on the old friendship between Attila and Aetius, no more buying time with hopeful diplomatic exchanges. If he wasn't stopped, he would go on until Rome itself fell.

# III

# DEATH AND TRANSFIGURATION

# 8

# A CLOSE-RUN THING ON THE CATALAUNIAN PLAINS

LOOKING BACK AFTERWARDS, WHEN PEOPLE KNEW WHAT A CLOSE call it had been for all Europe, they realized there had been signs, warnings, prodigies and portents of the coming threat: an earthquake in Spain, an eclipse of the moon, the Northern Lights casting their unearthly glow too far south, like spectres armed with flaming lances battling clear of polar regions. In May 451 a comet appeared vivid in the dawn sky – Halley's Comet, as we now call it, its glowing head and streaming tail as menacing as a flaming missile from a heavenly catapult. The threat that had been steadily building for 50 years – the Visigoths grabbing Aquitaine, Alans, Vandals and Suevians scattering across northern Gaul, Burgundians in Savoy, Franks edging along the Meuse, North Africa lost, Britain cut off, Brittany a law unto itself, Bacaudian brigands roaming wild – seemed on the verge of climax.

In undertaking the invasion of the West, the Huns faced a problem similar to that which faced the Germans as they prepared to invade France in 1914, and again in 1939.

Approached from the Rhine, France has fine natural defences in the form of the Vosges mountains, giving way to the Eifel and Ardennes in the north. Practically the only way through is up the Moselle, through what is now Luxembourg, and then out onto the plains of Champagne. But it was no good making a thrust through the mountains into the heart of France (or Gaul) if the army could be threatened from the north – from Belgium or, in this case, the region occupied by the Franks.

Attila had a problem with the Franks. The Frankish king had died, and his two sons were disputing the succession. The elder one had approached Attila for help; the younger one, aged no more than fifteen or sixteen, sought Roman backing, and found it in Aetius. Priscus saw this young man in Rome in late 450, and was struck by his looks: 'His first beard had not yet begun to grow, and his flaxen hair was so long that it poured over his shoulders.' Aetius adopted him as a son – a common device to ensure a firm alliance – and the youth went away laden with gifts and promises. Obviously, he was about to receive the help he needed to secure the throne, and thus tumble into the arms of Rome. It would not do to have a Roman vassal on the right wing, any more than Germany in 1914 could afford to let neutral Belgium fall into the Allied camp. To invade France successfully, Germany had to take out 'poor little Belgium'. To invade Gaul, Attila first had to neutralize the poor little Franks.

Early in 451 Attila's main army advanced up the Danube along frontier tracks, spreading out on either side, crossing tributaries over fords or pontoons of logs cut from the surrounding forests. One wing seems to have swung south and then up the Rhine, via Basel, Strasbourg, Speyer, Worms, Frankfurt and Mainz, then meeting the main force, which followed the old frontier from the Danube to the Rhine. The Huns probably crossed near Koblenz, cutting trees along the bank to make rafts and pontoon bridges for their wagons.

From there, in March 451, Attila could have sent a small force to sweep up those Franks not already fighting for the Romans. Evidence in favour of this is that Childeric, the elder son who had approached Attila, later emerged among the Franks as a king of some stature. Certainly, Franks soon formed a contingent in Attila's army as well as in Rome's; and this would hardly have been possible if they were still wholly allied to Rome, ready and waiting to stab Attila from his rear.

The accounts of this campaign are all Christian, since it was Christianity that kept the flickering torch of civilization burning: all of them were written later, and most of them are hagiographies of martyred bishops, owing as much to spin and imagination as to historical truth. But it is possible, even so, to map Attila's progress. There was, perhaps, a secondary crossing near Strasbourg, and some opposition from the Burgundians. But the main assault came near the junction of the Rhine and Moselle at Koblenz. That spring, the Huns and their motley allies headed up both sides of the Moselle, two single files on the winding roads, linking up at the nine-arched stone bridge of Trier.

Really, they should have got no further. Trier had been the capital of Rome north of the Alps until the provincial government moved to Arles 50 years before, and it had been a fortress for three centuries. Its 7-metre-high walls linked four colossal gateways, of which one is still there, saved by a Greek monk who walled himself up in it in the eleventh century, protecting it with an aura of sanctity. When the Huns came by, this north gate was a shining soft yellow, but over the centuries it acquired the dark patina that affects all ageing sandstone, and became the Porta Nigra, the Black Gate. Nothing in Gaul, then or now, could better state Rome's power than this Schwarzenegger-ish guardhouse, 30 metres high, 36 long and 22 deep. Its stone blocks, some bearing names and dates inscribed by proud masons, weighed up to 6 tonnes each. Cut by bronze saws powered by water from the Moselle, they were bound not with cement but with iron clamps into three storeys of 144 arched windows and two squat towers. Two arches, gated and portcullised, led through it into the old city and its 80,000 inhabitants. This was Rome in miniature. Its marbled palace, built on Constantine's orders in 300–10, was made with 1.5 million tiles brought from the Pyrenees and Africa. The city's bath-house was the empire's largest, except for those of Diocletian and Caracalla in Rome itself, complete with exercise-room, hot, cold and tepid rooms, coal-fired furnace and two-storey cellars. In the stadium, 20,000 people could see gladiators fighting, criminals fed to lions, and plays on a stage cranked up from the floor (all there in today's ruins).

So Trier should have stopped the Huns dead in their tracks. But they passed it with hardly a pause. We have no idea what happened. The lack of an account suggests that its garrison, depleted since Arles became Gaul's capital, just shut them-selves up and let the barbarians flow around them. The Huns moved on, no doubt leaving a rearguard to block the valley upriver in case Trier's soldiers regained their nerve.

In any event, the only information we have concerns the next town on their line of march, Metz. According to one account, the Huns hammered in vain at the walls of Metz with a battering-ram, and advanced on to a fortress upriver, where, just before Easter, news reached them that a portion of Metz's weakened walls had collapsed. A quick night-time gallop back downriver brought them straight into the breach, and the town fell on 8 April. A priest was taken hostage, others had their throats cut, and many died in their burning houses.

On then, down the gentle limestone slopes of the Ardennes

foothills, and out on to the flat expanses of the *campi*, the open savannahs that give their name to Campania, Champagne as it became. The region was known then as the Catalaunian Plains or Fields, after the Latin name for a local tribe, still recalled in the name of the present-day town of Châlons. There was, it seems, a small diversion north of Châlons, to Reims, the central city of Gaul, where all major roads met. The ancient town, with its triumphal arch built by Augustus and its forum, was almost empty, its inhabitants having taken to the woods, but there remained a small crowd hoping for the best, along with its archbishop and some priests. According to legend, the prelate, Nicasius, was singing Psalm 119 when the Huns reached him. Perhaps he hoped that this longest of psalms, with its 176 verses, would provide some special protection. It didn't. He had just reached verse 25 – 'My soul cleaveth unto the dust: Quicken thou me according to thy word' – when a Hun sword struck off his head. He was later beatified as St Nicaise.

The main thrust, though, lay westward, towards Orléans, where Attila's old enemies, the Alans, prepared for assault. The Huns, with their wagons, were moving with less than *Blitzkrieg* speed, covering no more than 20 kilometres a day, through a countryside emptied by fear. Those with possessions buried them; the rich trembled in their fortified mansions; the poor fled to the woods and mountains.

They even began to flee a little town to the north, way off the Hun line of march. The Parisians didn't want to be trapped on their river-island. It was (of course) a saint who brought them to their senses. Genevieve, like another later saintly maiden, had kept sheep as a child, before taking the veil at fifteen and becoming noted for her self-mortifying austerity and visions, the one no doubt producing the other. She was good at miraculous cures and at seeing the future, both talents that came in handy when the Huns invaded.

This, she saw, had to be the will of God, who could be mollified only by prayer and repentance. She made a dramatic appeal to the townsfolk not to abandon their homes, but instead to look to God for salvation. The men reviled her and went on fleeing, but courageous women put their cowardly men to shame, and the exodus stopped. Lo and behold, the Huns came nowhere near Paris. They had no need to, of course, because it wasn't on their route. But Paris remembered this simple country girl who reversed the panic that could have turned the future French capital into a ghost town, and made Genevieve the city's patron saint.

Where, meanwhile, was the imperial army? When the Huns had first invaded, no-one knew their destination. Perhaps it was Italy. Valentinian had ordered most of the army to remain at their home bases. Aetius, as a precaution, was sent off with a small force to Arles, at the mouth of the Rhône, where he awaited developments, no doubt in increasing impatience.

Now the Huns were heading south-west, aiming to go over the open lands of Champagne, across the Loire, then south towards the Visigothic capital, Toulouse. This would keep them well away from the Massif Central, and, once free of the Loire's forests and out in the open, allow their cavalry to operate to full advantage.

On the way, though, were two major cities, Troyes and Orléans.

Orléans would be the key, as it had been for centuries. Its original name, or rather the Latin version of its original Celtic name, was Genabum, since it sat on the *genu*, the knee, of the Loire, where the river kinked at its most northerly point. In winter the Loire was a torrent; but in summer it became a river-road, the best way of travelling through the thick oak forests either to the coast or to the high heartland and on down the Rhône to the Mediterranean. But it was also a meeting point for roads, one of which led south over a stone bridge. It was, in brief, the gateway to the north-west. Caesar having burned it, Marcus Aurelius rebuilt it, naming it after himself, Aurelianum, which later transmuted into Orléans. In the fifth century it was rich, big and sophisticated, far out-doing little Paris, and not bothered by the presence in the surrounding forests of an Alan clan.

It would have taken the Huns three weeks to cover the 330 kilometres from Metz to Orléans, assuming a clear run. They would be there by early May. The citizens locked themselves within their solid walls and prepared for a siege. Meanwhile, a Christian leader, Anianus – later sainted for his services as St Aignan (or Agnan) – had already hurried off to contact Aetius, to check for himself what help might be available, and when. Aetius was in Arles, at the mouth of the Rhône, a long haul for Anianus, whether by road or by river, perhaps a com-bination of the two, riding upriver beside the Loire's springtime current for 300 kilometres (two weeks), over the watershed at St Etienne to the Rhône (a day), then fast down-river for 200 kilometres (another five days). It would take at least the same again for Aetius to move north: say, five weeks in all – a close-run thing, especially as the Huns were not the only danger. The local Alans suddenly recalled that their kinsmen were Hun vassals, and were part of the approaching army. Their chief, Sangibanus, sent a message to Attila, say-ing that he would help take Orléans in exchange for fair treatment.

Attila's route led across the rivers Aube and Seine through Troyes, and around it, for this was a large army, with wagons, which would have used every available road. He would have noted the landscape north of Troyes, today's Aube *départe-ment*, the chalky savannahs of Champagne, where the Seine and Aube meander towards each other across the Catalaunian Plains. Troyes, a pretty place of wood-and-thatch houses and perhaps a stone-built villa or two, had no

walls – easy prey for the advancing Huns. There was a substantial church, which rated a bishop, Lupus, famous for
having been part of a mission to post-Roman Britain 20 years
previously, and about to become much more famous – briefly,
infamous – as a result of Attila's arrival.

Attila's troops would have entered Troyes. It was too good
a source of supplies to ignore. No doubt looting had already
started, inspiring a legend in which fact and fiction are hopelessly mixed, but which is often presented as history.
According to Lupus' official biography, he saved his city and
his people by confronting Attila, a meeting that involved one
of the supposed origins of a famous phrase. Assuming the
meeting took place, how Lupus introduced himself is not
recorded, but it presumably included something like: I am
Lupus, a man of God. At this, Attila came up with a smart
one-liner, in impeccable Latin:

'*Ego sum Attila, flagellum Dei*' – 'I am Attila, the Scourge
of God.'

This was, of course, a Christian interpolation, made
because Attila's success demanded explanation. It would have
been inconceivable that a pagan could prevail over God's own
empire, against God's will. Therefore, pagan or not, he must
have had God's backing, the only possible explanation being
that Christendom had not lived up to divine expectations and
was being punished for its lapses. A folk tale tells of a hermit,
captured by the Huns, foretelling doom: 'You are God's
Scourge, but God may, if it pleases Him, break his instrument
of vengeance. You will be defeated, so that you may know
that your power has no earthly origin.' Isidore of Seville, an
encyclopedist of the sixth and seventh centuries, also used the
phrase to describe the Huns. Within two centuries it was a
cliché: one to which we shall return in chapter 12.

Precisely the same argument would be used by a later pagan
leader against another monotheistic religion, when Genghis

Khan swept into the Islamic world in 1220. He is said to have told the citizens of Bukhara: 'I am the punishment of God. If you had not committed great sins, God would not have sent a punishment like me upon you.' In both cases, the historian who recorded the leader's words served an agenda, to remind the faithful of the need for piety. Thus churches make pagan leaders serve a divine purpose, despite themselves.

As the story goes, the bishop was intimidated. Since Attila was, it seemed, divine retribution, appeasement, rather than defiance, was in order: 'What mortal could stand against God's scourge?' he replied. So the two found each other useful. Attila agreed to spare Troyes – not so much as a chicken taken from it – with the proviso that Lupus must stay with him until Attila saw fit to let him go. The bishop could prove a handy lever should his flock think of offering resistance, or if he, Attila, needed a bargaining chip at some time in the future. It was a deal that rather took the shine off Lupus' reputation. Was he a hostage, as he would no doubt have claimed? Or more of a guide, an early example of what is now known as Hostage Syndrome, when the victim, in self-protection, becomes complicit in the crime?

Meanwhile, Anianus was in Arles, doing his best to persuade Aetius to move. Orléans could hold out for a month, no more. According to the account of his life, he sets a deadline: 'Thus shall the prophecies by the Spirit be fulfilled, that on the 8th day [before] the *kalends* (i.e. the 1st) of July, the cruel beast shall resolve to tear the flock to pieces. I beg that the Patrician shall come to our aid by the predicted date.' Any later than mid-June and all would be lost. Aetius gave his word, and Anianus headed for home.

Aetius now faced the unpleasant task of going to war with the people he had known from childhood, whose soldiers he had used as mercenaries, with whom he had sought nothing but peace for the last fifteen years. To fight them, he would have to make friends with Attila's enemies, the Visigoths, the strongest of the many barbarian forces scattered across the face of Gaul, and Rome's traditional enemy.

Theodoric had been resigned to war with Attila. Over the last 20 years, he had got used to being Aetius' foe as well, and had no hopes of any help. He was therefore preparing to defend his land, his people and his capital, Toulouse. It had not occurred to him to take the war to Attila through the hostile territory of Gaul. Aetius knew all this. To bring Theodoric on board would take some very astute diplomacy, for which he obtained backing from the Emperor Valentinian himself.

As it happened, there was a man who could undertake this task quite nearby, in Clermont-Ferrand. It was, of course, Avitus: patrician, scholar, diplomat, future emperor and friend of Theodoric. Having retired from public office, for the past eleven years he had enjoyed the life of a wealthy aristocrat, supervising Avitacum and its huge estate, with its pines, waterfalls and delightful lake, pursuing not just the pleasures of the senses and the mind, but also a political and cultural agenda. He knew from personal experience that military power alone could not preserve the empire. He had seen wandering barbarians settle and change. The idea was this: that peace would grow from education in the ways of Rome. As O. M. Dalton put it in his edition of Sidonius' letters, he probably believed that peaceful 'understanding with the most civilised of the barbaric peoples might save an empire which Italy was too enfeebled to lead'. If this was so – and his later life's work suggests it was – he would have dreamed 'of a Teutonic aristocracy more and more refined by Latin influences, which should impart to the Romans the qualities of a less sophisticated race and to their own country-men a wider acceptance of Italian culture'. Theodoric and his Visigoths were the proof that such an aim could be successful.

Having led his people to an end of wandering, Theodoric now had ambitions to rival, if not Rome, then at least its provinces in the arts of civilization. He was flattered to have the friendship of a man admired even in Rome. From his estate by the shores of Lake Aydat, Avitus had brought silky sophistication to Theodoric's untutored, fur-clad chieftains and his capital, Toulouse (Tolosa as it was then), 250 kilometres away to the south-west. Young Goths were now studying the *Aeneid* and Roman law. The patrician had even offered personal guidance on the tutoring of the youngest and brightest, another Theodoric. Of all Rome's nobles, Avitus was the only one guaranteed to get a good reception from Theodoric. They were friends, almost equals.

The fate of Gaul, perhaps of the empire, now rested on the personal links between three men: Aetius, the commander; Avitus, the peaceful patrician; and Theodoric, the barbarian king wary of Rome's motives, yet eager for Rome's culture. Two days after Anianus' departure, Aetius was with Avitus, putting his case. I imagine the two of them in the scroll-filled library overlooking the pines, the hot baths and the surrounding mountains. It was not an easy case, because Aetius wanted Avitus to use his peaceful links with Theodoric to convince him of the need for war. Attila was no Theodoric. It would be useless to think of talking settlement, peace and education. Sidonius' poem suggests what was said, the gist of which ran like this: 'Avitus, it is no new honour to have me make a plea to you. At your command, enemies become peaceful and if war is in order, you produce it. For your sake, the Goths stay within their frontiers, and for your sake they will attack. Make them do it now.'

And Avitus went, bearing an urgent request to Theodoric from the Emperor Valentinian himself, which Jordanes turns into ringing words, delivered, we can assume, by the patrician in person:

Bravest of nations, it would be prudent of you to combine against Rome's oppressor, who wishes to enslave the whole world, who needs no cause for war, but thinks that whatever he does is right. He grabs whatever he can reach, he takes pride in licence, he despises law both human and divine, he shows himself an enemy of all nature. Indeed, he who is the enemy of all deserves such hatred. I beg you to remember what you surely cannot forget: that the Huns do not win by fighting wars, in the results of which all share, but, more disturbingly, by treachery. To say nothing of ourselves, can your pride bear this to go unpunished? Being mighty in arms, heed your danger, and join hands with us.

Theodoric responded like a hero, declaiming his reply to Avitus in front of his chiefs:

Romans, you shall have what you desire. You have made Attila our foe as well. We will follow him wherever he summons us, and however puffed up he may be by divers victories over mighty peoples, the Goths know how to fight off these overbearing people. I call no war a burden, unless it lack good cause; for he on whom Dignity smiles fears no ill.

And so diplomacy and charm produced what no war could have achieved: a force that could confront the greatest barbarian army yet to threaten the empire. 'Will future races and peoples ever believe this?' commented Avitus' son-in-law Sidonius later, eager to assert the primacy of negotiation over force. 'A Roman's letters annulled a barbarian's conquests!'

For his hero's words, Theodoric received a just reward. 'The nobles shouted their acclaim, and the people gladly followed' – no longer in defence but forward, to stop Attila in his tracks, with Theodoric leading 'a countless host', flanked by two of his sons, Thorismund and Theodoric, the four others being left to guard the home front. 'O happy array,' comments Jordanes, who was himself a Goth. 'Sweet comradeship, to have the help and solace of those whom he chooses to share his dangers!'

And now, with little time to spare, Aetius sent messengers to every major city and every barbarian clan that had found new land and new life in Gaul. The greater threat of Attila's Huns won new allies: the Swabians of Bayeux, Coutances and Clermont, the Franks of Rennes, the Sarmatians of Poitiers and Autun; Saxons, Liticians, Burgundians and other clans of yet greater obscurity; even some of the wild Bacaudae from Brittany. Many had their own insights into Attila's progress, for traders brought news, and barbarian clans had friends and relatives fighting for Attila. Information leaked back and forth – so it was not too surprising that Aetius heard of Sangibanus' offer to side with Attila in the coming siege of Orléans.

After the Roman and barbarian armies linked up, somewhere unrecorded, they raced the Huns to Orléans, a race that Aetius won by a whisker, a day perhaps, or more likely several days, with enough time to suck Sangibanus, the vacillating Alan chief, into his ranks and 'cast up great earthworks around the city'.

Some say that the Huns beat them to it, which is unlikely, but it made a great story that continued the drama of Anianus, now back in the city after his frantic journey to Arles.

With the Huns at the very gates and the townspeople prostrate in prayer (of course, this being a Christian account), Anianus twice sends a trusty servant to the ramparts to see if help is coming. Each time he returns with a shrug. Anianus despatches a messenger to Aetius: 'Go and say to my son Aetius, that if he does not come today, he will come too late.'

Anianus doubts himself and his faith. But then, thanks be, a storm brings relief from the assault for three days. It clears. Now it really, really is the end. The town prepares to surrender. They send a message to Attila to talk terms. Terms? No terms, he says, and sends back the terror-stricken envoys. The gates are open, the Huns already inside when there comes a cry from the battlements: a dust cloud, no bigger than a man's hand, recalling the coming relief from drought in Elijah – the Roman cavalry, eagle standards flying, riding to the rescue. 'It is the aid of God!' exclaims the bishop, and the multitude repeats after him, 'It is the aid of God!' The bridge is retaken, the riverbanks cleared, the invaders driven from the city street by street. Attila signals the retreat. It was of course the very day – remembered as 14 June – that Anianus had given Aetius as the deadline.[1]

Such a close-run thing makes good Christian propaganda, and therefore is not much favoured by historians. But it may contain an element of truth, because Sidonius mentions it, and he was a contemporary. Writing to Anianus' successor, Prosper, in about 478, Sidonius refers to a promise he had made the bishop to write 'the whole tale of the siege and assault of Orléans when the city was attacked and breached, but never laid to ruins'. Whether or not the Huns were actually inside the walls when Aetius and Theodoric arrived, there can be no doubt that their arrival saved the city. The event would remain bound into the city's prayers for over 1,000 years, St Agnan's bones being revered until they were burned by Huguenots in 1562, at which point the city gave its affection to its even more famous saint, Joan of Arc, who had saved it from the English in another siege a century before.

In a sense, it didn't matter whether Attila actually assaulted

---

[1] Not exactly. The actual date he mentioned was *viii kal. julii*, i.e. 1 July minus eight days: 23 June.

the city or not. His scouts would have told him of the city's newly made defences and its coming reinforcements. There was no bypassing Aetius and the Goths; no chance of easy victory against this well-fortified city; no succour from Sangibanus, after all; nothing for it but a strategic withdrawal from the Loire's forests to open ground, where he could fight on his own terms.

A week and 160 kilometres later, the Huns approached Troyes once again, the wagons trailing along the dusty roads, the foot soldiers forming a screen over the open countryside, the mounted archers ranging all around, and Aetius' army hungry on the flanks, awaiting its moment.

There had to be a showdown, and the place was perhaps dictated by an encounter between two bands of outriders, pro-Roman Franks and pro-Hun Gepids leading the way in the retreat. They met and skirmished, possibly near the village of Châtres, which takes its name from the Latin *castra*, a camp. Châtres is on the Catalaunian Plains, the main town of which was Châlons – Duro-Catalaunum in Latin ('The Enduring Place of the Catalauni') – and the coming battle is often referred to by later historians as the Battle of Châlons. In fact, Châlons is 50 kilometres away to the north; Latin sources closer to the time refer to it as the Battle of Tricassis (Troyes), 25 kilometres to the south, which, they say, was fought near a place called something like Mauriacum (spellings vary), today's Méry-sur-Seine, just 3 kilometres from Châtres.

Now it was time for a decision. Attila was on the defensive, and his army tiring. Which was better: to risk all in conflict, or continue the retreat to fight another day? But there might not be another day. An army retreating through hostile territory was like a sick herd, easy prey. Besides, to cut and run, even were it possible, was no way for a warrior to live, certainly no way for a leader to retain his authority. Was this perhaps the prophesied moment of national collapse, from which young Ernak would rise as the new leader? His shamans would know. Cattle were slaughtered, entrails examined, bones scraped, streaks of blood analysed – and disaster foretold. The shamans had some good news among the bad. An enemy commander would die. There was only one enemy commander who mattered in Attila's eyes: his old friend and new enemy, Aetius. So Aetius was doomed. That was good, for 'Attila deemed the death of Aetius a thing to be desired even at the cost of his own life, for Aetius stood in the way of his plans'. And how was Aetius to die if Attila avoided combat?

Attila had with him an immense throng of semi-reliable contingents from subordinate tribes, and his unwieldy, essential wagons full of supplies. But he also had the Hun weapon of choice, his mounted archers. If he could strike fast, as late as possible in the day, the onset of night could allow a chance to regroup and fight on the next day.

It was 21 June, or thereabouts, 1500 hours. The battle-ground was the open plain by Méry, which undulates away eastwards and northwards. The Huns would have to avoid being forced to the left, where they would be trapped by the triangle of waters where the Aube and Seine came together. They would fight as the Goths had at Adrianople, with a defensive laager of wagons acting as a supply base, and mounted archers launching their whirlwind assaults on the heavily armed opponents. The Huns put their backs to the river, and faced the pursuing Roman armies as they spread out over the plain. Attila placed himself at the centre, his main allies – Valamir with his Ostrogoths and Ardaric with his Gepids – to left and right, and a dozen tribal leaders ranging beyond waiting for his signal.

On the Roman side, Aetius and his troops took one wing,

Theodoric and his Visigoths the other, with the unreliable Sangibanus in the middle.

Across the gentle undulations of the plain, all of this would have been in full view of both sides, and each would have seen the strategy of the other. Attila would hope his archers would break through the Roman centre; Aetius would hope his two strong wings could sweep in behind the archers and cut them off from their supply wagons.

Just nearby the plain rose in one of its slight billows, offering an advantage, which perhaps Attila had not spotted soon enough. When he did, and ordered a troop of cavalry to seize it, Aetius was ready. Aetius, either by chance or by shrewd planning, was closer. The Visigoths, with cavalry commanded by Theodoric's eldest son Thorismund, reached the summit first, forcing the Huns into a hasty retreat from the lower slopes.

First round to Aetius. There was nothing for it but a frontal assault. Attila regrouped, and addressed his troops, in a brief speech (in Hunnish, of course) that Jordanes, a Goth, quotes in Latin as if verbatim. It's fair to conclude the king said something, and perhaps the words were indeed remembered and found their way into folklore; but Jordanes was writing a century later, when the Huns were long gone, so what Attila actually said is anyone's guess. If Attila recalls Henry V here, it is Shakespeare's version, not the real thing. Here's the gist:

> After you have conquered so many peoples, I would deem it foolish – nay, ignorant – of me as your king to goad you with words. What else are you used to but fighting? And what is sweeter for brave men than to seek vengeance personally? Despise this union of discordant races! Look at them as they gather in line with their shields locked, checked not even by wounds but by the dust of battle. On then to the fray! Let courage rise and fury explode! Now show your cunning,

Huns, your deeds of arms. Why should Heaven have made the Huns victorious over so many, if not to prepare them for the joy of this conflict? Who else revealed to our forefathers the way through the Maeotic marshes, who else made armed men yield to men as yet unarmed? I shall hurl the first spear. If any stand at rest while Attila fights, that man is dead.

The words cannot be genuine, of course. Jordanes was keen to capture something of the fight-to-the-death spirit that has infused warriors down the ages: the Sioux's battle cry 'Today is a good day to die!', Horatius in Macaulay's Victorian epic ('How can man die better than by facing fearful odds?'), and the ageing Anglo-Saxon who urged his fellows on against the Vikings at the Battle of Maldon in 991:

> Courage shall grow keener, clearer the will,
> The heart fiercer as our heart faileth.

And the battle itself? Jordanes rose to the occasion, with grand phrases that echo in the evocations of many battles in many languages. In translation, it even falls easily into free verse:

> Hand to hand they clashed, in battle fierce,
> Confused, prodigious, unrelenting,
> A fight unequalled in accounts of yore.
> Such deeds were done! Heroes who missed this marvel
> Could never hope to see its like again.

A few telling details with the smack of truth survived the passage of time, pickled by folklore. A stream ran through the plain, 'if we may believe our elders', that overflowed with blood, so that parched warriors slaked their thirst with the outpourings of their own wounds. Old Theodoric was thrown and vanished in the mêlée, trampled to death by his own Visigoths or (as some said) slain by the spear of Andag, an Ostrogoth.[2]

Dusk was falling, on the evening of what could have been the year's longest day. The whirlwind tactics of the Hun archers had not had enough impact on the Roman and Visigothic lines, which forced their way forward, breaking the Hun mounted formation, slashing their way into the rear lines protecting the wagons. Surrounded by his personal guard, Attila pulled back through the heaving lines to the circle of wagons that formed a wheeled fortress in the rear. Hard behind him, through the gap, came Thorismund, who got lost in the gloom and thought himself back at his own wagons, until a blow on the head knocked him off his horse. He would have died like his father, if one of his men had not hauled him to safety.

With the coming of night, the chaos stilled. Troops found comrades and settled into scattered camps. The night was fine: if it had rained, Jordanes would surely have mentioned the fact. But there were, I think, clouds, because it would otherwise have been a peculiarly dramatic sight. It would have been lit by a half-moon, as we know from the tables of lunar phases. Consult Herman Goldstine's *New and Full Moons 1001 BC to AD 1651*,[3] and you learn that the new moon had fallen on 15 June, a week before the battle. So imagine a balmy summer night, darkened by cloud, ghostly figures, the snorts of horses, the clank and creak of armour, the groans of the wounded. Men mounted and on foot wandered in search of comrades, unable to tell friend from foe unless they spoke. Aetius himself was lost among the Huns, unnoticed by them,

---

[2] . . . and thus a distant kin of his Visigothic victim. His claim was not believed by enough people to turn him from footnote into hero.
[3] American Philosophical Society, Philadelphia, 1973.

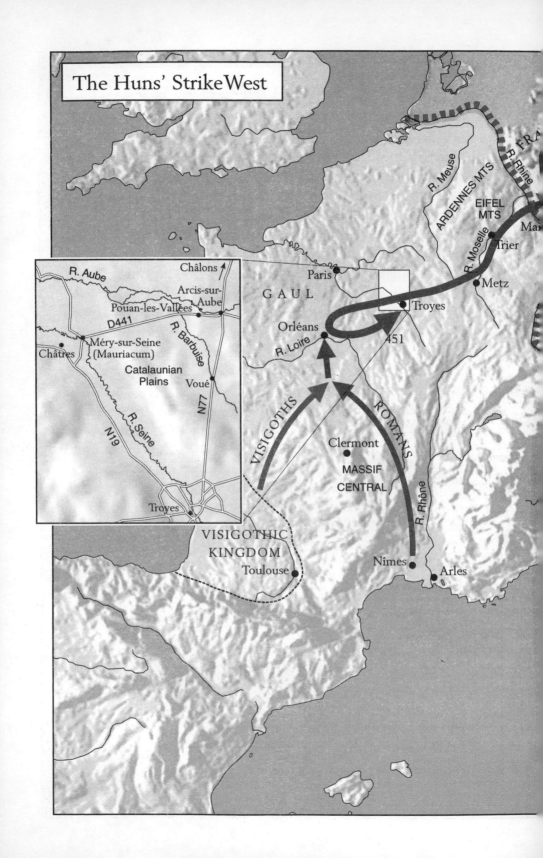

The Huns' Strike West

R. Aube
Châlons
Arcis-sur-Aube
Pouan-les-Vallées
D441
R. Barbuise
Méry-sur-Seine
(Mauriacum)
Châtres
Catalaunian
Plains
Voué
N77
R. Seine
N19
Troyes

GAUL
Paris
Orléans
R. Loire
Troyes
451
R. Meuse
ARDENNES MTS
EIFEL
MTS
R. Moselle
Trier
Metz
Ma
R. Rhine
FRA

VISIGOTHS
ROMANS
Clermont
MASSIF
CENTRAL
R. Rhône
Nîmes
Arles

VISIGOTHIC
KINGDOM
Toulouse

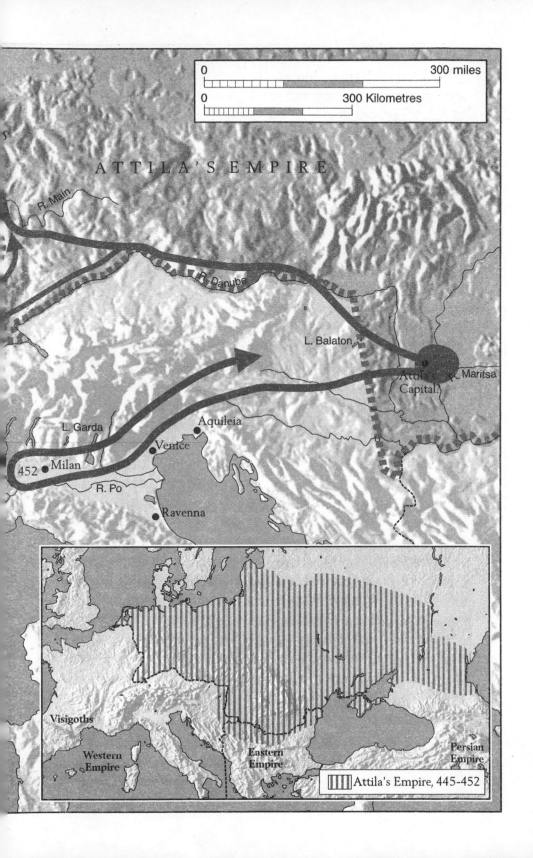

0
300 miles

0
300 Kilometres

ATTILA'S EMPIRE

R. Main

R. Danube

L. Balaton

Attila's
Capital?

R. Maritsa

L. Garda

Aquileia

Venice

452    Milan

R. Po

Ravenna

Visigoths

Western
Empire

Eastern
Empire

Persian
Empire

||||| Attila's Empire, 445-452

until his horse, stumbling over corpses, came to a Goth encampment and delivered him to safety behind their wall of shields, and perhaps to a couple of hours' sleep for the rest of the short night.

There is something else that Jordanes does not mention. The early-morning twilight should have witnessed a wonderful sight – Halley's Comet rising in the north-east, tail first, like a searchlight scanning the sky ahead. It was there all right, as astronomers have known since the orbit of Halley's Comet was accurately calculated in the mid-nineteenth century. Since then calculations have been refined.[4] The comet was noted by Chinese astronomers on 9 or 10 June, and became visible in Europe by 18 June. A vision like this would have imprinted itself on the minds of warriors as sharply as an arrowpoint, for nothing would more forcefully have marked the significance of the occasion. Many other sightings did. In their cuneiform records, Babylonian astrologers remarked that the comet's appearance in 164 BC and 87 BC coincided with the death of kings. Embroiderers stitched it into the Bayeux Tapestry to record its appearance when William the Conqueror invaded England in 1066. In the early fourteenth century, Giotto painted its 1301 return into his *Adoration of the Magi*. Surely, if it had been seen, men would have marvelled, and written, and sung.

They didn't. The only person to mention the comet was the Spanish bishop and chronicler Hydatius, and that was only in passing. Of the battle itself being marked by an event of astronomical significance – nothing.

It is dangerous to draw conclusions from the absence of evidence, but this absence, combined with the other absences of storm and moon, strongly suggest that the day after the

[4] For further details, see Gary Kronk, *Cometography*, vol. 1 (Cambridge, 1999).

battle dawned dry, drab and cloudy. If so, imagine the surviving Romans staring over their shields at a scene of dusty desolation – corpses everywhere, riderless horses grazing, the Huns sheltered in silence by their wagons, the course of the Aube marked by a line of trees across the treeless plains rolling away into grey twilight.

Stalemate – with the advantage to the Romans, for they were on home ground of a sort, could keep supplies coming, and could keep the Huns penned up until starvation drove them out. It would take time. Attila showed no sign of giving up, inspiring a Homeric image from Jordanes. 'He was like a lion pierced by hunting spears, who paces to and fro before the mouth of his den and dares not spring, but ceases not to terrify the neighbourhood by his roaring. Even so this warlike king at bay terrified his conquerors.' The Romans and Goths re-formed, closer, and began their siege, forcing the Huns to keep their heads down with a steady rain of arrows.

Attila saw a possible end. His shamans had predicted the death of a commander, who might turn out to be not Aetius, but Attila himself. He prepared for a hero's death by immolation, as if about to enter a Hunnish version of Valhalla, the abode of slain warriors. He ordered a funeral pyre of saddles – an indication, by the way, that the Huns had wooden saddles, Mongol-style, not leather ones – ready for an overwhelming Roman assault. They would never take him alive, never have the satisfaction of killing him or seeing him die of wounds.

Meanwhile, the Visigoths had been surprised not to find their king leading the besiegers, just when victory seemed certain. They looked for and found him, a corpse among a pile of corpses. As the siege continued, they raised the body on a bier and, led by Thorismund and his brother, carried him off for a battlefield burial, with ritual laments – dissonant cries, as Jordanes calls them. It seems they made their slow procession in full view of the Huns, to display their pride in their fallen chief. 'It was a death indeed, but the Huns are witness that it was a glorious one.'

Jordanes says that 165,000 died in the course of the two-day battle, and another 15,000 in the Frank–Gepid skirmish the night before: 180,000 dead. It is a ludicrous number, at a time when towns counted their populations in the low thousands. The countryside could not have supplied food enough to sustain such numbers. No-one can know how many actually did die, but if the losses had been one-tenth Jordanes' numbers they would still have been massive. From armies that may have numbered 25,000 each, perhaps one-third died: some 15,000 at a guess; and among them, as the shamans had predicted, a commander, though the two main protagonists, Aetius and Attila, had been spared to fight another day.

Trying to identify the site of the battle is, as Maenchen-Helfen snootily puts it, 'a favourite pastime of local historians and retired colonels', as if the matter were beneath the notice of serious academics. But this was a turning point in European history. It matters, if only because, were it to be found, archaeologists could, perhaps, find some evidence of what really happened.

In August 1842 a workman was quarrying sand some 400 metres east of the village of Pouan, 30 kilometres north of Troyes, when he found about a metre down a skeleton, lying on its back in a grave apparently dug so hastily that it was not even flat. The skeleton lay on its back in a gentle curve, as if in a deck-chair. Alongside were two rusty sword blades, some gold ornaments and a ring engraved with four enigmatic letters, HEVA. Jean-Baptiste Buttat might have kept his finds a secret, or disposed of them privately. Luckily, he sold the two sword blades to the Troyes museum, even though it could not afford Buttat's full asking price, and the decorations to a local jeweller, who in 1858 sold them to Napoleon III. The regional government then offered the swords to the emperor, so that the treasure could be all together. Napoleon III saw the wisdom of the offer, but then, in a fit of generosity, turned it on its head. 'National antiquities belong where they were discovered,' he wrote, and sent the jewels to join the swords, re-creating the original find in Troyes' museum. There, in the excavated Roman basement, the Treasure of Pouan has pride of place.

Actually, there's not much to it – the two swords; a torque, or neckring; a bracelet; two buckles and some decorative plaques; the ring. These few items were made to assert wealth and dignity. The settings and the sword handles are covered in gold leaf, the jewels are garnets. The larger sword, a double-edged blade almost a metre long, is of three pieces of steel turned, hammered and welded in the technique known as Damascene. Yet it is light enough to be used in one hand. Its pommel is of a unique shape, an oval piece of wood inlaid with garnets. The shorter sword is a single-edged weapon known as a scramasax.

In 1860 a local antiquarian, Achille Peigné-Delacourt, published his conclusions about the treasure. 'A chance discovery may have unexpected consequences,' he begins, 'and may furnish the means to resolve long disputed historical questions.' This is a case in point. Perhaps – Peigné-Delacourt quotes an eminent historian, a certain Monsieur Camut-Chardon – these were the remains of a warrior who, overtaken by some disaster, had fallen into the river, the course of which had subsequently changed? No, replies Peigné-Delacourt, that cannot be, because the soil in which the items were found long pre-dates the appearance of man on earth. M. Camut-Chardon had reported another bolder hypothesis, only to reject it. Peigné-Delacourt picks it up and runs with it: 'I am going to declare that I am one of the bold who attribute the skeleton and ornaments found at Pouan to Theodoric, king of the Visigoths, who was killed fighting Attila in 451.

'This conclusion impels us to fix the battle-ground to the spot where these remains were recovered.'

The geography of the place seemed to fit well with Jordanes' account. Roman roads bypassed and converged on Troyes. One road from Orléans, now vanished, led past Troyes 25 kilometres to the north-west, through Châtres (originally *castra*, the camp). It was here that the Franks and Gepids could have skirmished. A road ran north from Troyes, straight as an arrow, and so it remains today, the N77, still running as the Romans built it over a plain as big as an ocean. It's all agribusiness now, a patchwork of pastel browns and greens and yellows, but 1,500 years ago its chalky grasslands would have been terrific galloping country. A ten-minute drive brings you to Voué, which in Roman times was Vadum. It is on a stream, the Barbuise, with low, firm banks, no obstacle at all to a galloping horse, just a few centimetres deep, which runs off to your left to Pouan, with the Aube just beyond. The ground rises gently to the east of Pouan. Here, suggests Peigné-Delacourt, was where the Romans gathered, blocking the Huns from crossing the river.

I had no great hopes that Pouan would offer any revelations. On the map, it looks to be just one among the villages loosely scattered across the Catalaunian Plains north of Troyes. I went there early one spring morning, expecting drabness and insignificance, and was charmed. The Barbuise, flowing in over flat chalky fields and past trees speckled with balls of mistletoe, trickles right through the village, past a half-timbered mill and a solid grey church and houses with exposed beams. There is a public tennis court. Pouan is a comfortable dormitory for commuters to Troyes – or so I imagined, because there was no-one around to ask. It was time for breakfast. There seemed to be no square, no central shopping area, no focus to the village's bourgeois rambling. Ah, a bakery. It had tables, and there was a woman setting out chairs, and it advertised coffee. No, I was too early. All I could hope for was information. I hoped I did not derange her, but could she tell me – did people round these parts know about Attila? She looked politely puzzled. '*Attila le Hun*,' I explained. 'The great battle, near here, sixteen hundred years ago. Romans and Huns. And the treasure . . . ?'

'*Pardon, m'sieur, je ne sais rien.* Have you tried the *mairie*?'

Well, I couldn't wait for the town hall to open. That was that. I turned the car, paused to consider a lane leading along the Barbuise, backed up beside a half-timbered house to check my map, and saw a woman hurrying towards me.

'You want to know about Attila, *m'sieur*?' She was panting after her run from the bakery. My strange question had become a matter for instant gossip. 'My husband knows about Attila. Excuse me, my child, the bus, but this is our house, go and ask him.'

There was an entrance into a courtyard, the house on one side, a barn on the other – guarded, to my surprise, by a lion made of white stone. From the barn's shadowy interior stepped a slim figure in jeans and a green sweater – 'Raynard Jenneret. *Sculpteur*', as a sign on the barn proclaimed. We explained ourselves to each other. Jenneret mostly works metal into angular creations that look like toys, or science-fiction machines, or tribal totems, but the lion suggested more traditional interests. He likes history. Attila and Aetius were old acquaintances of his. He knew all about the treasure, and had himself dug around the site in the hopes of finding more. So he could take me there? He was delighted. We drove down a track, bumping past a field of winter wheat to our right which rose like a soft billow in this ocean-plain to a cross, an odd thing to mark the middle of a field. To our left, the slope levelled into an ancient flood plain, across which the Aube wound out of sight a kilometre away. Now I saw what gave Pouan its advantage. As well as having its own charming little river, it stood a crucial metre or two clear of the Aube's flood plain. Once, this sloping wheatfield had been a gentle riverbank, which accounted for its economic significance as a source of sand. Builders had always used it, Jenneret said; still do, as some yellow mounds further along the slope revealed. That also explained the cross – 20 years before, a *sablier* had been quarrying when the sand fell in and suffocated him. Right there, in waste ground coarse with grass clumps and straggly dogwood, was where the treasure had been found. Oh, no doubt that it was Theodoric's burial, and this was where Attila fought Aetius. Everyone knew that.

This, I could well believe, was the setting for a scene imagined by Peigné-Delacourt, a conspiracy theory of ambition, intrigue and murder. In his book, he wonders if Thorismund, eager to claim the throne over his brothers, might have had an interest in finding a corpse, any corpse, that could be identified, rightly or wrongly, as his father's, and buried quickly, with a show of grief and instant acclamation for Thorismund as king. And then, given the uncertainty of the battle's outcome and the knowledge of where the tomb was, would it be likely that those who conducted the burial would be allowed to live? It all sounds a bit over the top, given that the burial would have been so quick, almost in the heat of battle, with no burial mound to mark the spot. But it is not entirely the fruit of his imagination, because there have been other finds in the area of Pouan and its neighbour Villette, a couple of kilometres to the east – two small bronze vases, a cup, a gilded bronze ewer, three blades, horse-trappings: all sustaining the idea – for Jenneret, the certainty – that this was the battle-ground, and this the site of Theodoric's burial.

French scholars tend to agree. Others, on the other hand, point out similarities with the artefacts of other cultures in Russia or across the Danube, undermining any Visigothic links. Estimated dates range from the third to the seventh century. It is all infuriatingly vague, though when they try for greater accuracy archaeologists are drawn back to Peigné-Delacourt's suggestion, to the mid-fifth century, to a rich Goth, and, in the end, to Theodoric.

Of course, the letters HEVA engraved on the ring would settle it, if only anyone had a clue what they meant. The ring and the script are Roman. Scholars agree that it must be sheer coincidence that Heva is a common Latin spelling for Eve, unless we adopt the romantic idea that this noble had the ring engraved in honour of some Roman mistress. Scholars of Gothic have thrown up several possibilities, circling around *heiv*, 'house' or 'family', as in *heiva-franja*, 'head of a household', possibly connected to the Old High German, *hefjan*, to raise or educate. Old Saxon has *hiwa*, a husband. Or it means 'Strike!', the imperative of *heven*, to strike. There is no sense to be found in any Gothic or Germanic solution. Latin, though, might work. The inscription is, after all, in fine Latin lettering, which justifies a little speculation. Suppose this was a royal ring, and engraved accordingly: what might Theodoric have wished it to record? Remember that he aspired to things Roman. He was a friend of one of Gaul's most eminent scholars and politicians, Avitus. He knew that Rome proclaimed its authority with four letters: SPQR, *senatus populusque romanus*, the Roman Senate and People. I like to think that HEVA is a four-letter phrase, recalled by initials. But this is not a ring of royal authority, because it was not taken from him in death. It's personal, as personal as his sword. Perhaps he wished to state his own claim not in terms of government, but of personal achievement. HIC EST ('This is') fits; but 'This is' who, or what? We have several possible initial As: Aetius, Avitus, Aquitania. Theodoric had conquered Aquitaine. How about HIC EST VICTOR AQUITANIAE – 'This is the Victor of Aquitaine'? Or perhaps he liked to look forward to ever greater success – HIC EST VICTORIAE ANULUS, 'This is the Ring of Victory'? A totally different possibility was suggested to me by David Howlett, editor of the Oxford University Press's *Dictionary of Medieval Latin*. An inscription on an Anglo-Saxon lead pendant, found in the village of Weasenham All Saints in Norfolk, suggests that some in Europe shared with Jews a mystical interest in the names of God.[5] In that case, perhaps the initials stand for *Ha'shem Elohim V' Adonai* – The Name of God is 'Lord'. How odd if this were so. A Hebrew phrase recalled in neat Roman letters? But why, and whence? The questions fire the imagination – was this a war trophy, a gift or purchase from a Romano-Jewish community, a talisman with a meaning hidden from its owner, who looked on it as a Tolkeinian Ring of Power? Well, this is all wishful thinking. But it keeps open the hope that Raynard Jenneret, or some future *sablier*, will stumble on a bit of armour or a coin which will tell us once and for all, as clearly as if incised in a fine Roman typeface, that Theodoric was here, and so therefore HIC ERAT ATTILA.

Thorismund now wanted to finish the job. But Aetius, older and wiser, had a longer-term strategy in mind, which involved doing something quite astonishing.

He decided to let the Huns off the hook.

It takes some effort and some tortuous logic to see why. The Visigoths were Rome's traditional enemy, drawn into alliance only to face the great danger posed by Attila. If Attila

[5] The find is described by Elisabeth Okasha and Susan Youngs, 'A Late Saxon Inscribed Pendant from Norfolk', *Anglo-Saxon England*, vol. 32, Dec. 2004. The suggested interpretation is Howlett's.

were now overwhelmed and wiped off the face of the empire, that would leave the Visigoths in a position of some strength, and as much of a threat as the Huns had been – more, in fact, because Aetius knew the Huns of old and thought he could deal with them again. He knew the Visigoths as well, and did not trust them, whatever Avitus claimed about their ambitions to be considered civilized. Aetius was getting on. He was set in his ways, and was certain the Visigoths would remain a threat; as always in the past, he would need the help of the Huns to restrain them. Better an uncertain balance of power now than the risk of total collapse later. Attila had asked only for half the empire; the Visigoths would want the lot.

Of course, he couldn't tell Thorismund all that. Instead, he reminded the Visigoth prince of his brothers at home. Once they knew of their father's death, who knew what disputes over the succession might break out, if Thorismund, the eldest, were not around to claim the throne? Better for him to swallow his anger, break off the engagement and head for home to secure the succession. He was not to worry – the Romans would handle the Huns from now on. He made a similar argument to his Frankish allies. The surviving Huns would be on their way soon, cutting through or round the Ardennes, which would put them in a good position to extend their control over the area, unless the Franks were strong enough to put them off. Better for the Franks as well to head home.

Both agreed. And so, to the astonishment of the Huns, the rain of arrows ceased, the Visigoths filed away south-west on the 350-kilometre journey back to Toulouse, the Franks left for Belgium, and silence fell. Attila's troops, in their laager of wagons, wondered what it meant. They knew about retreats like this, for their archers had used similar tactics many times in the last century. It had to be a trick. They sat tight.

'But when a long silence followed the absence of the foe,

the spirit of the mighty king was aroused at the thought of victory, and his mind turned to the old oracles of his destiny.' A commander had died; he, Attila, was therefore destined to live. But there was no point in fighting on. Granted safe passage, the Hun wagons began to roll away, along the roads past Troyes to the Moselle, the Rhine and distant Hungary.

It is just possible that Lupus had something to do with Attila's escape. All this while, he had been hostage and guide, whether forced or voluntary. Perhaps, working for his own survival and that of his town, he had advised on the battle site. Now, having survived, he would advise how best to retreat, and get the battered Huns away from Troyes as fast as possible. If so, it worked; though not to Lupus' advantage, if there is any truth in his life-story. After seeing Attila safely back to the Rhine, he was allowed to return, as promised – to a less than rapturous reception.

> He received from his people only rejection for all the benefits he had brought them; for instead of being welcomed by the citizens, as he deserved for having delivered them from the loss not only of their livelihood but even their lives, seeing as how he had led Attila to the Rhine, he received defiance and discontentment as if he had been at one with him, on account of which the saint withdrew to Mt Lassoir, near Châtillon-sur-Seine.

Then, penitence done, he returned to Troyes to live for another 25 years, dying forgiven, famous and much honoured, and in due course canonized as St Loup, memorialized in the names of dozens of towns, peaks and churches all across France.

Gaul was saved.

And Attila lived to fight another day.

# 9

# A CITY TOO FAR

THE BATTLE OF THE CATALAUNIAN PLAINS IS OFTEN SEEN AS ONE of the great decisive battles in world history, the battle that saved western Europe from Attila. It was not that simple. This was not a Stalingrad, a turning point that stopped a barbaric invader in his tracks; more of a Hunnish Dunkirk, at which a great army escaped to fight on. Orléans had been the turning point, as Attila had seen when he avoided action and turned around; but it led to no definitive conclusion. Thereafter, for a couple of weeks, he was working to keep his army intact. The Catalaunian Plains was a rearguard action, forced upon Attila when he was already in retreat.

What if he had been victorious? After losing the initiative at Orléans, he would have had at best a bridgehead in Gaul. The open fields of Champagne would have offered valuable pasture and suitable territory on which his mounted archers could operate. But that would have been of use only if he managed to hold Metz, Trier and the Moselle corridor to the Rhine. That was his supply line, the artery that would feed him in some later advance that would seize all Gaul, the half of the empire he had so speciously claimed as Honoria's dowry. Now all that was lost, at least for the present. He had escaped by the skin of his teeth, and by pure chance – there was no way he could have known that Aetius would decide to let him go for political reasons to do with the death of Theodoric.

No-one in these confused times accorded the battle the importance it later acquired. In that very year, in Marseille, a chronicler was at work recording what he learned of these events. This unnamed sage, known only as the Chronicler of 452, was a devout Christian, his aim being to continue the history written by Jerome, which ended in the late fourth century. Yet when he came to the events of the last chapter, all he wrote was: 'Attila invaded Gaul and demanded a wife as if she were his by right. There he both inflicted and received a serious defeat, and withdrew to his own country.' Scholars find it interesting that he already knew of the Honoria scandal, and apparently did not doubt it. They are also interested by what he did *not* say. Since this was not narrative history, more a chronological list, we have to guess what he approved and didn't. He finished writing his account in 452, when Aetius was still one of the most powerful men in the empire (and might well be returning to Arles, a day's ride from Marseille, any time), but he does not say that this was a decisive victory for the great Aetius, because at the time of writing Aetius did not look like much of a saviour. 'At this time, the condition of the state appeared to be intensely miserable, since not even one province was without a barbarian inhabitant, and the unspeakable Arian heresy, which had allied itself with the barbarian nations and permeated the whole world, laid claim to the name of Catholic.' On top of that, Attila was still alive and kicking, which was very bad news, because he was, at that very moment, mounting yet another and possibly far more serious invasion. In brief, the world was going to the dogs and *it was all Aetius' fault*.

By autumn 451 Attila was back in his Hungarian headquarters, with its wooden palace, its stockaded houses, Onegesius' bath-house, and its encircling tents and wagons. Would he then have been happy to sit there, enjoying the loot brought back from the campaign in Gaul? A different character might have been. He might have learned his lesson, settled down to consolidate an empire that, if nurtured, would have created a lasting counterpart to Rome and Constantinople, trading with both. But Attila was no Genghis, willing to plan for stability and impose his vision on his minions and vassals. He was trapped by his circumstances. There would not have been much left in the way of silks, wine, slaves and gold after several weeks of enforced and ignominious retreat. His multi-tribal chieftains would have been restless.

No-one recorded what he did that winter. But we can infer that it was not good. In the summer of 451 the Emperor Marcian had called his 520 bishops to meet at Nicaea in the autumn, to sort out the vexed matter of Christ's nature, saying that he himself hoped to be there 'unless some urgent affairs of state should detain him in the field' – which in fact they did, the field in question being Thrace. Something had drawn him to the Danube frontier. Something forced the venue of the Fourth Ecumenical Council to be changed from Nicaea to Chalcedon, safe the other side of the Hellespont from Constantinople. And something prevented bishops from the Danube border area going to Chalcedon. If that something was Attila, back from failure in Gaul, it would not have been enough to keep the funds flowing, for these were the same regions the Huns had pillaged time and again. They were milked dry.

By now Attila knew that his main enemy, Rome, had an

unreliable ally in the Visigoths. The two would unite only in defence of Gaul. If he could ensure that his enemy was Rome, and only Rome, surely victory would follow, as it would have done at Orléans had it not been for Avitus, Theodoric and the Visigoths. Like all dictators, he must have known that his precarious confederation could be held together only with ever grander visions, and the promise of ever greater victories. What greater prospect than Rome itself – vulnerable, as everyone knew, because it had already been taken by barbarians, namely the Visigoths themselves, 40 years before?

But there were other enticing prospects along the way, in particular the town that guarded the main high road into Italy from Hun-occupied Pannonia. First in line was a minor prize, the Slovenian town of Ljubljana (Emona in Roman times), which, once taken, opened the road to the small but significant Isonzo river, Italy's traditional frontier (and for that reason the site of no fewer than twelve battles in the First World War). It was what lay at Isonzo's southern end that interested the Huns.

The fortress-town of Aquileia had a proud history of defending the homeland's north-eastern corner. Almost two centuries before, its women had joined in to fight off a rebel, Maximin, by donating their hair to make ropes for the town's defensive machinery. A temple had been built to 'Venus the Bald' in their honour. One of the richest, strongest and most populous of cities on the Adriatic coast, it had been built as a gateway to the east, a nodal point linking the land routes from Rome to the south and the Alpine pass to the north with the sea routes from the Adriatic.

So it was much more than a military base. Its thriving commercial life owed much to the presence of a large community of Jews, 'Orientali' in Latin sources, who may have been the original settlers. In any event, they introduced silk-weaving, dyeing and in particular glass-making, which had been practised in the Middle East for 2,000 years. It was they, therefore, who inspired the creation of a 5-kilometre canal leading across the Isonzo's swampy mouth from the sea. The result has been analysed in a paper by Samuel Kurinsky,[1] a Jewish American businessman, philanthropist and scholar with a specialist interest in the history of glass-making. 'The Jewish community', he writes, 'may have been one of the largest and most economically influential of the Diaspora, exceeded only by those of Rome and Alexandria.' Naturally, given the town's large Roman majority and the growth of Christianity, the Jews suffered repression, principally under a late-fourth-century bishop, Chromazio. It was he, it seems, who sanctioned the burning of the synagogue in 388, excused by St Ambrose, in standard antisemitic style, as 'an act of providence'. Over time, Christian buildings replaced the Jewish ones, some of which were unearthed by archaeologists from the 1940s onwards, often being described as 'paleo-Christian' or 'pagan' despite their Jewish iconography. Among the finds are several lavish mosaic floors, one right under the bell-tower of a later Christian basilica, another huge one – over 800 square metres, making it one of the largest of its time – under the basilica itself. Alongside is a marble-lined, octagonal *mikvah* (ritual bath), fed by a spring, with the six steps required by Jewish law.

The glass-makers of Aquileia are worth a small diversion, under Kurinsky's guidance. The art was still a mystery to Europeans when the Jews arrived among the bays of the Adriatic coast, so their products were in demand over a wide area, to the resentment of some Christians. St Jerome, briefly a resident of Aquileia, complained that glass-making had

---

[1] Samuel Kurinsky, 'The Jews of Aquileia: A Judaic Community Lost to History', Hebrew History Federation
(www.hebrewhistory.org/factpapers/aquileia28.html).

become one of the trades 'by which the Semites had captured the Roman world'. Recent finds have astonished experts, because they are some of the earliest produced in Europe. Surprise on surprise – a few preserve the names of their proud makers, some of whom were slaves, at least one being a woman. Two glass vessels emerged in Linz, the Danubian town on the Roman trade route over the Dolomites. The mouldings include the phrase *Sentia Secunda facit Aquileiae vitra*: 'Sentia No. 2 makes Aquileian glass'.

The stout walls of this rich and important city had often been besieged, but never taken – except once, when Alaric led the Visigoths towards Rome in 401. If Alaric could do it, so could Attila. And, as Attila's spies would have told him, Aetius, certain that he had shut the Huns back in their cage, had not ordered the town to prepare for action.

Action came in late June 452. We can infer this thanks to the pope and some birds. Pope Leo I, who wrote letters in May and June, made no mention of an invasion of Italy, so it is unlikely to have begun earlier; and Attila's siege could not have started much later, according to an unlikely source: the storks which nested on Aquileia's roofs.

The storks come into the story because this was no quick siege. Aquileia's citizens did not need orders from Aetius: they knew how to withstand an assault, having good access down-river to the open sea. After nearly two months of waiting, with Aquileia living up to its reputation, Attila must have begun to hear murmurs from his generals. How long was this going on? Vineyards and orchards and grain-rich fields would sustain the troops through the late summer, but where was the loot? Priscus, quoted by Jordanes, takes up the story:

> The army was already muttering and wishing to leave when
> Attila, as he was walking round the walls deliberating whether

he should break camp or remain longer, noticed some white birds, namely storks, which make their nests on rooftops, taking their young away from the city and, contrary to their custom, conveying them out into the country. Since he was an extremely shrewd inquirer, he had a presentiment and said to his men: 'Look at the birds, which foresee what is to come, leaving the doomed city, deserting endangered strongholds which are about to fall. Do not think this is without meaning; it is certain; they know what is going to happen; fear of the future changes their habits.'

Gibbon, always good for a quote, described the scene thus:

[Attila] observed a stork preparing to leave her nest in one of the towers, and to fly with her infant family towards the country. He seized, with the ready penetration of a statesman, this trifling incident which chance had offered to superstition; and exclaimed, in a loud and cheerful tone, that such a domestic bird, so constantly attached to human society, would never have abandoned her ancient seats unless those towers had been devoted to impending ruin and solitude.

Could there be any truth in this charming tale? Possibly, because the Huns would have sought and respected auguries, both natural and man-made (like the omens read into blood-marks before the battle on the Catalaunian Plains). For Romans and barbarians alike, birds were portentous creatures, especially ravens, owls and storks, as magpies are to us: 'One for sorrow, two for joy.' Now, storks are indeed creatures of habit, about which Attila would have been rather better informed than Gibbon; as, thanks to two and a half centuries of ornithology, are we. Storks in general – unlike Gibbon's lone mother in her Disneyesque devotion – do not have ancient seats. They migrate, heading south for winter.

The white stork, *Ciconia ciconia*, leaves its European summer nests between mid-August and early September, heading for Africa overland. Juveniles leave first, trailed by their parents. Western populations take one flight path, easterners another, both circling the Mediterranean, the two groups being divided with remarkable precision along latitude 11°E, a mere 200 kilometres west of Aquileia. Westerners fly over Spain, easterners, including those of Aquileia, over Turkey and the Dead Sea to the Nile valley and points south. Attila, coming from Hungary, would have been familiar with the habits of eastern white storks; and so would his shamans, who, as we know from the Catalaunian Plains, accompanied his entourage. A smart shaman might have been looking out for a reliable sign to buttress whatever Attila had in mind. It seems unlikely that the storks knew much about the ins and outs of siege warfare; but it is just possible, I suppose, that smoke and the collapse of their nesting-places drove them out early, which places this moment during the siege of Aquileia, with stork-like precision, a few days before mid-August. It is not too far-fetched to imagine a shaman, knowing Attila's hopes, coming up with an excuse to continue the siege. How better to inspire trust than by claiming inevitable victory? What better backing than the forces of nature, proclaiming the fall of the city as surely as rats proclaim the imminent sinking of a ship?

Whoever said what to whom, it did the trick. Hun spirits revived, inspiring a return to the tactics developed in the taking of Naissus in 447, only five years previously. 'Why say more?' comments Jordanes. 'He inflamed the hearts of the soldiers to renew the assault on Aquileia.' A siege train took shape – slings to throw boulders, 'scorpions' (heavy cross-bows firing metre-long arrows), battering-rams swinging beneath shells of shields – which in a remarkably short time broke through Aquileia's walls, with awful consequences for the city, 'which they despoiled, smashed asunder and devastated so savagely that they left hardly a trace of it to be seen' – an exaggeration to which we shall return later.

What, meanwhile, of Aetius and the Romans during Attila's advance? Not much, according to our main source, Prosper, a chronicler and theologian from Aquitaine who became one of Rome's leading religious and literary figures, possibly working as an official at the court of Pope Leo I. He was a man of abrupt and succinct opinions. To him, Aetius was idle and a coward. He made no provisions. He did not look to the Alpine defences. He would have scurried for safety with the emperor, if shame had not braced him. There is no need to take this as gospel, though. Prosper had an agenda, which was to downgrade Aetius in order that his master the pope should take the spotlight, centre stage, hand in hand with God, in the coming events. The fact was that the empire never did defend the Alpine pass, because it was too wide an entrance for easy defence. Italy was invaded six times in the fifth century, and not once were the invaders opposed until they got to the valley of the Isonzo and Aquileia.

What actually happened after the fall of Aquileia is vague. Attila apparently raided half a dozen smaller towns – Concordia and Altinum among them – in the surrounding area, but did not head for the seat of imperial government in Ravenna. Perhaps he judged it too tough a target, or perhaps he knew that the emperor was in Rome; in any event, he kept instead to the north, following the edge of the Po valley. Rather than suffer the fate of Aquileia, cities simply opened their gates: Padua, Vicenza, Verona, Brescia, Bergamo and, finally, Milan. There the Huns burned and looted so much that the citizens had time to flee. According to one account, Attila took up residence in the imperial palace, where he saw a painting of Scythians prostrate before the two Roman emperors of East and West. He liked the idea, hated the subject matter, and ordered a local artist to paint a similar scene with himself on a throne and the two emperors pouring out gold at his feet.

Now the advance faltered. A conqueror would have headed south across the Apennines to Rome, sweeping all before him. Priscus says that Attila, following closely in Alaric's footsteps and with the same intentions, was warned by his shamans that he might suffer the same fate should he take Rome, namely death immediately after victory. Certainly death was in the air, in the form of heat, food shortages and disease. High summer was over, but September in the north Italian plains is oppressive; and the area was home to malaria-carrying mosquitoes. Others experienced a similar fate later. In 540 the Franks were 'attacked by diarrhoea and dysentery, which they were quite unable to shake off because of the lack of proper food. Indeed they say that one third of the Frankish army perished in this way.' Another Frankish army failed for the same reasons in 553.

Possibly an army headed by Aetius also had an effect, though there is only one brief and confusing sentence by the Spanish chronicler Hydatius, writing in about 470, to support the idea. Instead of an all-out military response, though, Rome opted for a diplomatic one, written up by Prosper, who was keen to record the role played by his master, Pope Leo I.

Leo was a genuinely significant figure, made more so by Prosper in what would today be regarded as appallingly right-wing terms. Leo's election, delayed by his absence in 440, was awaited with 'marvellous peace and patience'. He rooted out heresy with admirable zeal, burning books as a divinely inspired holy man should. He showed himself to be a strong pope just at the moment when the greatest threat to the church, Attila, murdered his brother Bleda and assumed absolute power beyond the Danube. Worldly leaders like Aetius were examples of pride, ambition, injustice, impiety and imprudence, from all of which Leo, by comparison, was free. He even opposed the eastern emperor Theodosius II, who at the Second Council of Ephesus in 449 allowed that Christ did not share in the human nature of his mother, but was only apparently human. When Theodosius died in 450, Marcian, brought in to rule by Theodosius' sister, came as the saviour of orthodoxy, Leo's orthodoxy; hence the Fourth Council in Chalcedon in 451. Women, to Prosper, were irrelevant. Marcian's wife, Pulcheria, to whom he owed the crown? Galla Placidia, mother of the Emperor Valentinian and the erratic Honoria, one of the most powerful women of her age? Not a mention. And of course, now that Attila was threatening the very heart of the empire, Aetius was worse than useless and everything was down to Leo.

Where Aetius relied on his own judgement, Leo relied on God. His mission to Attila was from the Senate and Valentinian III. 'Nothing better was found than to send an embassy to the terrible king and ask for peace.' He took with him two colleagues: Trygetius, former prefect and experienced negotiator with Gaiseric the Vandal in Africa, and the ex-consul Avienus, now one of the two most powerful senators in Rome. Possibly, Leo's main role was to negotiate the ransom of captives. This, then, was a mission of top envoys. Yet in Prosper, Leo and God are Rome's real saviours. As a result, later accounts wrote out the other two entirely, or transformed them into something very different.

Attila was apparently quite ready to meet the three envoys, perhaps seeing in them a mirror-image of his own elite *logades*, headed by Rome's most senior shaman. As Prosper puts it, 'The king received the whole delegation courteously, and he was so flattered by the presence of the highest priest that he ordered his men to stop the hostilities and, promising peace, returned beyond the Danube.'

Just like that. Magic. Because Leo was in Prosper's eyes a

living embodiment of Christ working through man. 'The elect receive grace,' he said in another context, 'not to allow them to be idle or to free them from the Enemy's attacks, but to enable them to work well and to conquer the Enemy.'

What really happened at the meeting no-one knows. Perhaps, as some sources say, it occurred on the shore of Lake Garda, 'at the well-travelled ford of the River Mincius' (now the Mincio, which flows out of Lake Garda at Peschiera), though what Attila would have been doing travelling east prior to an invasion of Rome, I can't imagine; he should have been heading south. Certainly, there would have been some hard bargaining. Quite likely, Attila would have threatened Italy with a terrible fate, as Jordanes says, 'unless they sent him Honoria, with her due share of the royal wealth'. That would open the way for a counter-offer: no Honoria, who was now either safely married off or 'bound to chastity' (perhaps the same thing, given Honoria's raging rejection of her husband); but on the question of the royal wealth a deal could be done. Prisoners would have been released, cash paid, honour satisfied.

In the absence of any hard information, legends soon arose claiming a miracle. The version in the thirteenth-century Hungarian codex (*Gesta Hungarorum*), in which Attila is terrified into compliance by a vision of an angry, armed angel, is one among several examined in chapter 12 below. Certainly Attila was not a man to take much notice of popes. He had problems enough to stop his advance. Disease, famine, a sudden appreciation of what he was really up against: Attila must have now seen how much more he had bitten off than he could chew. In addition, he was now dangerously exposed, deep in Italy, with Rome's other half, Constantinople, closer to Hungary than he was himself.

He headed back across the Isonzo, and home to Hungary.

In the autumn of 452, as the ice re-formed over the

Danube, he sent off yet more ambassadors to Marcian threatening devastation 'because that which had been promised by Theodosius was in no wise performed, and saying that he would show himself more cruel to his foes than ever'.

But this was bluster. He had lost thousands on the Catalaunian Plains, thousands more to disease in Italy. He had not returned home in time to catch the full benefit of the summer grass. Even if the Italian campaign had paid for itself with Leo's ransom money, nothing was coming from Marcian, and now, once again, he had an exhausted army and expectant commanders to keep happy. There were no more embassies. That winter, an ominous silence descended on the Danubian frontier, leaving Marcian 'disquieted' at what Attila might be planning. Come the spring, something would have to be done.

Back in Italy, a dozen towns had suffered the Hun assault, or later claimed they had. Nothing, apparently, was as bad as the fate of Aquileia. Jordanes' words echo down the centuries, rewritten by Gibbon: 'The succeeding generation could scarcely discover the ruins of Aquileia.' Other writers, without looking too closely, claimed that the city suffered total and everlasting destruction.

Well, not exactly. It is possible to make a guess at the truth, because something is known of Aquileia post-Attila.

Six years later the town, supposedly so flattened that its ruins were hardly visible, was reviving well. It had a good flock of Christians, and a bishop. His name was Nicetas, and in March 458 he wrote to Leo, whose reply survives in a collection of his letters. Nicetas was coping with a crisis caused not simply by the destruction but by the business of recovery. It had all been terrible: families had been broken up, the men taken prisoner, the women forsaken; but now, with

God's help, things had improved. At least some of the men had returned. So Attila had indeed released prisoners, presumably because Pope Leo had ransomed them. How many did not survive to be ransomed? What happened to those who survived, but were not ransomed? Enslaved, for sure, and by now either dead or working for some Hun chief in Hungary.

Nicetas had two problems. The first was this: some of the women had remarried, thinking their husbands dead. What was the status of their marriages now? It was a terrible question to answer, for a ruling either way would throw hundreds of families into turmoil. Leo, however, was not a pope much given to doubt: he replied that second marriages should be annulled, and the first husbands reinstated. No mention, by the way, of the *women* taken by the Huns; they were lost for ever, and posed no theological problem.

The second matter concerned the status of the returnees as Christians. Some had, while prisoners, apparently been forced to adopt the ways of heresy, taking heretical communion, or (if they were children) being baptized by heretics. To describe Huns as heretics sounds odd indeed. In fact, the problem is evidence that Attila's army was still a very mixed bag, and included Goths, who had been converted to Arianism a century before. Nicetas might not know a Goth from a Hun, but heresy was a red rag to a papal bull. Leo ruled that enforced conversion was no conversion: they would be welcomed back, forgiven and reinstated.

Eventually, the domestic dramas played themselves out, and the reviving town was soon rich enough for its Christian community to build its basilica over the ruins of the synagogue. The Jews, it seems, had already left. True, the place went downhill. A century later, another barbarian attack, by Lombards this time, underscored its decline, and many of its inhabitants chose to drift west to a new settlement in the unpromising but safer lagoons and islands of the Laguna Veneta.

This connection became for many a simple statement that Aquileia's surviving inhabitants fled from the Huns to found Venice, which was supposedly a secure haven because the Huns dared not ride their horses into the surrounding mud. Perhaps the Jews of Aquileia had led the way, but for the Christian majority it was all much more stretched out than that. Not until 569, after another barbarian invasion, did Aquileia's bishop, Paulus, take his relics and regalia to the port of Grado, 10 kilometres south of Aquileia, and about as far out into the Adriatic as you can get without drowning. From there, after another century of rivalry, authority finally jumped to Venice. It was not until the ninth century that Venice proper began to turn channels into canals and link islands with bridges, and create something new and grand that would inspire later writers to turn the inconvenient, extended mess of historical fact into short, sharp folk tales.

Venice still retains a link with its Aquileian roots and traditions, to the benefit of its tourist industry. On the nearby islands of Murano and Burano, they still make glass, thanks in part to the slave Sentia and her co-workers in Aquileia before Attila turned their world upside down.

# 10

# A SUDDEN DEATH,
# A SECRET GRAVE

SELDOM HAS A GIRL BECOME SO FAMOUS FOR DOING NOTHING. IN Greek and Latin, she was Ildico, which historians equate with the German name Hildegunde. She could have been a Germanic princess, sent by some distant vassal to secure Attila's blessing. Attila already had numerous wives, not so much because he was a man of huge sexual energy, but because the presentation of high-born women was a form of tribute, and their seizure a way of asserting dominance over distant and unreliable vassals. Jordanes, quoting a lost passage of Priscus, says that Ildico was a very beautiful girl. No-one else mentions her. Anyway, she was Attila's latest wife, picked up or delivered in the spring of 453.

What happened on the night of Attila's wedding to Ildico was told by Priscus, who had been with Attila himself four years before and would have taken a passionate interest in these events. For the past three years he had been with his old chief Maximinus up the Nile, sorting out another sub-chapter in the long-running dispute about the balance of divinity and humanity in Christ. This fuss had been re-ignited in 448, when an elderly priest named Eutyches claimed that Christ was of a single nature, all divine, not human at all. Disputes had been vicious, with the authority of Rome and Constantinople again in dispute. The Fourth Ecumenical Council in Chalcedon in 451 tried to draw a line under the argument, stating that Christ was one *person* with two *natures*, allowing him by a sleight of baffling terminology to be both God and man. But the council also in effect proclaimed equality with Rome for Constantinople, which would henceforth have authority over the Balkans and all points east. Rome was furious, and so were the monophysites of Egypt – those who stuck to the idea that Christ had just one nature. Priscus and Maximinus were negotiating peace with two wayward Egyptian groups when Maximinus died. In early 453, then, Priscus had just returned to Constantinople, to find the place still in a chaos of religious dispute. He may even have advised the city's military governor on the best measures to control the riots. Apparently, there were still good links between the Greeks and the Huns, perhaps through some multi-lingual Gothic intermediary, who brought the shocking news from Hungary.

Priscus' original does not survive, but it was copied by Jordanes. Here is Jordanes' account of what happened after the wedding, when Attila retired with his new young bride:

> He had given himself up to excessive merry-making and he threw himself down on his back heavy with wine and sleep. He suffered a haemorrhage, and the blood, which would ordinarily have drained through his nose, was unable to pass through the usual passages and flowed in its deadly course down his throat, killing him. Thus drunkenness brought a shameful end to a king who had won glory in war. On the morrow, when most of the day had passed, the king's

attendants, suspecting something was amiss, first shouted loudly then broke open the doors. They found Attila without any wounds but dead from an effusion of blood and the girl weeping with downcast face beneath her head-scarf.

The details are convincing – a young girl, a good deal of drink, no hint of ill health, a night of lusty consummation, the body, the weeping girl, the concealing *velamen*. What could have gone wrong? Later, imaginations worked overtime on the subject of Ildico – a wronged princess set upon vengeance, a hidden dagger, poison, who knows what skull duggery? Similar tales arose after the death of Genghis Khan, claiming that he was the victim of a revenge attack by his latest wife. Lesser mortals do not like their kings simply to die; there should be comets and portents and high drama. But there was no hint of that at the time, and Ildico's shocked state is against it. More likely Attila, now in his mid-fifties, suffered a catastrophic collapse of some kind.

But what? I think the question can be answered, with recourse to some medical detail.

The report spoke of blood, flowing out through nose and mouth. So much for one dramatic suggestion – that the king died while in the full flow, as it were, of his creative energy, i.e. of a heart attack or stroke brought on by sex. Neither strokes nor heart attacks cause external bleeding. The blood could only have come from some organ with a connection to the mouth – lungs, stomach or oesophagus. Lungs do not suffer sudden haemorrhage (only slow bleeding after years of debilitating disease, like TB). This leaves stomach and throat.

Take the stomach first. He could simply have choked on his own vomit. But there is no mention of vomit; it was the blood that seized the attention of his attendants. One possibility is that the blood could have come from a peptic ulcer, which could have been developing for some time, without necessarily causing any symptoms (ulcers are not always painful). One component in the growth of an ulcer is stress, and of that Attila had borne more than most. The effect of years of tough campaigning might now have been compounded by the painful awareness that he had done all he could, that there never would be a Great Hunnic Empire encompassing Gaul and the Hun homelands, let alone all the eastern and western realms of Constantinople and Rome. If he ever had believed he was destined – by the Blue Heaven or the God of War or whatever deity his shamans worshipped – to rule the world, he now knew for sure he would have to settle for less. It was, actually, the end. So perhaps what happened was that an ulcer broke, causing him to vomit, which would normally have woken him, except that he lay unconscious from drink and exhaustion.

There is another and, I think, slightly more convincing possibility. The Huns were great drinkers, not only of their own barley-beer but of the wine that they imported from Rome. It was wine that Priscus mentioned at his supper with Attila. For 20 years Attila had been consuming alcohol, perhaps in large amounts (remember the Hun habit of draining the cup after each toast). There is a condition caused by alcoholism known as *portal hypertension*, which produces *oesophageal varices*, which in plain language means varicose veins in the gullet. These swollen, weakened veins can burst without warning, producing a sudden rush of blood, which would, for a man lying on his back in a drunken stupor, run straight into his lungs. If he had been awake, or sober, he would have sat up, bled, and probably recovered. Drink, hypertension and weakened veins in his throat – that was probably the combination that killed him. He drowned in his own blood.

Poor, innocent Ildico awoke next to a corpse, and could only weep, too shocked and apprehensive to go for help, or even open the door when attendants concerned at the strange silence knocked and shouted.

Jordanes takes up the account. The word spread. Distraught attendants called others. People trooped in aghast. As the terrible truth struck them, they began their ritual mourning, which all cultures express in their own way. In this case, they drew knives and sliced off chunks of hair – a habit which may have survived for three centuries from the days of the Xiongnu, in whose royal graves archaeologists have found plaited hair cut off at the roots. The men also cut their cheeks, an act that explains the scarring to which several authors referred in their descriptions of the Huns. As Jordanes writes, they 'disfigured their already hideous faces with deep wounds to mourn the famous warrior not with womanly tears and wailings, but with male blood'. This ritual was common to many tribes from the Balkans across Central Asia, and was already well known in the West. Sidonius recalls it to praise the courage of his hero Avitus: 'In the bearing of wounds, you surpass the one to whom wailing means self-wounding and furrowing the cheeks with iron and gouging red traces of scars on menacing features.'

The body was placed out on the grassland, lying in state in a silken tent in full view of his mourning people. Around the tent circled horsemen, 'after the manner of circus games', while one of Attila's senior aides delivered a funeral dirge, which seems to have been repeated to Priscus word for word, though of course translated from Hunnish into Gothic and then Greek, from which Jordanes produced a Latin version, from which at last this version comes:

> Chief of the Huns, King Attila, born of his father Mundzuk, lord of the bravest tribes, who with unprecedented power alone possessed the kingdoms of Scythia and Germany, and having captured their cities terrorized both Roman empires

and, that they might save their remnants from plunder, was appeased by their prayers and took an annual tribute. And when he had by good fortune accomplished all this, he fell neither by an enemy's blow nor by treachery, but safe among his own people, happy, rejoicing, without any pain. Who therefore can think of this as death, seeing that no-one thinks it calls for vengeance?

These lines have inspired much scholarly analysis, even some brave attempts to reconstruct a Gothic version, to little effect. It is impossible to prove if it had a genuine Hunnish source, let alone if it captured anything of the original. But Priscus surely believed it did, or why would he have quoted it so exactly? Perhaps he was eager to do a good job of reportage that does something to record the Huns' grief, albeit nothing much for their poetic abilities. The best Attila's people can say of him, apparently, is that he pillaged on a massive scale, and died without giving them an excuse to kill in revenge for his death. As Maenchen-Helfen says, it sounds 'like an epitaph for an American gangster'.

The description continues with a ritual lamentation, a sort of wake, a display of both grief and celebration of a life well lived.[1]

Then, when night fell, the body was prepared for burial. The Huns did something to which we will return in a moment, 'first with gold, second with silver and third with the hardness of iron'. The metals, Priscus says through Jordanes, were

[1] Jordanes, or Priscus, says that the Huns called the rite a *strava*, which, as the only single surviving word that could perhaps be Hunnish, has been the cause of much hopeful speculation. Scholars arguing for over a century agree on one thing: Turkish it isn't, which means almost certainly that it was not after all Hunnish. According to several experts, it is a late-medieval Czech and Polish word for 'food' in the sense of a 'funeral feast', though whether the Huns had adopted it 1,000 years earlier, or whether Priscus' informant used the term in passing, is a mystery.

symbols – iron because he subdued nations, gold and silver for the treasures he had stolen. And then 'they added the arms of enemies won in combat, trappings gleaming with various special stones and ornaments of various types, the marks of royal glory'.

What was it that was done with the metals? Most translations say they bound his 'coffins' with them, from which flows a ludicrous but often-repeated story that Attila was buried inside three coffins, one of gold, one of silver, one of iron. Gibbon accepts the legend as fact, without comment. As a result, generations of treasure-hunters have hoped to find a royal tomb containing these treasures.

This idea is widely accepted in Hungary – it was even taught as hard historical fact in schools – partly thanks to the account in Géza Gárdonyi's novel, *The Invisible Man*. As Attila lies in state,

> the head shamans sacrificed a black horse behind the catafalque, and the blind Kama questioned the departed Hunnish souls as to how Attila should be buried.
>
> 'Put him in a triple coffin,' was the reply. 'Let the first coffin be made of gold, like the sunshine, for he was the sun of the Huns. Let the second coffin be made of silver, like the tail of a comet, for he was the comet of the world. Let the third coffin be made of steel, for he was as strong as steel.'

It's nonsense if you give it a moment's thought. How much gold would it take to make a coffin? I'll tell you: about 60,000 cubic centimetres. This is $15 million worth in today's terms, a solid tonne of gold: not much in terms of modern production or in terms of the empire's annual gold output, but still the equivalent of a year's tribute from Constantinople (which, remember, had dried up long before). If the Huns had had that much gold, Attila would never have needed to invade the west, and he would by now have had a good deal more than a wooden palace and a single stone bath-house. And, if they had it, is it really conceivable that they would do anything so dumb as to bury it all?

And there are still two more coffins to go, each bigger than the last. Two hundred thousand cubic centimetres of metal! No emperor was ever buried with wealth like that. Besides, it would have taken months to cast and make them, and then they would have weighed over 3 tonnes. Handling them would have been a considerable operation – 60 people to lift them, a hefty wagon, a team of oxen – and this was a ritual that was supposedly performed secretly, at dead of night. The whole thing is as daft as anything that can be spun from a single word.

And spun it was, not by Gárdonyi, but by his sources, examined in detail by the eminent director of Szeged's museum, now named after him, the Mora Ferenc Museum. He traced the story back to a nineteenth-century writer, Mor Jokai, who in turn took it from a priest, Arnold Ipolyi, who in 1840 claimed he had it from Jordanes, at a time when very few people had access to Jordanes. More likely, he had heard of Gibbon's account. Anyway, Ipolyi either failed to understand, or deliberately improvised for the sake of a good story.

If you look at what Jordanes actually wrote, there were no metal coffins. The Latin suggests a more realistic solution: *coopercula . . . communiunt*, 'they fortified the covers'. No mention of *arcae* (coffins), although the word is used in verbal form later in the account. Now it begins to make sense. We may, at the most, be talking of a wooden coffin, into which are placed a few precious items like the slivers of gold used to decorate bows. The lid is then sealed with small, symbolic golden, silver and iron clasps. As it happens, there are precisely such coffins among the Xiongnu finds in the Noyan Uul hills of Mongolia.

What, then, of the riches supposedly buried with the body? As Peter Tomka writes, 'The dead man would have been laid in his coffin in ceremonial clothing. He would have been furnished with gifts of food and drink, sometimes with simple tools, like knives or tweezers.' But nothing of much great value would have been placed in the coffin itself. If the Pannonhalma treasure – cult objects decorated with gold flake, but no body – is anything to go by, the body and the king's prize possessions would have been buried separately. What treasure-seekers and archaeologists are looking for is a corpse in a wooden box, which might by now have vanished into the Tisza's flood plain, and a hoard of small personal objects.

In Szeged's museum, you feel you are as close to Attila as you are likely to get, especially in the company of its current director, Bela Kurti, who routinely handles objects that could well have been handled by Attila himself. Kurti, a burly man with a greying beard who has been at the museum for over 30 years, explained how this had come about.

The hero of this story is an octogenarian who lives in a hamlet on the flood plain of the Tisza, about 12 kilometres south-west of Szeged. Balint Joszef – Joseph Balint, if you like – is a former farm worker who is famous locally because of what he found when he was five. The place is too small to show up on a map, but there's a lake that bears the same name – Nagyszéksós (pronounced Narj-sake-shosh). It was a fine day in the early summer of 1926. Little Joszef was out with his family, playing while they planted pumpkins. He saw something hard sticking up from some newly turned earth, scratched at the soil, and pulled out a strange-looking metal pot, which seemed to be all holes – 39 of them to be precise, in three rows. He showed it to his mother. As a pot, it was completely useless, being filthy and full of holes, so she took a hammer and flattened it out, and made it into a rough-and-ready circle, like a crown. 'Now you're going to be king!' she said, and he took it away to play in the pig-sty. It was a heavy thing. He couldn't wear it. So, having rolled it like a hoop around the farmyard, he forgot about it, and lost it.

Six months later, one of the farm labourers found it again, and this time it occurred to one of the family that it might be important. He cleaned it, and saw to his astonishment that he was holding gold. He cut it into three pieces and took it to a jeweller in Szeged to see what it might fetch. The jeweller, wary of the law, reported the find to the police, who took it to Szeged's museum, where it came into the hands of the director, Mora Ferenc. Mora at once drove out to the farm and spoke kindly to little Joszef, who pointed out where he had made his discovery. The other two bits of the bowl appeared. There followed an official request: could the museum's archaeologists please dig up the Balints' pumpkin field? Balint senior was appalled at the idea, and wouldn't hear of it.

Eight years passed. Mora died. His successor, rather more determined, returned to Nagyszéksós, overruled Mr Balint, excavated the field, and discovered the greatest Hun treasure ever found – 162 pieces: belt buckles, neckrings, gold jewellery inlaid with precious stones, horse harnesses, saddle decorations, boot clasps, decorative bits of swords and daggers, handles of wooden tools, bits of saddles and whips, bows and pots. Further finds have raised the total to over 200 pieces, mostly small, amounting to a kilogram of gold. From the boot clasps, archaeologists know that these items belonged to one or more members of the Hun elite. Experts like István Bóna and Peter Tomka agree: this was a funeral offering, and it was – crucially – not part of a burial. No bones were found in the Balints' field, no ashes, no trace of any washed-away burial mound.

The bowl, by the way, is now back together again, and in

the National Museum in Budapest, the centrepiece of a trove on which Kurti is expert. A copy stands in the Szeged museum. Similar finds in Persia show that the holes once held decorations of glass or semi-precious stones, which suggests it would have been used for toasts at formal dinners like the one described by Priscus. It is, frankly, a pretty coarse piece of work. But it is intriguing to think that this object may come down to us from that place, that man, that particular occasion when Attila was at the height of his power, just four years before the bowl became a funeral offering.

Meanwhile, there would have been the mournful funeral procession, and a secret burial 'in the earth'. There is no mention of a burial mound. If the burial was in line with Xiongnu royal burials, there might have been a deep pit, a wooden room and a wooden tomb, into which the coffin would have been placed, the hole then being refilled.

The word 'secret' is important. Genghis Khan was buried in secret, and so were his heirs. The secrecy had a double purpose. The obvious one was to foil grave-robbers (both knew the dangers, the Mongols from the Noyan Uul burial mounds in the hills of their homeland and the Huns from the attentions of the Bishop of Margus a few years before Attila's death). The second one was to preserve the sanctity of the site, and thus protect the divine aura that surrounded the emperor. In the case of the Mongol rulers, their attendants had a problem, in that everyone knew roughly where the burials were – on the sacred mountain of Burkhan Khaldun, now known as Khan Khenti, in northern Mongolia. To solve the problem, the Mongols disguised the graves thoroughly by churning the ground with galloping horses, placed guards around the whole area, and then allowed trees and grass to camouflage the place. After a generation, no-one could find the exact sites, which remain secret to this day.

Attila's case was rather different. There would, it seems, have been traditional rites to honour the passing of the leader of a tribe of wandering pastoral nomads. But the Huns, wanderers no more, had been in Hungary for only a couple of generations. There was no traditional sacred site that would have been suitable as a burial-ground for Hun chiefs, and, even if there were some distant folk memory of their (unproven) Xiongnu ancestry, no mountains around that would act as a bridge between earth and heaven. There was not much option except a simple earth burial.

That is what Hungarians believe, with a slight twist added by Gárdonyi. Where was the king to be buried?

> Old Kama answered, following the heavenly council. 'The River Tisza is full of tiny islands. Divert the waters from the narrower branch in one of the places where the river divides. Dig the grave there very deep in the exposed bed, and then widen that bed so that it will be the greater. After the king has been buried, let the waters flow back again.'

As a result, in Hungary today many believe, and state as a fact, that Attila was buried in the River Tisza.

However the burial was made, it would have had to be in a place kept secret, something of a problem in Hungary's gently rolling or dead-flat *puszta*. Priscus, according to Jordanes, tells us how this was supposed to have been achieved. 'That so great riches might be preserved from human curiosity, they slaughtered those appointed to the work – a dreadful reward, which engulfed in sudden death both buriers and buried.'

This is worth a closer look. It was common practice across all Eurasia to mark the death of a king with the ritual slaughter of animals and slaves. In Anyang, China, tourists can now view a remarkable burial-site, in which a small army was buried along with its royal commander, leaving human skeletons, horse skeletons and a score of chariots. Not that it was a universal custom, for slaves and soldiers were valued assets, and so increasingly models were used instead: hence the famous terracotta army of Xian.

Now to the business of killing grave-diggers to preserve secrecy. As far as I know, Jordanes' is the first mention of such an idea. Perhaps this should not be surprising, considering that usually the burial of a great king involved a rather obvious memorial, in the form of a burial mound, of which there are hundreds across Hungary, the Ukraine and southern Russia, all the way over Asia to the royal tombs of the Xiongnu in Mongolia. Secrecy had never been an issue. It became so again only with the burial of Genghis Khan, which, perhaps not by coincidence, spawned a similar idea: that, to preserve the secret of the great khan's death, all living creatures along the route of the funeral cortège were killed. Marco Polo was told this about the burial of Genghis's grandson, Mönkhe, and it soon became a truism applied to the cortège of Genghis himself. In the case of the Mongols, it simply doesn't make practical sense. Nothing could be better designed to make the route of a cortège visible than a trail of dead bodies and grieving families.

But in Attila's case perhaps it was different. This was a unique circumstance. Never before had a barbarian ruler achieved so much. There was no precedent to draw on. A night-time burial, no mound – that sounds real to me. If Priscus had made up the whole thing, or if he had responded only to his own classical models, he would surely have gone on about lamentations and the death of victims and burial mounds.

So how do you keep the secret? Maenchen-Helfen, again, is somewhat snooty about the idea. 'To kill the labourers who buried the king was an inefficient means to prevent the robbing of the tomb, for thousands must have known of it. Besides, who killed the killers?' I'm not so sure. It would not have been all that hard to organize, because the Huns had an expendable labour force of slaves taken in a dozen campaigns, from among the Germanic tribes, from the Balkans, from Gaul, from Italy. Priscus had seen some of them on his trip, and contrasted the successful Greek businessman with the other grim-faced and depressed prisoners employed around Attila's headquarters. The Huns had no compunction about killing (remember the two princely refugees punished by impaling). It is as easy to kill a man as a sheep – easier, actually, because with a sheep you have a slight extra worry about the quality of the meat. It would not have been a great leap from self-inflicted cuts to cutting the throats of house-servants.

I can imagine a crowd of prisoners, about 50 of them, led off to dig a burial-pit, utterly unaware of their coming fate, because the plan was known only to a few *logades*; then the approaching procession, and the crowd of mourning Huns, thousands of them, being told to return to their homes by the small group of *logades*; the slow advance with a guard of 50 or so Hun soldiers and pall-bearers, the reverential entomb-ment, the slow work of filling in the grave and the careful raking of the spot, perhaps even an area that would be soon covered by the spring-time floods of the River Tisza; then the prisoners formed up, the march off into the darkness; and then, with the first glimmer of dawn in the eastern sky, the separation of the prisoners into groups, and the quick cutting of throats, with each Hun guard performing one or two executions, all over in a minute. Of course, there would be Huns who knew the secret, but they would be the guardians of a sacred trust. The secret was safe with them, until the passing seasons and the Tisza's annual floods had disguised the spot for ever.

# 11

## TRACES OF THOSE
## WHO VANISHED

ALMOST INSTANTANEOUSLY, THE EMPIRE THAT HAD SEEMED SO
grand turned into a house of cards. Attila, the greatest leader
to emerge from the steppes until Genghis, had never made
proper provision for the succession. Priscus had seen him
lavishing affection on his younger son, Ernak, and responsi-
bility on his eldest, Ellac, but it takes more than wishful
thinking to hold an empire together. Genghis got it right,
establishing a bureaucracy, and written laws, and a formal
statement of who should take over when he died a good eight
years before the event. Attila was like a parent who dies
intestate, with the result that his sons – and by now, with all
those wives, there were so many that they were almost a sub-
tribe – squabbled his inheritance to bits. Each one claimed his
share, arguing that the vassal peoples should be divided
equally, as if they were family servants. The Mongols had
stories about chiefs (Genghis, of course, but also others) who
showed their sons how, while a single arrow can be easily
broken, a bundle remains unbreakable: unity is strength!

Attila and his family had no such wisdom. In Jordanes' words, 'A contest for the highest place arose among Attila's successors – for the minds of young men are wont to be inflamed by ambition for power – and in their heedless rush to rule, they all destroyed his empire.'

If the sources for what happened while Attila was in power are thin, now the links to the outside world were cut to bits, and we have nothing but the baldest of generalizations. Chiefs of once independent tribes would not be treated like servants, and rose in fury. First, perhaps, the Ostrogoths, but the main rebellion was led by the leader of the Gepids, Ardaric, one of Attila's greatest allies. He had supported his new lord on the Balkan campaign of 447 and formed the right wing on the Catalaunian Plains. It was he who now formed an alliance to win back the freedom of the Germanic tribes from their Hunnish overlords.

In 454, according to Jordanes, there was a great battle. Its details are unknown; all we have is a name, the Nedao river in Pannonia – but no Nedao river is mentioned in any other source, and the name and location have since vanished from memory. Even the most ardent of Hun experts, Maenchen-Helfen, can say no more than that it was probably a tributary of the Sava, which flows into the Tisza at Belgrade. Anyway, it was a great victory for Ardaric, who, it was said, killed 30,000 Huns and Hun allies – a figure that should be cut to a tenth, as usual, if it is to be brought within the realms of possibility. Among the dead was Attila's eldest, Ellac. 'Thus did the Huns give way, a race to which men thought the whole world must yield.'

And thus did the Gepid Alliance take over the Huns' lands, and their vexed relationship with the empire. Ambassadors were despatched to Constantinople, where they were well received by Marcian, who had stood up to Attila and had been waiting apprehensively for his next move. He must have been hugely relieved by events beyond the Danube, and happily granted Ardaric aid to the tune of 100 pounds of gold a year – one-twentieth of the sum his predecessor had paid Attila.

With Attila's death, the imperial world became a marginally better place. Divided, the barbarians were easier to handle. There were large-scale resettlements of minor tribes: the Ostrogoths were granted land in Pannonia, and the remaining Huns broke into two groups, one on the Black Sea coast, another straddling today's Serbian–Bulgarian border. Smaller struggles continued, especially between the western Huns and their old enemies, the Ostrogoths. Jordanes mentions a battle in which the Huns, 'regarding the Goths as deserters from their rule, came against them as though they were seeking fugitive slaves', and got a severe beating. A new Hun leader emerged, Tuldila by name. Sidonius mentions him in another of his grovelling panegyrics, this one to the Emperor Majorian in 458: 'Only one race denied thee obedience, a race who had lately, in a mood even more savage than their wont, withdrawn their untamed host from the Danube because they had lost their leader in warfare, and Tuldila stirred in that unruly multitude a mad lust for fight.'

In 465–6 they tried again. One of Attila's sons, Dengizich, who had a base on the Sava, somewhere within 75 kilometres west of Belgrade, joined with Ernak (Attila's favourite, still alive) and sent an ambassador to Constantinople, asking the emperor, now Leo I,[1] to reinstate the market on the Danube. Leo refused.

There was one final outburst of bellicosity when Dengizich and the last of the European Huns crossed the frozen Danube in 467, forcing himself upon a community of Goths in a

[1] Reigned 457–74. Not the same as Pope Leo I (440–61). For four years (457–61), both pope and emperor were called Leo I.

desperate bid for an area to resettle. In a message to the local imperial commander, Anagastes, Dengizich said his people were even prepared to surrender, if only they had somewhere to call their own; and he had to have an answer a.s.a.p. because 'they were starving and could no longer wait'. The emperor's reply favoured the Huns; the Goths, in fury, turned on them; the Huns defended themselves; the Romans joined in; and that was pretty much it for the Huns in Europe. They fought on, hopelessly, until the end just two years later, in 469, recorded by a laconic early-seventh-century source, the *Eastern Chronicle*. Dengizich was killed by Anagastes and his head brought to Constantinople, where it was 'carried in procession through the Middle Street and fixed on a pole at the Wooden Cross. The whole city turned out to look at it.' No-one knows Ernak's fate.

A few Huns survived, merged with other tribes or scattered slowly eastwards, dissipating like dust after an explosion, sinking back into the dreamtime from which they had emerged a century before.

As the remains of Attila's empire faded away in the East, so did those of Rome's in the West. For historians, the western empire's decline was a messy business. For years, the Roman army had not been one of true-blue Romans. Aetius may have been called the 'last of the Romans', but his army on the Catalaunian Plains would have been nothing without Visigoths, Franks and Burgundians, among others. What he would have done without them the gods alone knew. Attila's disappearance removed a major threat, but left many others scrapping over Rome's decaying body. Yet he did not disappear completely, for his influence reached beyond the grave, his name weaving through events and personalities as the western empire brawled and murdered its way to extinction.

For some, and for a few years, Aetius had been Rome's saviour, its bastion against barbarism, until all his efforts were reduced to nothing by an astonishingly melodramatic end. It came in Rome, where the hopeless Valentinian had re-established his court. Since his mother and his anchor, Galla Placidia, had died in 450, Valentinian had had no-one to talk sense to him. He had, in Gibbon's words, 'reached his thirty-fifth year without attaining the age of reason or courage', and was open to all sorts of nonsense, much of which was whispered into his ear by a prominent senator and two-times consul, Petronius Maximus. Aged 60, Petronius was described by the prolific Sidonius as one of Rome's leaders, of insatiable ambition, 'with his conspicuous way of life, his banquets, his lavish expense, his retinues, his literary pursuits, his estates, his extensive patronage'. He was also, it seems, extremely suspicious of the famous Aetius, with his wealth, his friends in high places and his own private barbarian army, all of which made him the western empire's most powerful official. As Petronius hinted to the emperor through his favourite eunuch and adviser Heraclius, Aetius could well be on the point of staging a coup. He could even be planning a new dynasty, for his son Gaudentius was engaged to Valentinian's daughter Eudoxia. It was up to Valentinian, Petronius implied, to strike first, or be struck.

One day in September 454, when Aetius was in conference with the emperor, the eunuch Heraclius by his side, the general began to argue the case for a quick marriage between their two children. Perhaps he was too insistent, and perhaps this seemed proof of a plan to seize power. In any event, Valentinian, whether in sudden anger or a prearranged attack, jumped from his throne, accused Aetius of treason and drew his sword – 'the first sword he had ever drawn', in Gibbon's overheated words. At this, Heraclius drew his as well, other guards followed his lead, and the unarmed Aetius died where he fell beneath a dozen blades.

With his death, Rome itself fell faster. A Roman is supposed to have commented to Valentinian: 'You have acted like a man who cuts off his right hand with his left.' A friend of the Huns, possibly of Attila, and then their enemy, Aetius had spanned the Roman and barbarian worlds, and held the uncertain balance between the two. There was and would be no-one to replace him.

So far so good for Petronius, then; and so bad for Rome, with worse to follow. Heraclius the eunuch, with ready access to the emperor's ear, urged his master to avoid replacing one ambitious man (Aetius) with another (Petronius), and Petronius received no thanks or reward for his scheming. Gibbon has a good story about the emperor raping Petronius' wife, but there is no need to repeat it, because Gibbon does not give his source, and Petronius already had quite sufficient reason for wanting revenge on Valentinian.

Incensed, Petronius hatched another plot. He approached two barbarian guards, Optila and Thraustilla, who had served with Aetius and now served his murderer Valentinian, which does not say much for the emperor's vetting procedures. Six months after Aetius' murder, in the spring of 455, Valentinian went to the Campus Martius, the Field of Mars, once marshy flatlands to the north of the city, in the bend of the Tiber, now drained and mostly built up. Accompanied by a small contingent, he was going to practise archery in one of the open areas. Dismounting, he strolled to the mark with Heraclius and the two barbarian guards. As the emperor prepared to shoot, Optila struck him on the temple, and, as he turned, Thraustilla delivered a second blow – I should imagine with a mace – which killed him. Another blow killed Heraclius. It seems the weak and cowardly emperor, murderer of Rome's star Aetius, was so loathed that the imperial guard made no move to defend him. The two assassins leaped on their horses and galloped off to Petronius to claim their reward.

Valentinian had no heir; with him, a dynasty died, and so did the final basis for the transmission of power. The Senate proclaimed Petronius emperor. But Petronius, having achieved the heights, found only despair. He was suddenly and utterly alone, without a valid claim to the throne, unpopular, and powerless in the face of events beyond his control.

Across the Mediterranean, the Vandal ruler Gaiseric was watching. Gaiseric's grandparents had migrated in a vast sweep from north of the Alps through Spain to Africa, and now he was set on completing the circle with a seaborne invasion of Italy from the south. Gaiseric had long taken a keen interest in events on the mainland, because, you will remember, his son had antagonized the Visigothic king Theodoric by doing dreadful things to his daughter, and Gaiseric had hoped that Attila might be able to deal with both the Visigoths and the Romans. That hope had died on the Catalaunian Plains. But now, with Aetius and Valentinian dead and their murderer precariously on the throne, Gaiseric had his chance. Three months after Petronius Maximus had himself proclaimed emperor, a huge Vandal fleet anchored at the mouth of the Tiber.

Poor Petronius. He had been nicknamed 'the most fortunate' because of his success. Ten years later, Sidonius wrote about his supposed good fortune: 'Personally, I shall always refuse to call that man fortunate who is poised on the precipitous and slippery peak of office.' Petronius had had his every wish fulfilled, yet now, having reached the heights, he was overwhelmed by vertigo. 'When the supreme effort brought him to the yawning gulf of the imperial dignity, his head swam beneath the diadem at the sight of that enormous power, and the man who once could not bear to have a master could not bear to be one.' With no legitimate claim to the throne, opposed by the bureaucrats, he felt a prisoner in his palace, and 'was rueing his own success before the first evening fell'. His only major act was to reappoint Avitus to be, in effect, ruler of Gaul, in the hope that he could use his diplomatic skill to control half a dozen barbarian tribes. At home, Petronius was useless. If he knew of the approach of the Vandal fleet, he could do nothing about it. When it anchored in late May, he saw defeat staring him in the face.

He panicked and fled the palace, right into the arms of a mob, which, incensed by his impotence and cowardice, stoned and stabbed him to death, tore him apart and tossed his bloody bits into the Tiber.

And who should try to save the city? Why, the man who was Rome's expert in handling these barbarians, Pope Leo, who had gone out to meet Attila four years before. This time, he was only half successful. Gaiseric spared the people, but in a two-week operation stripped the city of its wealth, including the Capitol's gilt bronze roof, the gold table and candlesticks originally seized from Jerusalem in AD 70, the palace furniture, the imperial jewels, and prisoners by the hundred, including the empress herself, her two daughters and Aetius' son.

A few days later the news of this catastrophe reached Avitus, who was in Toulouse at the time with his friends the Visigothic royals, minus old Theodoric, who had fallen on the Catalaunian Plains, and also minus his son, Thorismund, who, at Aetius' urging, had returned home to secure the succession he claimed. For three years all had gone well, even though there were those who did not accept him. Then Thorismund fell sick, and luck played into his enemies' hands. He was letting blood from a vein, sitting on a stool, when a treacherous servant sent word that he was alone and unarmed. Assassins stormed in. Thorismund grabbed the stool and – according to Jordanes – slew several of his attackers with it before they killed him. His brother, Theodoric the younger, widely believed to have masterminded the murder, took over. So it was this Theodoric who was presiding over the Visigothic court when news arrived of the second seizure of Rome by barbarian hordes (the first, of course, having been by Theodoric's ancestor, Alaric, on the Visigoths' long march westward half a century earlier).

Avitus was clearly fond of this athletic young man, for his son-in-law Sidonius paints him in a flattering light, making him sound like a superstar. Above average height, solidly built, long curly hair down over his ears, bushy eyebrows and long lashes, hook-nosed, well muscled, with thighs 'like hard horn', slim-waisted and well groomed (a barber shaves him every day, and trims his nose-hairs as well). A good administrator, he starts his day with a prayer (like most Visigoths, he professes Arianism, but probably doesn't take it very seriously), then holds audiences for petitioners and foreign envoys. Mid-morning is time for hunting, with Theodoric practising his archery. Lunch is served simply, with no great show of silver to overwhelm the conversation. Toasts are few, drunkenness unknown. Afterwards, a short nap, then a board-game, in which self-restraint combines with good fellowship. At supper, there may be some entertainment: no musicians or singers – Theodoric seems to be totally un-musical – just a mime-artist, without anything satirical or hurtful. More petitions, then bed, with armed sentries on guard.

Somehow, at this refined barbarian court, the idea arose that there was a possible new emperor right there with them in Toulouse. Sidonius described the scene in obsequious verse.

The Gothic elders assemble, an unkempt crowd, in tarnished and greasy linen tunics and skin cloaks and horse-hide boots, an obvious contrast to their elegant prince. Avitus addresses them, urging a renewed commitment to peace from young Theodoric – 'you, as the old men here can witness, whom these hands held weeping against this breast, if perchance the wet-nurse sought to bear you off against your wishes'. Who can resist? All urge the cause of peace, and Theodoric, whose rough ways had been smoothed away in childhood by Avitus himself, swears to redress past wrongs by avenging the Vandal assault on Rome, if only – now comes the punch-line – 'if only you, renowned leader, would take upon yourself the name of Augustus'.

Avitus looks down, acting modest and unworthy.

'Why do you avert your eyes?' asks Theodoric. 'Your unwillingness becomes you all the more ... with you as leader, I am a friend of Rome.'

A month later, the magnates of Gaul also rallied to the cause, and proclaimed Avitus emperor. In September he was in Rome, winning grudging support from sceptical senators. Sidonius delivered his panegyric in fawning praise of the new emperor, asserting his past successes, his present legitimacy and his inevitably glorious future.

But in this tattered realm, past success conferred neither present legitimacy nor any guarantee of future glory. Most of Gaul was lost to Franks, Burgundians and freebooting Bacaudae. The Visigoths held the south-west, and would soon seize most of Spain. Germans of various tribes ran the Rhineland. The Vandals had North Africa. Ostrogoths dominated the Danube. It didn't leave much: just Italy itself. Power was not now with either emperor or Senate, but with the army, the only defence against assault. As Aetius had shown, who ruled the army ruled the (diminishing) western empire. With Aetius gone, Avitus gave the position of commander-in-chief to a non-Roman, Ricimer, who was a Visigoth on his mother's side and a Suevian on his father's. It was Ricimer who managed to save Italy from another seaborne invasion by the Vandals in 456, and thus proved himself the true, if temporary, power in the land.

Avitus, the patrician from Gaul with a private army of barbarians, was never popular in Rome. Almost at once he was out of his depth. In 456 the harvest was bad. Famine threatened. Avitus said that to reduce the number of mouths to feed he would dismiss his private army, but to pay them off he melted down some of the few bronze statues that the Vandals had not taken. Crowds took to the streets in protest. Ricimer and the army made no move to protect their emperor. Avitus fled back to Arles, regathered contingents of his own, returned with them, and was defeated by Ricimer near Piacenza. Ricimer was magnanimous in victory, and let Avitus retire gracefully. He died on his way home.

Our subject, Attila, is almost lost in the next 20 years of Rome's collapse. Seven more emperors; an interregnum; assassination and usurpation in Rome; murder and conflict among the barbarian kingdoms – all this, which would take a book to recount in detail, leads to a sort of end of the western empire in 476, when the last Roman emperor, Romulus, was deposed by a barbarian, Odoacer.

It was not a neat end, however, because the barbarians had been at and inside the gates for so long that the change from Roman to barbarian at the head was more a symbolic than a practical switch. And suddenly it becomes easy once again to see Attila's influence at work, because both the last Roman emperor, Romulus, and the first barbarian emperor, Odoacer, owed their lives to him. By a strange coincidence, their respective fathers, Orestes and Edika, had both been officials at Attila's court, and colleagues in 449 on the ill-fated embassy written up by Priscus. Romulus would have heard all about it from his father, Attila's Roman henchman, Orestes; and so would Odoacer, from his father, Edika, the Skirian whom Chrysaphius tried so disastrously to recruit as an assassin.

How had this come to pass? After Attila's death, Orestes had returned to his estate in Pannonia, from where he was plucked to lead an army against the Goths, now on the warpath once again. Orestes, with the army behind him, became king-maker, and, after making a few others, the last he made, in 475, was his own child, little Romulus, known contemptuously not as Augustus, but Augustulus, 'baby Augustus'.

The army was itself now fatally infected by decay. With no outlying empire and a collapsing bureaucracy, the taxes dried up and the pay stopped, and at last the barbarian troops had had enough. Odoacer, thanks to his father, was in command of Skirians who, after Attila's death, had taken service with Rome. At first they backed Orestes, who promised cash, then land. Cash was in short supply; and of land there was none. So it was Odoacer and his Skirians who finally revolted against the very symbol of Roman power, and replaced the son of Attila's right-hand man with the son of one of his generals.

One-third of the western empire was now in barbarian hands, and at its centre sat a barbarian ruler. Was this deplorable? For conservatives, of course. But in the very long run a new Europe would emerge, a Europe with a new diversity of cultures and nations. Rome itself endured in many ways: its institutions, its culture, its traditions, its Christian faith. Only in Britain did barbarian invaders forget Rome, looking upon its buildings, walls and roads as upon alien artefacts and asserting their own pagan origins. On the mainland, barbarian rulers saw themselves as proud heirs to an ancient power, and paid lip-service to their nominal overlord in Constantinople. In Gaul, non-Romans took over Roman villas, learned Latin and adopted Christianity. Great Roman cities remained great. Latin remained the *lingua franca* for educated Europeans for 1,500 years, a tradition faintly echoed today in the ceremonies of ancient European universities, and across Christendom, for which AD – *anno domini*, the year of our Lord – still divides history in two.

And Attila himself? He remains one of history's great might-have-beens. With a little more diplomacy, better sense, less war and a commitment to administration he could have had so much. He could have seized all northern Europe, had Honoria in marriage, created a dynasty that ruled from the Atlantic to the Urals, from the Alps to the Baltic. Perhaps, in some parallel universe, Britain would have fallen to the Huns rather than to the Angles and Saxons, and Chaucers and Shakespeares would have written in Hunnish, and we would all have ended up worshipping not the Christian God but some shamanistic Blue Heaven. As it was, Attila's contribution to Europe's history remained bound by barbarian migration and Roman collapse, processes that were happening anyway. He tweaked both. In his rise, he drove tribes westward faster than they would otherwise have travelled. Once in power, having blotted up outlying tribes, he slowed down the same movement. In political and historical terms, Attila did little more than add a few speed bumps in the high road of Europe's history, allowing an acceleration here and a slowing down there. It all amounted to a perfect balance of pluses and minuses, signifying nothing.

Along the way there had been much sound and fury. But this, too, signified nothing. Thompson sums him up succinctly: 'Did the Huns make no *direct* contribution to the progress of Europe? Had they nothing to offer besides the terror which uprooted the Germanic nations and sent them fleeing into the Roman Empire? The answer is, No, they offered nothing . . . They were mere plunderers and marauders.'

Is that it, then? Not quite. There is more to Attila than plundering and marauding, because his name resounds still as an archetype of a certain sort of power. His influence is to be found not in his practical achievements, but in his appeal to the imagination. He broke the bonds of historical fact, and entered legend, a shift that is the subject of the final chapter.

# 12

## AFTERLIFE: THE GOOD, THE BAD AND THE BEASTLY HUN

EVEN IN HIS LIFETIME ATTILA WAS BOTH OPPRESSOR AND HERO, both symbol of paganism and instrument of God, depending on the beholder. Within years of his death, the truth was being encrusted with propaganda, legend, myth and pure hokum, flowing in a torrent of folklore that separated into three streams: the Christian West, the Germanic and Scandinavian borderlands, and Hungary.

Most of Attila's victims and most of those who wrote about him were Christian, and Christians had an official agenda: to show that, although existence was a battleground between good and evil, between God and Satan, the end result would be God's victory. Human history, therefore, was an unsteady progression towards Christ's second coming, and every event had to be examined for evidence of God's omnipotence and wisdom. The task of the Christian chronicler was to see through the murky flow of events to the underlying reality. Attila's grim advance across Europe was no credit to him. He was unwittingly God's instrument, a scourge laid upon Christian backs for past sins – or, in other metaphors, the wine-press of God's vengeance, the furnace for the purification of his gold – and an opportunity for God to reveal his power, not directly, but through his representatives, the higher the better, from ordinary priests and nuns to bishops and the pope, with victims being marked down not as failures but as martyrs. In this cataclysm, the old corrupt world of pagan Rome must be seen to vanish and a new age to dawn, a Christian renaissance, with yet greater glory to follow.

So there is a certain logic to the way in which Hunnish mayhem was exaggerated. Vandals gave their name to a type of routine marauder; Goths inspired 'Gothic', which was originally a term of cultural abuse before it acquired its flattering overtones; but the Huns were always beyond the pale. From the chronicles written in the 300 years after Attila's death, you would think he had left nothing standing in Gaul and Italy. He was even said to have destroyed Florence, killing 5,000 people, though the Huns never crossed the Po, 100 kilometres from Florence. As the *Life of St Lupus* puts it, 'no city, castle or fortified town anywhere could preserve its defences'. Attila left nothing but barren land behind him. He was the fulfilment of the apocalyptic prophecy in the Book of Revelation: 'And when the thousand years are expired, Satan shall be loosed out of his prison, And shall go out to deceive the nations.' The worse the image of destruction, the greater the influence of those who successfully stood against him.

The most admired writer of his time, Sidonius, made sure that praise went first and foremost to those with divine backing. Well, he would. He had friends in high Christian places, as his surviving letters show. Lupus, Gaul's most eminent cleric; Sidonius' own father-in-law, the future emperor, Avitus; Prosper, successor to Anianus as Bishop of Orléans, 'the greatest and most perfect of prelates'; and a dozen other bishops. He would himself become a bishop (of Clermont-Ferrant, when he was about 40). Who really saved Troyes, Orléans and Rome? Not Aetius and his army, but three godly men: Lupus, Anianus and Pope Leo – actually four, if you count Avitus, whose Christian commitment to peace enabled him to persuade his Visigothic friends to join Aetius.

The result of this agenda is that the real-life individuals and events were quickly hidden behind propaganda and symbols. Lupus and the rest became epitomes of saintliness, Attila the leader from hell – literally, in some portraits, which show him with devilish horns and pointed ears.

It's an insidious process, because historians – especially those trying, as I am, to write narrative history – are tempted to mix legends with history, simply because they make a good story. I did it earlier with St Agnan saving Orléans. See what happens to the story of Attila's retreat from Italy after the meeting with Leo (assuming it took place at all). By the eighth century it has become a miracle. Paul the Deacon, an Italian of that time who wrote a history of the Lombards, has Attila remarking: 'Oh! It was not the one who came [i.e. Leo] who forced me to depart, but another who, standing behind him sword in hand, threatened me with death if I did not obey his command.' After that, almost everyone repeated the story, in ever more imaginative variants. Ravenna, the temporary seat of imperial administration, became the usual venue, although Attila never approached it. In one version, Attila asks who is approaching. It is the pope, he is told, 'coming to intercede with you on behalf of his children, the inhabitants of Ravenna'. Attila takes this as a joke: 'How can one man produce so many children?'

That was in the ninth century. Four hundred years later, in newly converted Hungary, the *Gesta Hungarorum* has Attila taking the pope hostage, until he is terrified by a vision, 'namely, when the king looked up he beheld a man hovering in the air, holding a sword in his hand and grinding his teeth, who threatened to cut off his head. So Attila obeyed the Romans' request and released the Apostle's successor.' Others turn the vision into the war-god Mars, or St Peter; or transform the pope's colleagues into sword-wielding saints, Peter and Paul, a version portrayed in a fresco by Raphael, painted in 1514 for Leo's papal namesake, Leo X. That painting, moreover, in which Leo I has Leo X's features, is entitled *Attila the Hun Turned Back from Rome* – not from Ravenna, please note. So, in the course of 1,000 years, a legend invented 300 years after the event became accepted fact; and it remains so even today in certain quarters. One Christian website says with casual assurance: 'The man-like form Attila saw in the air holding a sword in his hand was probably an angel, as in similar Biblical accounts.'

The same thing happened with the epithet 'Scourge of God'. The first surviving reference is in the *Life of St Lupus*, written in the eighth or ninth century, but it would probably have already been doing the rounds orally well before that. There are many later versions of the story. Here is one.

Troyes is well defended with walls and troops, commanded by the bishop. Lupus is on guard. Attila, swollen with arrogance, approaches on horseback, and bangs on the town gate.

'Who are you,' demands Lupus from above, 'you who scatter peoples like chaff and break crowns under your horses' hooves?'

'I am Attila, King of the Huns, the Scourge of God.'

'Oh, welcome,' is the bishop's unlikely reply. 'Scourge of the God whom I serve! It is not up to me to stop you.' And he descends to open the gate himself, take Attila's bridle and lead him into the town. 'Enter, Scourge of my God, and go wherever you wish.'

Attila and his troops enter, wander the streets, pass churches and palaces, but see nothing, because a cloud conceals their gaze. Blinded, they are led straight through the town, miraculously recovering their sight on exit. Thus is the Beast tamed by God's servant.

And it worked. History slips away, legend sticks. Today, some histories simply refer to Attila as *flagellum dei*, the Scourge of God, as if that were how he was known at the time. You may even see the nonsensical statement that Attila adopted the phrase himself, as if he spoke Latin and consciously assumed the role of divine scourge.

Many places in western Europe have utterly spurious stories of Attila and Huns, so far removed from reality that the names should be in quotes. In the Friuli region of northeast Italy, folk tales distorted Attila's German name, Etzel, into Ezzel and mixed him up with a harsh twelfth-century ruler, Ezzelino: 'They said he was the son of the Devil or of a dog, he had black hairs on his nose that stood on end when he was angry and every speech he began with a bow-wow-wow.' In Metz, an oratory acquired defences of granite that broke Hun swords. In Dieuze (in Lorraine, eastern France), Huns were blinded because they captured a bishop, their sight restored on his release. Modena in Italy had its own version of St Lupus. In Reims, the Devil himself opened the town's gates to the Huns.

Cologne has the most famous of 'Hun' victims – St Ursula and her many virgins (I'll tell you the numbers shortly). You can see their bones to this day in Cologne Cathedral; not *their* bones, of course, because the whole thing is a myth from which sprang a tangle of variants. The unlikely seed for the tales is a fourth- or fifth-century inscription, still on view in the Church of St Ursula, according to which a senator called Clematius was impelled by visions to rebuild a basilica on this spot to honour some martyred virgins. No hint of how many virgins, no mention of Huns. Over the years, these victims acquired a story, pulled together in 1275 and first printed by

William Caxton in 1483. It concerns a princess, Ursula, from either Britain or Brittany, depending on the version, who is wooed by a pagan king. She refuses the match, dedicating herself to perpetual virginity and demanding a corps of ten virgins to attend her on a pilgrimage. The story becomes hopelessly complicated, with a journey down the Rhine to Rome and disputes between rival prelates, but the upshot is that on their return Ursula and her virgins reach Cologne, only to find it besieged by the Huns, who, on the orders from their unnamed prince, behead the lot.

It was never more than a legend, and soon became ludicrous. An early version recorded the eleven martyrs in Latin numerals as 'XI M', with the M standing for 'martyrs'. But M is also 1,000 in Latin script, which was how some unknown copyist understood it. Now, suddenly, there were *eleven thousand* virgins – not that it made sense, because Ursula was one of the eleven, so the 11,000 would have included 1,000 Ursulas. Never mind. The legend thrived, inspiring a cult and variants and paintings, all branching off one another like a hypertext fantasy. In one version, Attila himself offers to marry Ursula, allowing her to assert her virgin holiness: 'Get away!' she says. 'I did not disdain the hand of Caesar only to become the property of someone as cursed as you!' In 1143, bones which supposedly were those of some of the long-martyred virgins were sent to the Rhineland monastery of Disibodenberg, where they inspired the ascetic and intellectual Hildegard of Bingen to write a song ('O ecclesia') rejecting earthly marriage for the love of God. Later, in the fifteenth and sixteenth centuries, Ursula and her story were much painted: by two anonymous Dutch and German masters, by Caravaggio, and by Carpaccio, who portrayed her life in eight episodes, with the Huns in Florentine dress. Also in the sixteenth century, Lucas Cranach the Elder drew on the story for an altarpiece in Dresden, focusing not on the victims but on a dispassionate Hun prince leaning on his sword. In 1998 the British playwright Howard Barker used the myth to examine the meaning of a commitment to virginity (victims) and the nature of a moral detachment (the prince) that seemed to recall that of a Nazi SS officer. Meanwhile, the legend had spun off into another realm, having inspired a sixteenth-century Italian nun, St Angela, to found the Ursuline order of nuns, which by 1700 had 350 foundations in France alone, many of which were forcibly shut down in the French Revolution. In Valenciennes, eleven Ursulines were guillotined for teaching Catholicism, allowing those who like historical parallels to cast the atheistic revolutionaries as Huns. Stories, paintings, a play, music, nunneries, schools and colleges galore – it goes on, endlessly. As a result of the sub-cult of Hildegard and the boom in medieval chants, a quartet has recorded *11,000 Virgins: Chants for the Feast of St Ursula* (Anonymous 4, HMV 907200). Enough already: if you are looking for real-life Huns, this is about as much help as using *Hamlet* to research medieval Denmark.

Other traditions in the ex-Roman empire took root and flourished, perhaps the oddest being the tales of the 'good Attila'. Apparently, towns looking for their origins saw Attila as a force for renewal, as in the following fairy story.

Once upon a time, Attila was in Padua when there came a poet with a composition in praise of the great chief. Leading Paduans prepared a performance. The poet, following literary tradition, gave Attila divine origins. 'What's the meaning of this?' interrupts our hero. 'To compare a mortal man with immortal gods! I'll have nothing to do with such impiety!' And he orders the poor man to be burned on the spot, along with his verses. When the pyre is ready and the poet tied on top, Attila approaches: 'Enough. I just wanted to teach this flatterer a lesson. Let us not frighten poets who use truth to sing our praises.'

There might have been enough here for some great post-Roman epic in French or Italian. No writer took up the challenge with success. But there have since been quite a few failures, all of them revising history in vain attempts to make something worthwhile. In 1667 Pierre Corneille's *Attila* had 20 performances, then faded into well-deserved obscurity. A terrible German melodrama by Zacharias Werner, lawyer, philosopher, priest and playwright, performed a few times in Vienna in 1808, ends with Attila's murder (not a natural death, as per history) by the Roman princess Honoria (not the Germanic princess Ildico). An English version, put on in London in 1832, concluded with a line by Attila's brother Bleda (whom Attila murdered, but who is somehow still alive): 'Ha! Is he dead? The tyrant dead? Ha! ha! [Laughs hysterically].'

This dire creation was the basis for Verdi's 1846 opera *Attila*. Written when the struggle for Italian unification, the Risorgimento, was in full swing, it is full of enthusiastic expressions of Italian patriotism inspired by its hero's destructive ambitions. The first scene plunges right into the theme, when the maidens of Aquileia appear, alive, against Attila's express command. 'Who dared against my interdict to save them?' demands Attila of his Breton slave, Uldino, who replies that they are a worthy tribute for Attila: 'Warriors extraordinary, they defended their brothers . . .'

'What do I hear?' interrupts the king. 'Whoever inspired unwarlike women with valour?'

And Odabella, Aquileia's princess, daughter of her slain father, answers *con energia*, several repetitions and a shattering top C, 'The boundless holy love of our country!'

One line, a plea to Attila by Aetius – the baritone Ezio – quickly became a political slogan:

*Avrai tu l'universo,*
*Resti l'Italia a me.*
(You may have the whole world,
but leave Italy to me.)

The story-line is complete tosh, with Attila being stabbed to death by his intended wife Odabella, but Ezio's soulful plea for Rome's resurrection (*Dagli immortali vertici*/From the immortal peaks) was an instant hit, and the passion of the music has its admirers, which is why the opera is still occasionally performed.[1]

In a few places you can still hear the noise of Attila's passing echoing faintly. In Udine, not far from Aquileia, they say that the castle-topped hill dominating their town was built by Attila's hordes, using their helmets as buckets, so that their leader could relish the spectacle of Aquileia in flames. There is one name that acts as a memorial to the Huns: Hunfredus was its original form, a combination of 'Hun' and 'peace', denoting someone who could make peace with the Huns. Hunfroi, as it was in old French, was brought by the Normans into England, where it became Humphrey, and into Italy as Umberto. Near Châlons, at the northern edge of the Catalaunian Plains, a sign points north-east to 'Attila's Camp', which turns out to be no such thing. The tree-covered mound is a first-century hill-fort, attached to Attila simply because the arrival of the Huns was the biggest thing to happen around that time. If French schoolchildren know anything of Huns, it is Attila's supposed boast: *Là où mon cheval passera, l'herbe ne repoussera pas* (Wherever my horse passes, the grass will not grow). And, finally, his fame has also kept him alive in film, first in Fritz Lang's *Kriemhild's Revenge* (1924), and more recently in a couple

---

[1] The Royal Opera House in London did it in 2002.

of remakes that should not be mentioned except in a foot-note.[2]

The Germans – that is, the Germanic tribes – saw things rather differently, because they had formed part of Attila's empire. They remembered with greater respect. Between the Germanic-speaking communities of old Europe travelled bards and poets, who sang of past glories, carrying their creations from court to court, commuting from Lombardy in northern Italy to the Gothic capital of Toulouse, the Germanic enclaves in France, the emerging German-speaking lands east of the Rhine and all points northwards. Attila became a famous figure in Germanic lore, which means early English lore as well. He gets a passing mention in the oldest English poem, *Widsith*, probably written in Mercia in the seventh century. All these legends plundered history, distorting it out of recognition into a rag-bag of heroes and wonders and gods and literary motifs.

By the ninth century, Attila was part of Scandinavian sagas as well as Germanic ones. This is odd, because his brief empire hardly touched the Baltic. Yet the Hun imperium, though not Germanic, seems to have been powerful enough to capture folk memory and popular imagination. Until the last century, ordinary people in north Germany referred to funeral-mounds as *Hunnenbette*, 'Hun beds'. Thus, among Norwegians and Danes, Attila joined Ermanaric the Ostrogoth and Gundicarius (Gundahar or Gunther) the Burgundian, woven with them into stories to carry grand themes of honour, justice, vengeance and the workings of fate. Vikings carried Attila's name with them to Iceland in the tenth

[2] *Attila the Hun* (original title: *Attilo Flagello di Dio*), 1954, with Anthony Quinn and Sophia Loren; *Attila*, made for American TV in Lithuania, 2001, with Gerard Butler as Attila, Powers Boothe as Aetius, Siân Phillips as Attila's grandmother and Steven Berkoff as Rua (Ruga).

century, and then beyond, to Greenland, source of the tenth-century *Greenlandic Lay of Atli* (Attila). He went yet further, to the New World with Thorfinn Karlsevni and his 100 Vikings, who in 1018 founded a short-lived colony on the coast of Newfoundland. I imagine them huddling round fires in their turf houses, listening to their bard. No *skraeling* (as the Norsemen called the local Indians and Inuit) would have heard, but it is an odd thought that one of the first musical and poetic works heard in the New World told of Attila, the Huns and their fights with the Burgundians.

For that was the heart of the legends: a minor incident in written sources, but strong in folk memory, probably because it played well as a family feud. Only a few surviving fragments hint at its popularity – a ninth-century Latin epic, German and English versions of the same story, a few Norse sagas. The principal hero is a certain Walther, a hostage at Attila's court, and a favourite of the king. He flees with a princess, Hildegund (the original German form of Ildico). They have a treasure. The hero Hagen, who may be either a Burgundian or a Hun, pursues them, joined by King Gunther of the Burgundians. There is a great battle, after which the three heroes are reconciled. In the English version, *Waldere*, part of which survives, Hildegund urges Walther to fight Gunther:

> Companion of Attila,
> Even now, in this hour, let neither your courage
> Nor your dignity desert you.

This story overlaps with another set of legends, about the Burgundians themselves, a.k.a. the Nibelungs, or Niflungs. Here, as in other strands, poets treated the elements as components for a do-it-yourself epic: you can have Attila enticed by Siegfried (Sigurd in Norse) into Siegfried's treasure-chamber, where Attila dies; or Attila providing a maiden for Hagen, who begets Aldrian, who does the enticing. In other stories, Hagen also begets Niflung, after whom the whole collection of sagas is named. There is no unity to be found.

Here's one version.

Gunther the Burgundian (who in real life was killed by the pre-Attila Huns in about 437) has a treasure. He also has a sister, Gudrun, who is married to Attila. Attila, wishing to extort the treasure's hiding-place from Gunther, kills him by throwing him into a snake-pit. Then Gudrun takes a grisly revenge. In the greatest surviving version of the legend, the *Volsungsaga*, Gudrun holds a grand feast, which she says is to show that she accepts her lot. Far from it. She kills the two boys she has had by Attila, and then, at the feast—

'The king asked where his sons were. Gudrun replied: "I will tell you and gladden your heart. You caused me heavy sorrow when you killed my brother. Now you shall hear what I have to tell you. You have lost your sons – on the table both their skulls are serving as cups – and you yourself drank their blood mixed with wine. Then I took their hearts and roasted them on a spit, and you ate them."'

Taking on the role of Ildico-as-murderess, Gudrun kills Attila in his sleep and burns down the hall of the sleeping Huns.

To this you can add a back-story, that of Brunhild, who is won by Gunther with the help of the hero and dragon-slayer Siegfried, formerly married to Gudrun before Attila. It is from Siegfried that Gunther, having killed Siegfried, acquires the treasure, to get which Attila murders him.

Many of these tales of greed and vengeance play out with Attila as a sort of centre point. He may be a rival for the Nibelungs' treasure. Or, perhaps because originally he was the non-Germanic outsider, he may have the unlikely role of a powerful, kindly and victimized ruler. That is how he is portrayed in the most famous of medieval German epics, the *Nibelungenlied*, created in about 1200 by some anonymous Homer-like poet from the many current tales. But the Attila of the *Nibelungenlied* is a strangely unassertive figure. In the context of the epic's time, he exemplifies the two highest virtues of kingship: faithfulness and mildness. But this makes him rather useless in dramatic terms. He is ignorant of almost everything that matters. He doesn't know that his wife, Kriemhild, mourns her former husband Siegfried. He hasn't a clue about the tensions between the visiting Burgundians and his own Huns. He suspects nothing even when the Burgundians attend church in full armour. It is Kriemhild who dictates the action, keeping him in the dark. Nothing could be more at odds with the historical Attila, the cunning Attila whose careful records so embarrassed Priscus and his diplomatic mission, the Attila who built a nation and an empire, and challenged both Constantinople and Rome.

Faithfulness and mildness were not good qualities for blue-blooded heroism, which was part of the problem faced by nineteenth-century German writers who wrestled to adapt this national treasure. The philosopher Georg Hegel thought the whole thing should be dumped as reactionary, irrelevant, trivial and trite; better for writers in need of sources to focus on Germany's real roots, Christianity and the Roman empire. Writers took no notice. Besides Werner's lamentable drama, there were five more Attila plays in German in the nineteenth century, followed by another four in the twentieth. The playwright Friedrich Hebbel tried a Hegelian synthesis in a Nibelung trilogy performed in 1861, filling Attila with Christian virtues, so that his death leads on to a brave new Christian world.

It was Wagner who saw how best to handle Attila. In the four operas of his Ring cycle, he did what a good bard would have done: he cherry-picked what best suited him from Germanic and Norse legends, opted mainly for Norse mythology – a hoard of gold, a Ring of Power, a Helmet of Invisibility, gods, giants, a dragon, magical warrior-maidens – rejected history, and dropped Attila completely.

Perhaps the folk memories would have died, but for Europe's descent into new forms of barbarism in the late nineteenth and twentieth centuries. Given the right circumstances, outrage and prejudice had a ready-made symbol. Those circumstances first arose in the Franco-German War of 1870 (usually called 'Franco-Prussian' by British historians, but Prussia was already Germany, as near as made no difference).

In the summer of 1870 the Germans killed 17,000 French soldiers and took 100,000 prisoner at Sedan, and headed on south, towards Châlons and the Catalaunian Plains, for the same geostrategic reasons as Attila – open spaces, fast progress – except that their target was Paris. A widely syndicated newspaper article that October made the obvious equation between the invading Germans and the Huns, compared Kaiser Wilhelm I to Attila and recalled the tale of how St Genevieve saved Paris. Now, as then, God would help those who helped themselves; and so he did, apparently. Encumbered by prisoners – by the very weight of their success – then slowed by French guerrilla attacks, the Prussian army stuttered to a halt. The western limit of their advance, rather oddly, was Orléans, where Attila had turned back. The armistice that followed confirmed Germany in the French imagination as Europe's latter-day Huns.

For the next 40 years, the great powers stared at each other with narrowed eyes, each seeing treachery and barbarism in the others. The French, in particular, seethed in humiliation and impotence, waiting for a chance for *revanche* on these reincarnated Huns.

Actually, the Germans welcomed the comparison. When Germany sent off troops to China to confront the Boxers, the peasant rebels who in 1900 sought to drive all foreigners from China, Kaiser Wilhelm II told his soldiers: 'Let all who fall into your hands be at your mercy. Just as the Huns a thousand years ago under the leadership of Attila gained a reputation by virtue of which they live in historical tradition ... so may the name of Germany become known in such manner in China that no Chinaman will ever again dare even look askance at a German.'

German nationalism went hand in hand with German imperialism. Seeing rival imperialists all around – France, Russia, Britain – Germany seized new colonies and built a fleet to equal that of Britain, the world's superpower. It was Britain's ruling class, therefore, that felt the threat of German expansion most keenly. One among them was the literary guardian of empire and Englishness, Rudyard Kipling.

It was Kipling who first brought to English readers the French equation of German with Hun. In 1902 he was inspired by a long-forgotten incident in which Germany proposed a joint naval demonstration to collect debts from Venezuela. Kipling, incensed at the very idea of co-operating with Germany, put his anger into the mouths of oarsmen who symbolize those who toil worthily for king and empire:

> And you tell us now of a secret vow
> You have made with an open foe!

'The Rowers' now sounds obsessive, obscure, self-righteous and thoroughly blimpish, a rhyming harrumph from some peppery colonel.

> In sight of peace – from the Narrow Seas
> O'er half the world to run –

With a cheated crew, to league anew
With the Goth and the shameless Hun!

Twelve years later, Kipling's fears came true, without any recognition from him that British and German imperialism were opposite sides of the same coin. Germany, though, faced a unique problem: the near-certainty of war on two fronts, against both France and Russia. The key to victory was the rapid conquest of France, which meant a fast advance through neutral Belgium, any hint of opposition or delay to be dealt with ruthlessly. Thus, in Germany's case, war had to involve an unprovoked invasion of a neutral country and a readiness to use terror. It was virtually inevitable that theory would become practice, which it did a few days after Germany's advance into Belgium in August 1914. In the university town of Leuven (Louvain), a few Belgian snipers provoked a dreadful over-reaction, which proved a propaganda gift to Germany's opponents. Hundreds were killed, thousands imprisoned, 1,000 buildings burned, including the ancient library and its 230,000 books. On 29 August *The Times* deplored the loss of the 'Oxford of Belgium', at the hands of 'the Huns'. Kipling himself urged Britain into war:

> For all we have and are
> For all our children's fate,
> Stand up and take the war.
> The Hun is at the gate!

Nor was this reaction confined to the British. The 'Flames of Louvain' came to symbolize the fate of 'poor little Belgium', and nations not yet at war were horrified. Across Europe, outrage justified prejudice and self-righteousness. From Switzerland, the French poet and soon-to-be Nobel laureate Romain Rolland, formerly rather pro-German, wrote a letter of protest to the German writer and 1912 Nobel laureate Gerhard Hauptmann, making the German–Hun analogy and asking whatever happened to the legacy of Goethe? Hauptmann, formerly critical of Prussian nationalism, replied testily that right now Germans would rather be considered the sons of Attila than the sons of Goethe, an outburst that won him a decoration in the Kaiser's birthday honours.

The whole delicate network of treaties unravelled in two months, and once again Germans followed in Attila's footsteps. Their Third Army advanced on the Catalaunian Plains, and once again failed to achieve the instant victory they sought. This time the British were France's allies, and quickly adopted France's and Kipling's insulting analogy, as well as the less insulting epithet Boches.[3]

Kipling's glib equation – German = Hun – became a commonplace, almost always as a generalized singular, 'the Hun'. A quick internet search produces examples by the hundred. *War Illustrated* for 1 December 1917 entitled an article 'The Footprints of the Hun'. Robert Lindsay Mackay of the 11th Battalion of the Argyll and Sutherland Highlanders wrote in his diary: 'It was apparent in many ways that the Hun meant to hold his third line but our early move where we broke in and rolled up his flanks, upset him.'

But there is something odd about the term. No-one had ever talked about Attila's Huns as 'the Hun'. Yet – if you rely on the literary sources – for English-speakers everywhere, 'the Hun' came to stand for Germany, and Germans, and German barbarism. It was a peculiarly English thing: the French did not speak of *le Hun*, although the analogy was theirs

---

[3] Origin unknown. One derivation is from *Alboche*, supposedly a blend of *Allemand* and *caboche*, slang for 'head', but also a sort of hammer and a part of the tobacco plant. More research is needed.

originally. *Les Boches* or *le Boche* was enough, which seems somehow more human, more in line with the German term for the English soldier, Tommy, paralleled in English by Fritz and Jerry. Neither French nor German had a term with the satanic connotations of 'the Hun'.

You might think 'the Hun' was a universal English usage. Certainly the conditions were bad enough to justify its spread. When the Western Front settled into trenches, soldiers entered a nightmare in which any atrocity seemed likely and rumour was taken as fact. Ordinary soldiers 'knew' that Germans boiled down corpses to make tallow, crucified prisoners in no-man's-land, and fought with saw-edged bayonets, the better to rip open English bellies. As Paul Fussell writes in *The Great War and Modern Memory*, 'Such is the desire for these bayonets to bespeak nastiness in the German character that to this day the rumour persists that they were a specific instrument of Hun nastiness.'

Yet it never caught on in the front lines. Tommy felt some familiarity with the Boches or Boche (singular), and Fritz, and Jerry, trapped like him in a horror dictated by the top brass. Sometimes, Tommy referred to 'old Jerry', even 'poor old Jerry', the 'old' proclaiming familiarity, even affection. Fighting men did not talk about 'the Hun', because they did not hate as those at home might have wished. In the play *Journey's End*, by the ex-soldier R. C. Sherriff, the men in the trenches talk of 'the Boche', never 'the Hun'. Indeed, one character remarks, 'The Germans are really quite decent aren't they? I mean, outside the newspapers.'

*Outside the newspapers.* The term 'Hun' belonged to those back home with an interest in whipping up hatred, like Kipling, and official propagandists, and anti-German headline writers. E. A. Mackintosh, killed at Cambrai in November 1917, aged 24, recalled in 'Recruiting':

'Lads, you're wanted, go and help,'
On the railway carriage wall
Stuck the poster, and I thought
Of the hands that penned that call.

Fat civilians wishing they
'Could go and fight the Hun.'
Can't you see them thanking God
That they're over forty-one?

On Sunday, 10 November 1918, the day before the armistice, the *News of the World* proclaimed the end with HUN SURRENDER CERTAIN.

'The Hun' was of its time, and its time passed. By the early 1930s, it was slipping out of fashion and into mock-imperial speech, giving way before a greater horror, 'the Nazis'. Hitler's antisemitism unleashed an evil against which the beastliness of 'the Hun' paled into insignificance. Two books published in the 1940s – *The Hun in Africa* and *Harrying the Hun* – were last gasps. Today, the term is an archaism, used only to evoke a moment in time and its antique prejudices.

In Hungary, his homeland, Attila's rise to stardom began soon after the arrival of the Hungarians, the Magyars, in 896. For the best part of a century, these warrior-nomads acted like latter-day Huns, raiding into Bulgaria, France, Italy and Germany, until the Emperor Otto I put a stop to their bandit ways on the banks of the River Lech in 955. After that, with nowhere left to migrate to and no-one weaker to raid, they settled. In the 970s the current leader, Geza, did a deal with Emperor Otto II and the pope. The deal was this: he would have himself baptized, and release all Christian slaves, in exchange for recognition as king. To seal the agreement, he betrothed his son Vaik, renamed István (Stephen), to Gisela, daughter of the King of Bavaria, one of Otto II's subsidiary monarchs. The clause about releasing Christian slaves was not popular with Hungarian nobles, and the place was still seething when Geza died in 997. It was young Stephen, aged 22, who finally asserted royal authority, and had himself crowned king in 1001. To mark the occasion, Pope Sylvester II sent Stephen a crown, which by tradition was worn by all Hungarian kings for the next thousand years. It (or a replica: its authenticity is debated) is on view today in the Hungarian National Museum, a glittering symbol of Hungarian and Christian stability in the heart of central Europe. Stephen went on to found ten dioceses under two archbishops and act as patron for many monasteries. Fifty years after his death in 1038 he was canonized.

The point of all this? A Hungarian, Christian, landowning nobleman in (say) 1020 would have sprung from a grandfather who had been a pagan marauder, and from great-great-grandparents who had been illiterate nomads. Not much of an identity there, nor deep roots, nor any historic claim to the land. Now, people who lack these things like to acquire them somehow, which is what the Hungarians did, looking with relief back to the people and the leader whose successes seemed so remarkably to foreshadow their own.

Very quickly, folk tales sung by bards provided three great heroes: Attila, Árpád and Stephen. Stephen back to Árpád, a mere century, was an easy link. But between Árpád and Attila was a blank of four centuries and a thousand unrecorded miles. Such a blank, though, was a gift to poets, and quickly filled, with stories along the following lines.

When King Attila died, he left two sons. The first, Dengizich, died in battle. The second, Ernak, became known as Csaba, or Chaba (meaning 'shepherd', i.e. of his people). He was the son of Honoria, the Roman princess (whom Attila had married in some unexplained way). Chaba returned to Asia, leaving behind 3,000 warriors, the Szeklers, as border guards (*székel* = 'border guard' in Hungarian). Chaba prayed that whenever his people were in trouble Nature herself would tell him, and he would return to protect them. Twice he galloped back to save them. Years passed, and Chaba died. At long last, mighty enemies arose and threatened the Székely. Chaba returned one last time, leading an army across the starry skies to scatter the enemy. The path of the shining, ghostly army became a road in the Heavens. Hungarians call the Milky Way 'The Way of the Souls', and remember Chaba and his heroic father, Attila. From Chaba followed those generations during which Hun joined seamlessly with Magyar: Ugek, Előd, and then Álmos, who had his own cycle of epics, because it was he who, Moses-like, led his people back to the Carpathians, where he died, to be succeeded at last by Árpád. Now the Magyars were back in their homeland, where they formed an alliance with the Székely, who held fast to their duties as border guards; and that is why they remain to this day as a large Hungarian-speaking minority in central Romania, still claiming descent from Attila.

These tales were sung by pagan bards, who had no place in a Christian nation, with its corps of literate monks. As the oral tradition died, a written one took its place, hijacking the old stories and retaining their nationalist agenda. In the thirteenth century, in the *Gesta Hungarorum*, an anonymous Benedictine monk repeated the claim that Attila was a direct forefather of Árpád, whose Magyar invasion over the Carpathians in 896 was nothing more than a return to land that was his anyway, thanks to Attila.[4] Shortly after the *Gesta* were written, the Huns suffered a brief setback as heroes,

[4] This section is based on works by Bäuml and Birnbaum; Thierry; Cordt; and Daim et al.: for details, see the bibliography.

because Hungarians equated them with the Mongols, who devastated the country in 1241–2. Attila's reputation was restored by a chronicler named Simon Kézai, who portrayed his hero surrounded by wealth; even his stables were lined with purple velvet. Thereafter, Attila remained both ancestor and hero-king. It was even believed that Attila's sword, the Sword of Mars, had been owned by the Hungarian kings, until it was given to a German duke in 1063, who gave it to his emperor, Henry IV, who . . .

And so legends about legends could lead for ever onwards, if we let them. By the late fifteenth century Attila had become a sort of Hungarian Charlemagne, the forebear not simply of Árpád and Stephen, but of their successor, Hungary's greatest king, Matthias Corvinus, whose courtiers praised him as the 'second Attila' for restoring Hungary to power and glory under a strong, centralized monarchy. Matthias revelled in the comparison. His pet historian, the Italian Antonio Bonfini, cast Attila as a Roman and proto-Renaissance figure, inventing for him grand orations to mark the murder of Bleda and the Battle of the Catalaunian Plains. The comparison with Attila was not always flattering, however. One of Matthias' critics, Callimachus, an Italian aristocrat with an abiding love of the Polish monarchy, saw him as a threat to peace in Europe and attacked Matthias-as-Attila in a biography of the Hun, presenting him as a back-stabbing, land-grabbing tyrant. But even he did not deny that Attila was a Hungarian at heart, a myth which suited the Hungarian aristocracy as well as the king. In the eighteenth century, the Ésterházys – princes of the Holy Roman Empire, Haydn's patrons, owners of the castle known as the Hungarian Versailles – traced their proud but spurious lineage right back to Attila.

So it is not surprising that Hungarians today have a very different take on Attila from western Europeans. Nor is it an invalid one. Attila was in the end more plunderer than emperor; but he did no more than most leaders of his time would have done if they could have, namely gain as much as possible from victims and enemies. Only victory allows time and leisure for more civilized virtues to emerge; and Attila was not quite successful enough to afford them. He could have created an empire reaching from the Atlantic to the Caspian; he could have rivalled Rome at its height; his heirs could have seized Rome itself, turned on Constantinople and redirected the course of history. If he ever dimly glimpsed such a vision, he could not focus on it, let alone achieve it, because in the end he did not control his creature: it controlled him, and it drove him to death and itself to a hasty end. His legacy is his name, his image, and the mystery of what might have been.

# BIBLIOGRAPHY

Detailed bibliographies are contained in Thompson and Maenchen-Helfen. The following are the sources I found most useful.

Altheim, Franz: *Attila und die Hunnen*. Verlag für Kunst und Wissenschaft, Baden-Baden, 1951.

Ammianus Marcellinus: *The Later Roman Empire*, trans. and ed. Walter Hamilton. Penguin, Harmondsworth, 1986 (and later editions).

Ascherson, Neal: *Black Sea*. Jonathan Cape/Random House, London, 1995.

Bachrach, Bernard: *A History of Alans in the West*. University of Minnesota Press, Minneapolis, 1973.

Bäuml, Franz and Marianna Birnbaum: *Attila: The Man and his Image*. Corvina, Budapest, 1993.

Bierbach, Karl: 'Die letzten Jahre Attilas'. Dissertation, Friedrich-Wilhelms-Universität, Berlin, 1906.

Blockley, R. C. (trans. and ed.): *The Fragmentary Classicising Historians of the Later Roman Empire: Eunapius, Olympiodorus, Priscus and Malchus*. Francis Cairns, Leeds, 1981–3.

Bóna, István: *Das Hunnenreich*. Konrad Theiss, Stuttgart, 1991.

Boor, Helmut de: *Das Attilabild in Geschichte, Legende und Heroischer Dichtung*. Wissenschaftliche Buchgesellschaft, Darmstadt, 1962.

Bury, J. B: *The Invasion of Europe by the Barbarians*. Macmillan, London, 1928.

Byock, Jesse (trans. and intro.): *The Saga of the Volsungs*. University of California Press, Berkeley, 1990.

Cameron, Averil: *The Mediterranean World in Late Antiquity AD 395–600*. Routledge, London, 1993.

Campbell, Duncan: *Greek and Roman Siege Machinery 399 BC–AD 363*. Osprey, Oxford, 2003.

Cordt, Ernst: 'Attila: Flagellum Dei, Etzel, Atli'. Unpublished paper. Quaderni dell'Istituto di Filologia Germanica, University of Trieste, 1984.

Daim, Falko et al.: *Reitervölker aus dem Osten: Hunnen + Awaren*. Burgenländische Landesregierung, Eisenstadt, 1996.

de Guignes, Joseph: *Histoire générale des Huns, des Turcs, des Mogols et des autres Tartares occidentaux*. Desaint & Saillant, Paris, 1856–8.

Dingwall, Eric John: *Artificial Cranial Deformation: A Contribution to the Study of Ethnic Mutilation*. John Bale, London, 1931.

Gárdonyi, Géza: *Slave of the Huns*. Corvina, Budapest, 2000. Trans. from the Hungarian *A Láthatatlan ember* [*The Invisible Man*], 1902.

Gibbon, Edward: *Decline and Fall of the Roman Empire*, mainly vol. 3. 1776–88. Numerous editions.

Gillett, Andrew: *Envoys and Political Communication in the Late Antique West, 411–533*. Cambridge University Press, Cambridge, 2003.

Gordon, C. D: *The Age of Attila*. University of Michigan Press, Ann Arbor, 1960, 1966.

Grosvenor, Edwin: *Constantinople*. London, 1895.

Harries, Jill: *Sidonius Apollinaris and the Fall of Rome AD 407–485*. Oxford University Press, Oxford, 1994.

Jordanes: *see* Mierow.

Kassai, Lajos: *Horseback Archery*. Püski Kiadó, Budapest, 2002.

Kurinsky, Samuel: 'The Jews of Aquileia: A Judaic Community Lost to History'. Fact Paper 28, Hebrew History Federation, 2000 (www.hebrewhistory.org).

Macartney, C. [Carlile] A.: *Studies on Early Hungarian and Pontic History*. Ashgate, Aldershot, 1999.

MacDowall, Simon: *Adrianople AD 378*. Osprey, Oxford, 2001.

MacDowall, Simon: *Germanic Warrior 236–568 AD*. Osprey, Oxford, 1996.

Maenchen-Helfen, Otto: *The World of the Huns*, ed. Max Knight. University of California Press, Berkeley, 1973. An extraordinary labour of love, completed as far as possible from notes after the author's death by the editor, with a vast bibliography. Also contains a survey of the fifth-century Roman empire by Paul Alexander.

Mierow, Charles (trans. and ed.): *The Gothic History of Jordanes*. Princeton University Press/Oxford University Press, Princeton and Oxford, 1915.

Muhlberger, Steven: *The Fifth Century Chroniclers: Prosper, Hydatius and the Gallic Chronicler of 452*. Francis Cairns, Leeds, 1990.

Nicolle, David: *Attila and the Nomad Hordes*. Osprey, Oxford, 1990.

Nicolle, David: *Romano-Byzantine Armies 4th–9th Centuries*. Osprey, Oxford, 1992.

Peigné-Delacourt, Achille: *Recherches sur le lieu de la bataille d'Attile en 451*. Paris, 1860 (*Supplément*: Troyes, 1866).

Rudenko, S. I.: *Die Kultur der Hsiung-Nu und die Hügelgräber von Noin Ula*. Trans. from the Russian by Helmut Pollems. Rudolf Habelt, Bonn, 1969.

Selby, Stephen: *Chinese Archery*. Hong Kong University Press, Hong Kong, 2000.

Sidonius Apollinaris: *The Letters of Sidonius*. Trans. and ed. O. M. Dalton. Oxford University Press, London, 1915.

Sidonius Apollinaris: *Poems and Letters*. Trans. W. B. Anderson. Heinemann, London/Harvard University Press, Cambridge, Mass., 1963.

Sinor, Denis (ed.): *Cambridge History of Early Inner Asia*. Cambridge University Press, Cambridge, 1990.

Sitwell, Nigel: *Roman Roads of Europe*, Cassell, London, 1981.

Thierry, Amédée: *Histoire d'Attila et de ses successeurs*. Didier, Paris, 1856.

Thompson, Edward A.: *The Visigoths in the Time of Ulfila*, Oxford University Press, London, 1966.

Thompson, Edward A.: *The Huns*, Blackwell, Oxford, 1999. A revised and updated version by Peter Heather of Thompson's original 1948 edition.

Tomka, Peter: 'Der Hunnische Fürstenfund von Pannonhalma', in *Acta Archaeologica Academiae Scientiarum Hungaricae* 38, 1986.

Trever, Camilla: *Excavations in Northern Mongolia (1924–1925)*. Leningrad, 1932.

Underwood, F. A.: 'The Hun at the Gate: Kipling's Obsession with the German Threat', *Kipling Journal* 308, December 2003.

Whitby, Michael: *Rome at War AD 293–696*. Osprey, Oxford, 2002.

Wilcox, Peter: *Rome's Enemies (1): Germanics and Dacians*. Osprey, Oxford, 1982.

Yetts, W. Perceval: 'Discoveries of the Kozlov Expedition', in *The Burlington Magazine*, vol. 48, no. 277, April 1926.

# INDEX